Mehmet Sinan Birdal received his PhD in International Relations from the University of Southern California. He is currently Assistant Professor at Maltepe University in Istanbul, Turkey.

THE Holy Roman Empire AND THE Ottomans

From Global Imperial Power to Absolutist States

MEHMET SINAN BIRDAL

New paperback edition first published in 2014 by I.B.Tauris & Co. Ltd
6 Salem Road, London W2 4BU
175 Fifth Avenue, New York NY 10010
www.ibtauris.com

First published in hardback in 2011 by I.B.Tauris & Co. Ltd

Copyright © Mehmet Sinan Birdal, 2011

The right of Mehmet Sinan Birdal to be identified as the author of this work has been asserted by the author in accordance with the Copyright, Designs and Patents Act 1988.

All rights reserved. Except for brief quotations in a review, this book, or any part thereof, may not be reproduced, stored in or introduced into a retrieval system, or transmitted, in any form or by any means, electronic, mechanical, photocopying, recording or otherwise, without the prior written permission of the publisher.

ISBN: 978 1 78076 710 9

A full CIP record for this book is available from the British Library
A full CIP record is available from the Library of Congress

Library of Congress catalog card: available

Printed and bound from camera-ready copy edited and supplied by the author.

*To my parents,
İnci and İlker*

CONTENTS

List of Tables and Figures ... ix

Preface and Acknowledgements ... xi

1. Introduction ... 1

2. From Empires to Absolutist States: Political Change in Early Modern Europe ... 23

3. Institutions and World-Views ... 44

4. Legal Evolution and State Formation: A Comparison of Roman Law and Islamic Law ... 59

5. State Formation in the Holy Roman Empire ... 86

6. State Formation in the Ottoman Empire ... 117

Conclusion ... 149

Notes ... 156

Bibliography ... 187

Index ... 207

TABLES AND FIGURES

Table 2.1: The transition from empire to absolutist state   38

Table 3.1: Stages of moral and legal development according to Habermas   54

Figure 4.1: Positivation and the emergence of modern natural law   80

PREFACE AND ACKNOWLEDGEMENTS

This book was born out of my dissatisfaction as a young PhD student with the ahistoricism of international relations theory. My initial attempt to study historical change in international relations took me on a long journey through history, sociology, institutional economics, comparative law and history of political theory. Thus, the most important challenge for such an interdisciplinary project was to make accessible the diverse literatures with their own theoretical and methodological agendas to international relations theory. I hope this book can demonstrate how much international relations can be refined theoretically and enriched empirically through the interdisciplinary study of international change. I also believe that historical comparisons between Western and non-Western states are crucial for developing better and less Eurocentric theories.

My doctoral advisor Hayward Alker encouraged me to write a comparative history of the two last medieval empires in Europe and was very interested in the progress of the project throughout. Another formative experience was my close collaboration with Timur Kuran as his research assistant. His work made me aware of the importance of legal institutions for the developmental trajectories of states. Unfortunately, Alker passed away on August 24, 2007. Alker's intellectual orientation and vision enriched this project on many levels. He will always be missed. After Alker's passing, I was lucky to have Ann Tickner, Laurie Brand and Timur Kuran as my committee members. I owe them many thanks for their encouragement and support. Many others supported and motivated me in this process: colleagues Nicholas Onuf and Megan Reid, who read my chapters in their initial phases and gave me valuable comments. Zeynep Türkyılmaz relentlessly carried sources for me from the UCLA Library. İnci Birdal tirelessly read the whole book and helped me with important corrections.

The School of International Relations at USC provided valuable support for my project. In the summer of 2002 it granted me a pre-dissertation grant to conduct preliminary research in İstanbul. In the summer of 2004 I received a generous grant from the Berkes Family that enabled me to travel to Vienna. In 2006-07, the Center for International Studies at USC granted me a fellowship, which helped me to start writing my dissertation.

When conducting the research and writing this book I had the invaluable support of Mario Jose Trujillo who patiently tolerated my absence from domestic work and the pile of books, articles and papers occupying most of our apartment. My parents, İnci and İlker Birdal, always encouraged me in my studies. I dedicate this book to them.

1

INTRODUCTION

In 1519 Charles V was elected emperor of the Holy Roman Empire. Although Europe had been divided into multiple polities for some time, in the sixteenth century the legitimacy of political authority was still underpinned by the medieval world-view of a universal Christian community. Central to this world-view was the dream of Nebuchadnezzar in the Book of Daniel, in which the Roman Empire was prophesied to be the last empire of mankind on earth. The Holy Roman Empire was conceived as a continuation of the Roman Empire.[1] Charles, by inheriting vast dominions of the Iberian Peninsula and the Americas, the Netherlands, Sardinia, Sicily, the kingdom of Naples and Austria personified the revival of the empire. After crushing the anti-imperial Cognac alliance forged by the Medici pope, Clement VII, Venice, France, Florence and Milan, Charles consolidated his grip over northern Italy. At the height of his power he was crowned by Clement VII in Bologna on 24 February, 1530 with a spectacular procession of twenty cardinals, four hundred papal guards and three hundred knights.[2] This was one of the most significant ceremonial events of the sixteenth century. It was preceded by long protocol negotiations between the papal and imperial representatives and formalized the unity between the secular and spiritual heads of Christendom. Unlike medieval processional patterns, Charles's entry into the city in 1529 emulated the Roman practice for imperial entries by proceeding directly from the city limits to the center. The processional route was embellished not by conventional religious *tableaux vivants*, but by triumphal arches. Charles was presented as an ancient Roman emperor rather than a Habsburg emperor.[3] The Romanization of the city and the ceremony reflected the appeal of Habsburg public diplomacy to Renaissance art and humanism.

On the day of the coronation, the pope wearing the papal tiara with three crowns entered the basilica of San Petrinio, followed by Charles wearing the iron crown of Lombardy. While Charles kissed the feet of the pope and apologized for the sack of Rome by imperial troops not long before, Clement, humbled by the imperial victory, begged the emperor for his indulgence. 'I am reluctant to have you kiss my feet' the pope said 'but ceremonial law demands it.'[4] The emperor's unprecedented power was also reflected in the changes to the coronation liturgy. The *Laudes regiae*, homage to the high dignitaries of the church and state, had been a fixed component of coronation ceremonies since the eighth century. By the twelfth century the imperial *Laudes* included the formula: *Christus vincit, Christus regnat, Christus imperat* (Christ conquers, Christ reigns, Christ commands). Under Pope Innocent III in the early thirteenth century this formula was dropped from the *Laudes*, since it established a direct link between Christ and the emperor, leaving the pope merely a mediating role. The reintroduction of the formula into the coronation liturgy symbolized the rising authority of the emperor.[5] Thus, the imperial victory seemed to have put an end to the medieval controversy between the pope and the emperor.

The call for a universal empire was a leitmotiv for the great humanists of the Renaissance from Dante to Erasmus. Habsburg propaganda used this idea for legitimating Charles's rise to superpower. In order to commemorate the coronation, Parmigianino painted a portrait of the emperor being handed the globe by the infant Hercules while being crowned with laurel by Fame.[6] Hercules was a carefully selected ancient figure. In a book commissioned by the adventurous Duke Charles the Bold of Burgundy, Raoul Lefèvre claimed that both the ducal house of Burgundy and the royal house of Spain descended from Hercules. The Habsburgs also claimed descent from the legendary hero. In 1516 when Charles – following his Burgundian ancestors – became Master of the Order of the Golden Fleece, Luigi Marliano designed a coat of arms ornamented with symmetrically placed columns of Hercules with the motto *plus oultre*. The motto was a pompous challenge to both Dante's warning *non più oltre* and Erasmus's rendering of the Pindaric metaphor *ad Herculis columnas*. In both contexts, the Herculean columns referred to the borders of the known world. The order was founded in 1430 by Philip the Good to institutionalize the vow of his father, John the Fearless, who was imprisoned by the Turks during the Necropolis crusade of 1396 and pledged to avenge his capture and retake the holy places. Like Jason, who had to retrieve the Golden Fleece to recover his kingdom from the usurper, the order devoted itself to the recovery of the holy places by defeating the Turks. Thus, Charles's motto expressed the ideological backbone of his empire: to expand Christendom beyond the columns of Hercules into Africa, the Middle East and ultimately, to the Americas.[7]

Charles's claim to world dominance and his appeal to the Roman caesars, however, did not go unchallenged. Emerging during the disintegration of the Seljukid state and the Mongolian invasions, the Ottomans invoked Mongolian and Irano-Islamic conceptions of universal rulership. They claimed descent from the legendary Oghuz Khan. Sultan Bayezid the Thunderbolt, who fought Tamerlane, added the title *khan* to the sultanic seal (*tuğra*).[8] In their rivalry with fellow Turcoman emirates of Anatolia the Ottomans posed as holy warriors (*gazis*) allegedly invested by the last Seljukid rulers with sovereignty.[9] Finally, by conquering Constantinople, the seat of the Roman emperors, the Ottomans asserted the title of caesar.[10] They refused to address the Holy Roman emperors as caesars, on the grounds that there could be only one caesar on earth. Thus, they addressed Charles V simply as the king of Spain, and his successor Ferdinand as the king of Austria.[11]

The syncretism of Ottoman ideology is reflected in the portraits commissioned by Mehmed II, the conqueror of Constantinople. Circulating portraits among sovereigns was a common practice both in Renaissance Italy and the Timurid-Turcoman civilization. Mehmed II ordered medallions with his own image and hosted painters like Costanzo da Ferrara and Gentile Bellini in his capital. In Bellini's portrait the Sultan is represented as a Renaissance prince behind a pulpit with a Venetian arch and an inscription *victor orbis* (conqueror of the world). Mehmed also sponsored two palace painters: Sinan, trained by two Europeans, and his apprentice Şiblizade. In a rare portrait by the two painters the sultan is sitting cross-legged - a pose traditionally reserved only for Genghis Khan and his five sons. He wears a scholar's white turban and holds a handkerchief in one hand and a rose in the other. His face, however, is depicted in a realist manner copying Bellini's portrait. The portrait, combining Renaissance and Timurid traditions, embodies the universal ambitions of the Ottoman dynasty.[12]

Mehmed II's patronage of Renaissance painters was not maintained by his successors, but the Ottomans continued to propagate a syncretistic ideology. The claim for universal suzerainty reached its peak in the pomp of Süleyman and his publicists. In 1532, infuriated by Charles's ostentatious coronation, Süleyman ordered a golden helmet, horse furnishings, a scepter and a throne from a consortium of Venetian jewelers. Before being sent to Istanbul, some of these ceremonial items were put on public display at the ducal palace to demonstrate the wealth of the sultan to the rest of Europe. Although imperial regalia such as crowns, scepters, orbs and golden chains were not part of the traditional Ottoman iconography of sovereignty, the sultan carried them in his march on Vienna, the capital of Charles V's

Habsburg dynasty. The sultan entered Belgrade and Nish in processions full of pomp and circumstance, which the French and Habsburg diplomats were made to watch. Ottoman propaganda seems to have worked, since we have many descriptions of these processions in the Venetian reports of the time. As the historian Gülru Necipoğlu emphasizes, 'Süleyman's composite crown – with its combined elements from the pope's tiara, the emperor's mitre-crown, and Habsburg parade helmets with Islamic motifs – was an intelligible statement of Ottoman imperial claims.'[13] Süleyman referred to himself as shah, caesar, sultan, shadow of God over all nations, caesar of caesars and chosroes of chosroeses.[14] His letters to European monarchs usually began with a long section called *unvan* or *intitulatio*:

> I am the sultan of sultans, the proof of khans, the distributor of crowns to the chosroes of the world, the shadow of God on two worlds, I am the padişah of the Mediterranean and the Black Sea, Rumelia, Anatolia, the provinces of Rum and Karaman, the provinces of the Zulkadr and Kurdistan and Diyarbakır and Azerbaijan, and the provinces of the Tatars and Damascus and Aleppo and Egypt and the Holy Jerusalem, the honored Mecca and the respected Medina and Jidda and other Arabian lands and Yemen and Persian lands and the abode of peace, Baghdad, and the splendid province of Basra, and Luristan and Tunisia and Jerba and the lands of the east and the lands of the west, many lands and climates conquered by my noble ancestors and my glorious forefathers – may God enlighten their proofs – with overwhelming force and many lands conquered by my majesty with my flaming and victorious sword, Sultan Süleyman Khan, the son of Sultan Selim Khan, the son of Sultan Bayezid Khan. [15]

In contrast to this long list of titles, Süleyman's letters would usually address European monarchs in a section called *elkab* or *inscriptio* with humble honorifics, simply as king of Spain or king of France.

For a modern observer, the enormous investment in such expensive regalia and ceremony might seem irrational. Likewise, the official claim by a leader today to world supremacy would be considered unacceptable if not ridiculous. However, such expenses and claims were regarded as an essential – sometimes even indispensible – part of politics in a patrimonial government, in which a single individual ruled over the rest of the population. In contrast to bourgeois society, aristocratic societies valued unearned, inherited wealth and prioritized honor and prestige over economic profit since their wealth depended on their socio-political status.[16]

Thus, in aristocratic societies the strategies of acquiring, maintaining and enhancing political power – both domestically and internationally – were substantially different from those of modern industrial societies, which hold professionalism, economic profit and earned wealth in high esteem.

This book investigates how these different modalities of power determine the performance of a state in foreign politics and, ultimately, the emergence of the dominant unit in the state system. Its primary focus is the transition from medieval empires with claims to universal suzerainty to absolutist states recognizing the equality of all sovereign states. It studies two powerful imperial dynasties of the sixteenth century: the Habsburgs and the Ottomans. These cases have significant theoretical relevance. First, the study of these early modern superpowers contributes to the theoretical debate on continuity and change in international relations.[17] Second, the transition of empires is especially significant due to the incompatibility of the conception of the boundary and political authority of an empire and that of a territorially demarcated sovereign state.[18] Third, the inclusion of the Ottoman Empire as a case study has important implications for overcoming the Eurocentric bias of international relations theory. The English School, for instance, which emphasized the importance of cultural values of the state system, declared that the Ottoman state was not comparable to European states based on its Islamic identity.[19] From a different angle, Paul Kennedy argued that the decline of the Ottoman Empire was to be explained by successive incompetent sultans and cultural and technological conservatism.[20] Going beyond *ad hoc* explanations for the Ottoman state and integrating its history into a theoretical account of transition will not only enhance the empirical scope of international relations theory, it will also help to refine it conceptually. This refinement involves two processes: first, categorical concepts such as essentialized representations of Islamic and Christian values will be transformed into variable concepts. In order to compare distinct value systems, one needs to break down the compound concepts into their constituent elements. This constitutes the second stage of theoretical refinement: which aspect of the value system is significant for the performance of a state in the state system?[21] This book will focus on the aspect of political legitimacy in order to systematically investigate the effect of values on state formation. The Habsburg and the Ottoman dynasties that dominated central and eastern Europe between the sixteenth and eighteenth centuries provide a critical pair of comparative cases since both states are considered to be paradigmatic models of despotic rule. Thus, focusing on the legitimation needs of these states provides critical evidence for the proposed theory of transformation.

The temporal scope of the study is selected for several reasons. First, both Charles V and Süleyman achieved a level of power that none of their medieval predecessors could have imagined. In the sixteenth century, the Ottomans and Habsburgs were equally matched in the size of their respective territorial domains, population, agriculture, minerals, manufacturing, transport and economic organization.[22] Both dynasties legitimized their reigns with reference to a theologically inspired universal world-view. Some scholars might object to the selection of the sixteenth century, arguing that medieval empires had already lost the edge against territorial states in earlier centuries.[23] Such arguments, however, fail to explain the persistence of these imperial states.[24] In the words of Fernand Braudel, 'At the end of the fifteenth century the modern monarchies emerged: Aragon of John II and then of Ferdinand the Catholic, Castile of Isabella, France of Louis XI and England of the Tudors... However, the sixteenth century still bears the imprint of great empires.'[25] Immanuel Wallerstein adds that 'only after the failure of the empires did absolutist states become dominant in the eighteenth century.'[26]

The end of the rules of Charles V and Süleyman indeed marked the end of imperial ideals. Charles was the last emperor to be crowned by a pope. As James Reston stated: 'With this ceremony a seven-hundred-year-old tradition came to an end. Charlemagne and Charles V were to be the brackets of a dying ideal, the ideal of a universal empire joined with a universal religion.'[27] Similarly, soon after Süleyman's death, his rule became to be referred nostalgically as the Golden Age by the Ottoman ruling elite. One should, nevertheless, be wary in taking at face value the discourse of decline embraced by these statesmen. In the seventeenth century major transformations occurred in both empires. The rise of the territorial states in Germany, starting with imperial reforms in the fifteenth century, gained important impetus during the Reformation in the sixteenth century. The Counter-Reformation, the Second Reformation and the Thirty Years War (1618–1648) turned the German Empire into a confederation of semi-sovereign states. Thus, the German princes, including the imperial Habsburg dynasty, executed state formation separately within their own domains rather than collectively on the imperial level. Meanwhile the Ottomans themselves were busy fighting the Savafids in the East and the Habsburgs in the West. In the Treaty of Sitvatorok (1606) the Ottoman sultan abandoned his claim to superiority and accepted equal status with the Habsburg monarch. After a century of warfare on the western frontier, the Treaty of Karlowitz in 1699 and the Treaty of Istanbul in 1700 marked the greatest loss of territory in the history of the empire. By sealing the closure of the ever-victorious imperial frontier these treaties had a deep cultural impact on Ottoman society and paved the way for the reforms of the eighteenth century and, finally, comprehensive Westernization in the nineteenth century.

In both empires the failure of the imperial project led to crises on both the institutional and cultural planes. While the Habsburgs gave up pursuing the project of a universal empire and transformed their domains into an absolutist monarchy, thereby becoming one of Europe's great powers in the seventeenth century, intensive warfare in the seventeenth and eighteenth centuries did not lead to a centralized absolutist Ottoman state. The transformation to an absolutist state occurred much later with the early nineteenth-century reforms through which the Ottoman state was accepted into the family of European states, albeit with the reputation of being a sick man.

International Relations Theory and Conceptualizing Change System and Identity

The comparison of the two dynasties poses a problem for international relations theory. International relations is divided in the ontological debate between neo-realism and constructivism, disputing whether the sources of change in the international system are material, ideational or a combination of both. According to neo-realists, there has been no change in the fundamental dynamics of international politics (regardless of different kinds of states and state systems): states have always competed for power.[28] Constructivists argue that change in international politics occurs due to changes in ideas. However, neither a neo-realist focus on material capabilities nor a constructivist focus on ideas can fully explain the difference between the outcomes of the two state formation processes. The challenges faced by the Holy Roman and the Ottoman Empires in the seventeenth and eighteenth centuries demonstrate the importance of institutional path dependence and its impact on the state's capability of adaptation. This study concurs with the early constructivist critiques of neo-realism that legitimating social values inform the way actors define power and the strategies to achieve it. However, ideas cannot be studied apart from the institutional framework in which they are born, reproduced and transmitted. Otherwise, it would be impossible to distinguish idiosyncratic ideas from socially sanctioned values. In this context, Jürgen Habermas's synthesis of social and system theory and Avner Greif's approach to the role of cultural beliefs in institutional change offer a way to integrate the strengths of both sides of the ontological debate. The key to understanding the mechanism of change in international relations is the institutional mechanisms and related discourses that turn material and ideational resources into power. Thus, this work turns to insights from historical sociology to explain how domestic institutions influence state competitiveness and thereby the evolution of the state system.

Neo-realism emphasizes that the state system is made up of autonomous states competing to maximize their power. Devoid of a supranational authority, the prevailing logic of the state system is that of anarchy in which states are motivated by self-help. According to Kenneth Waltz, structural changes in the state system are brought about by changes in the distribution of power among sovereign states. Thus, the entire history of international relations is interpreted as an alternation among three structural modes: unipolarity, bipolarity and multipolarity. This conception of systemic change precludes any change in the logic of anarchy which remains the perennial structure of the state system.[29] In Waltz's view, one can talk about a transformation of the international system only 'when the international system is no longer populated by states that have to help themselves.'[30] As long as self-help or the autonomous way of life[31] of states remains intact, any talk about system transformation is superfluous.

Two aspects of neo-realism limit its grasp of historical change: First, neo-realism assumes that international politics is determined by the logic of anarchy. Any changes beyond the level of the state system, such as changes in domestic institutions and moral values, are excluded from the analysis for the sake of parsimony. Second, neo-realism presupposes that states as the units of the system are functionally undifferentiated. Regardless of their form and nature, all states throughout history have only one function with regard to the state system: the pursuit of power.[32] Power, however, can be pursued in a myriad of ways. Paul Schroeder points out that self-help is usually not an affordable strategy. States try to hide from threats, or transcend them by creating institutional arrangements or bandwagon with stronger states for protection. Schroeder also argues that states seek survival not only through balancing but also through specializing by fulfilling important international functions. Contra neo-realism, Schroeder emphasizes that functional differentiation is a consequence of survival strategies.[33] Although Schroeder discusses specifically modern examples such as Britain as the holder of European balance, specialization was certainly a feature of the medieval states system as well. One only needs to remember the specific functions of the Holy See, the knights of St. John or the Teutonic knights, the city states of Ragusa, Venice, Genoa, and lastly, the Holy Roman and Ottoman empires. In the transition to the modern state system these actors lost their specific functions.

Some balance of power theorists, particularly hegemonic stability theorists, go beyond the state-centric limitations of Waltzian theory. They not only focus on the distribution of power in the state system but also emphasize the states' political capacity for mobilization.[34] In this research tradition, the power transition theory has the most historical outlook and focuses considerably on the early modern state system. Power transition theory is concerned not only with a country's military, social and economic indices of power but also with its political capacity, i.e. the ability to extract resources from its population in order to advance the policy goals of the government. Thus, the theory focuses on endogenous dynamics of power generation: at the peak of its power the hegemon has already mobilized most of its social and economic resources and is facing increased costs for marginal addition. It can be challenged by rising dissatisfied states during a period of relative power parity (when the challenger develops 80 percent of the hegemon's power until it accumulates 20 percent more power than the hegemon). Power parity is followed by overtake in which the old hegemon is replaced by a new one.[35]

As a historian of great power politics, Paul Kennedy asserts that since the sixteenth century the rise and fall of great powers was predicated on their productive and revenue-raising capacities and military strength. Comparing the divergent trajectories of European states and Mughal India, Ming China, Tokugawa Japan, Muscovy and the Ottoman Empire, Kennedy claims that all non-European states suffered from having a centralized imperial authority. The political fragmentation of Europe sparked military and commercial competition leading to innovation.[36] The emergence of a system of sovereign states indeed had very important consequences for state formation in Europe, but not exactly for the reasons specified by Kennedy. It is hard to argue that – being a major part of European politics – the Ottomans did not feel the competitive pressure from European warfare and commerce as early as the Habsburgs. Although theories of power transition and hegemonic stability go beyond system level explanations and head attention to the process of power generation, they usually focus on problems of imperial overextension and lack a theory of institutional change.

Constructivist critics argue that such a theory of institutional change needs to account for changes in ideas and rules. In this context, they criticize neo-realism for its inability to explain the transformation of the European feudal system into the modern international system, which attests to the changing legitimation principles of international politics.[37] Neo-realists dismiss this criticism simply by asserting that legitimating principles are mere justifications of power-holders and have no effect on power politics. Despite the medieval communal discourse, feudal actors behaved in the same way as modern states.[38] The realist approach to legitimacy equates it with political order and hence with the factual possession of force.[39] As a result, it explains system maintenance but neglects system transformation.[40] Constructivists object to this neglect of normative power in politics.[41] Indeed, neo-realism cannot explain the particular rationale behind feudal survival strategies. Merely stating that states pursue power is tautological, since states are power-containers, 'circumscribed arenas for the generation of administrative power.'[42] In order to overcome this tautology one needs to incorporate what political actors define as power or power-enhancing strategies and how these definitions change over time. In this regard, constructivists argue that neo-realism is indeterminate with respect to the emergence of particular state forms such as absolutism. Absolutism was the outcome of the struggles between feudal units and indicated the rise of the sovereign state which entailed a functional differentiation of the units of the state system. What neo-realism misses is the historical fact that the autonomous state itself is a product of modernity. The investigation of the historical conditions of the autonomy of the state and thus, the conduct of self-help politics constitutes the core issue of historical and political sociology. Historical changes in the form and nature of states matter because the neo-realist concept of the sovereign state is itself a product of historical circumstances.

In line with their criticism, constructivists are concerned with the emergence of the rules of the modern international system and especially the principle of sovereignty. Some studies trace the changes in ideas about legitimate statehood among states and argue that legitimacy constitutes states as actors in international politics.[43] Core states can play an important role in producing and reproducing values of legitimate statehood in international politics.[44] These values are also shaped by the interaction between domestic collective identities and international legitimating principles.[45] Constructivist studies demonstrate that, while changes in domestic identities lead to changes in the definition of state interests and the fundamental institutions of the state system, changes in the legitimating principles of statehood lead to changes in the self-definitions of states. These accounts emphasize the role of ideas in historical change, but do not provide an alternative conception of system or systemic change to that of neo-realism.

Alexander Wendt attempts to formulate a constructivist theory of systemic change. Claiming to provide a social systems theory of international politics Wendt bases his argument on three premises: states are the principle actors in international relations; key structures in international relations are inter-subjective rather than material; identities and interests are constructed to a large extent by these structures and hence, are endogenous to the international system.[46] He distinguishes between two kinds of state identity: corporate identity, the Weberian state with legitimate authority over the means of violence in a territory; and social identity, which emerges out of the interactions between states. Corporate identity involves the needs of a state for physical security, ontological security, recognition by others, and development. It motivates a state to engage in interaction with other states, through which it develops its social identity, i.e. its role in the state system.[47]

Wendt restricts constructivism by focusing solely on inter-state culture and ignoring the cultural processes within these states. In his view, theorizing social construction at the level of the state system necessitates a foundation – what he calls the essential state - exogenous to the system.[48] The essential state has five properties: '(1) an institutional-legal order, (2) an organization claiming a monopoly on the legitimate use of organized violence, (3) an organization of sovereignty, (4) a society, and (5) territory.'[49] Thus, Wendt also takes the modern state as the basic unit of his systems theory. Although he is aware that state identities and interests are determined partly by domestic processes, he argues that 'relative to the international system states are self-organizing facts.'[50] Therefore, Wendt asserts that systemic theory has to exclude processes at the domestic level. Eventually, Wendt, like Waltz, ends up with an ahistorical theory starting with the premise of the sovereign state.[51]

Wendt uses the identification theory of Herbert Mead to account for the construction of social identities among states. However, Wendt's rendering of Mead neglects the latter's own approach to international politics. Like constructivists in international relations, Mead argued that the consciousness of international society was essential for national self-consciousness.[52] However, he also recognized the need of the state to legitimize its political conduct.[53] As a social activist and social psychologist, Mead was careful to distinguish between the international identification process and domestic legitimization. With respect to internationally inspired domestic reform movements, such as the labor movement or the peace movement, he asked 'How far may the reform go without weakening the fixed order of society? ... *The reformer stands in the position of the man urging concessions in the interests of humanity, and at the expense of the state.*'[54] When reform proposals contradict the organizational principles of a state, which draw the limits of a society to learn without losing its collective identity, crises will ensue.

Wendt's anthropomorphic conception of the state is untenable since the state, unlike the individual, has to face both outward with respect to other states, and inward with respect to its population.[55] Moreover, as recent critics in sociology and history pointed out, the concept of identity is either too hard and essentialist or too soft, which hardly serves any analytic purpose. They argue that taking social constructivism seriously means distinguishing among external categorizations, self-understanding, objective communality and subjective groupness. Lumping together all these different processes in a single concept of identity impoverishes the analytical strength of social constructivism.[56]

Thus, a proper application of Mead's social-psychological analysis cannot dismiss the domestic identification process as Wendt does. Mead was aware both that social actors inspired by international identification had to legitimize themselves domestically, and that the foreign conduct of a state had to be in line with its domestic political legitimation.[57] Rather than state identity one should study political legitimation, which implies that a state contains several social actors with multiple collective identities, that often these social actors compete over the definition of a certain identity, and, finally, that the state can make use of multiple collective identities to secure legitimacy.

William Bloom demonstrates that people do not identify with a national identity simply because they are externally identified as a nation at the level of the state system. Identification requires the internalization of national symbols so that people *en masse* experience a transformation into a psychological group, i.e. a group of humans sharing a sense of belonging based on identification.[58] The capability of a state to generate this identification process has a direct impact on its capacity to mobilize its material and human resources, provide public goods, and facilitate collective action and ultimately, its performance in the state system. Thus, investigating the identification process within a state brings two important questions to the fore. First, how can one explain the variance in the success of different state forms in generating mass identification? Second, how do states undergo major changes in their master discourses without losing their legitimacy? As the transitions from medieval to modern state forms attest, the mechanisms through which political discourses legitimized state authority varied throughout history. Therefore, a constructivist explanation of historical change needs to outline how and why some ideas have more compliance pull than others. It needs to account for how certain ideas gain and lose their legitimating power.[59]

Jeffrey Legro studies why and how foreign policy ideas of great powers change over time. His analysis emphasizes the importance of normative conceptions of foreign policy within a state:

> We may know what societies desire, we may know the balance of power among them, and we may know the prevailing domestic and international rules. Yet, unless we also understand how states conceive of appropriate action – and when such conceptions are likely to change – we cannot understand how interests will be achieved, how power will constrain or enable such efforts, and which rules are likely to be violated.[60]

Legro defines foreign policy ideas as collectively held strategic ideas reflecting national conceptions about the nature of international politics and identifies three ideal types: integrationism (acceptance of and cooperative participation in the prevailing international society), separatism (desire to remain aloof from the extant system), and revisionism (rejection of the dominant norms of interaction in a given international society and belief that overturning these norms serves the national interest). New foreign policy ideas are shaped by pre-existing dominant ideas and their relationship to experienced events, either reinforcing the continuity of concepts or leading to their radical change. Collective ideas shape their own continuity or transformation by setting the terms and conditions of when change is appropriate and by constituting the most likely options for the new orthodoxy. When established strategies do not yield the expected outcomes, there is pressure for collective reflection and reassessment. The wider the gap between expectations and outcomes, the more intense the crisis experienced by societies and thus the stronger the incentive for collective reorientation. Legro calls this first stage of ideational change collapse. However, reorientation of ideas depends on the second stage called consolidation. The prospects for the consolidation of new ideas are shaped by the number of available prominent ideas and their perceived efficacy. The more dominant an idea, the less available alternative ideas will be and the more likely a society will stick to the old orthodoxy. Also the less new ideas are perceived as efficient, the less attractive they become and the more likely the society will turn to old ideas.[61] Legro, however, does not offer a theory on the ideological and institutional context of dominant ideas. As explained below, sociology and institutionalist economics can offer important insights in this respect.

Legro's purpose is to explain policy changes but not polity transformations. The transition from empires to absolutist states in early modern Europe involves significant social transformations irreducible to changes in strategic beliefs. Historical sociology demonstrates that the transition was accompanied by changes in the relations between social actors, or what has been characterized as the transition from *Gemeinschaft* to *Gesellschaft*. Compared to territorial states, the political discourse in medieval empires was addressed to a small and limited cosmopolitan elite that was legally superior and separated from the rest of subject populations that were only loosely and indirectly connected with each other. Thus, medieval empires could not mobilize their populations without upsetting the established social order and causing a legitimation crisis. The differences between empires and absolutist states reveal how ideas have different impacts on different types of states.

Thus, international relations can gain important insights from the sociology of state formation and its relation to the generation of power in the state system. This, however, requires a rejection of the presumption that state centricism is a prerequisite of system theory. Both Wendt and Waltz focus on the international level and take the modern state for granted. Conflating the question of level of analysis with system theory conceals alternative conceptions of the system. Waltz invokes a rather obsolete conception of the system borrowed from cultural anthropology and focuses exclusively on equilibrium among states. This is apparent in Waltz's preoccupation with changes in the balance of power. Alternatively, bio-cybernetic systems theory emphasizes boundary-maintenance as a central feature of systems.[62] The boundaries of the international system are political boundaries separating not only one state from another but also domestic politics from international politics. Hence, the maintenance of the international system does not depend solely on the equilibrium among its major elements but also on the maintenance of its boundaries against its environment – the boundaries between the domestic and the international.

The historical emergence of territorial boundaries marks the emergence of an international system functioning relatively autonomously from its units. Hence, constructivists assert aptly that 'an examination of the shifts in the function of boundaries is particularly helpful for a better understanding of the origins and the evolution of the present international system.'[63] The emergence of the modern state with territorial boundaries as emergent properties of the international system lies at the center of systemic change, which is neglected by both Waltz and Wendt.[64] Thus, the transition from empire with the claim of universal suzerainty to territorially bounded absolutist states recognizing other states as equal sovereigns constitutes the core problematique of the emergence of the modern international system.

In this context, Wendt's distinction between materialistic and idealistic ontologies in international relations is misleading.[65] The prevailing Weberian approach in historical sociology studies the effects of war-making on state-formation. Thus, it adopts a realist view of international politics, but with a completely different ontological stance that has escaped the attention of scholarly debate. The Weberian argument conceptualizes war-making as superstructure to complement the Marxist focus on class-relations. However, the main theoretical cleavage in international relations, which Wendt maintains, is between a materialist ontology that focuses on war-making and an idealist ontology prioritizing social factors. Consequently, as its stands, the historical sociological debate appears confusing to international relations scholars; it prevents inter-disciplinary communication. Thus, before articulating the connections between international relations theory and historical sociology, one needs to resolve the apparent contradiction between a system theory and a social theory of international politics.

Jürgen Habermas, Institutionalist Economics and the Ontological Debate

Jürgen Habermas's discussion of the concept of social crisis combines both survival imperatives of systems theory and identification processes of social theory in a single theoretical framework. From the perspective of systems theory, 'crises occur when the structure of a social system allows fewer possibilities for problem-solving than are required for the maintenance of the system.'[66] This conception focuses exclusively on external or environmental factors as causes of crises but ignores internal crises tendencies. Analogous to Ruggie's critique of Waltz, Habermas asserts that the systems-theoretic conception cannot recognize changes in the identity of the social system.[67]

In contrast to systems theory, idealist historiography defines identity changes as historical moments when meaning systems that secure identity lose their social integrative power. Historians within this perspective study the meanings of group identification. The constructivist research program in international relations falls largely into this category. Habermas criticizes the idealist approach by asserting that crises do not occur simply because members of a society say they do.[68] The survival imperatives of the state system influence social identification when they cannot be solved within the abstract range of possibilities for social change defined by organizational principles.

Similar to Habermas, institutionalist economist Avner Greif also criticizes one-sided approaches to institutional changes, which either focus merely on the actors' intentions or systemic pressures. According to New Institutionalism with its emphasis on intentions, institutions are created by forward-looking individuals to serve certain functions. This perspective reduces institutional change to the actors' perceived costs of reform and neglects how existing institutions and rules can influence the individuals' cost-benefit calculations. In contrast, evolutionary institutionalism (Old Institutionalism) defines institutions as behavioral patterns reflecting unintended consequences of individual interactions. Rationally bounded individuals are backward rather than forward-looking since they act on inherited cultural traits. Systemic forces of mutation and selection determine the direction of change in the distribution of cultural traits, while inertia sets the rate of change. This perspective, however, ignores the fact that individuals through social interaction can and often do change the social environment.[69] Greif combined the insights of both perspectives by arguing that 'individuals look forward through the prism implied by past institutions.'[70]

Both Habermas and Greif emphasize the need to combine an actor-centered approach with a system-centered approach to studying social change. Institutional change requires human initiative, but humans are constrained by extant institutions. In the words of Karl Marx: 'Men make their own history, but they do not make it as they please; they do not make it under self-selected circumstances, but under circumstances existing already, given and transmitted from the past.'[71] There are, however, important differences between Habermas and Greif. Greif operates with a narrower definition of rationality than Habermas, but provides useful analytical tools for the study of institutional change. How the two approaches can complement each other will be elaborated in the third chapter. In order to appreciate the strengths of both, however, a glimpse at the historical sociological studies in international relations is indispensable.

Historical Sociology and International Relations

Historical sociology provides a useful literature to study the institutional sources of changes in the state system.[72] Several attempts have been made in this direction. Stephen Hobden explores the insights of historical sociology in international relations by reviewing the works of Theda Skocpol, Charles Tilly, Michael Mann and Immanuel Wallerstein. He concludes that three elements from historical sociology are useful for the development of an account of international systems to match the analysis of the state: 'the historicisation of social forms; the analysis of change in international systems; and the lack of a dichotomy between domestic and international.'[73]

Certain scholars of international relations question the prevailing understanding of the emergence of the modern state system by following the Weberian and Marxian approaches in historical sociology. Justin Rosenberg bases his critique of realism on the social analysis of different forms of polity and how different class structures produce different geopolitical systems. He asserts that the state system created at Westphalia was an absolutist system and not the modern international system composed of states as 'purely political institutions.'[74] Building on this insight, Benno Teschke invokes a theory of social property relations to explain geopolitical processes. He claims that the spread of capitalism entailed not just the penetration of pre-capitalist states by cheap commodities but also political and geopolitical processes in which pre-capitalist states designed counter-strategies against the penetration.[75] An important contribution of this approach is its insistence on situating state formation within a larger social context than the Weberian approach, which writes the history of the state as a history of administrative rationality.[76] Thus, these studies question the prevailing dogma in international relations marking the Peace of Westphalia as the moment of the birth of the modern international system and emphasize that the modernity of the international system does not lie in the plurality of the units comprising the system but in the social structure of the units.

Hendrik Spruyt's institutionalist work on the evolutionary dynamics in the transition from feudal to modern state system also uses the historical sociological approach. Spruyt criticizes Waltz by arguing that the structure of the system is also determined by the type of the dominant unit.[77] He explores why sovereign states became the prevailing political organizations in the international system. In his view, the success of the competing units in pre-modern Europe, such as city-states, city-leagues and sovereign states depended, among other things, on their international legitimacy, i.e. their recognition by other units as credible committers.[78] However, Spruyt does not include empires in his list of available institutional options. In his account, the 'imperial solution had failed by the early fourteenth century.'[79] Thus, Spruyt excludes two major actors in the European states-system – the Habsburgs and the Ottomans – and does not exhaust the range of political alternatives.[80]

The recent book by Daniel Nexon applies network analysis to account both for changes in ideas and the formal structure of institutions. Nexon criticizes both realist and constructivist theories of international change, in particular in early modern Europe. The states-under-anarchy model of realism presumes that collective mobilization within states faces far fewer obstacles than among states. This presumption can be seriously challenged by the composite states prevalent in early modern Europe. Composite states ruled over various political communities linked to central authorities through distinctive contracts specifying rights and obligations. These communities enjoyed limited autonomy through their customs but were not directly linked with each other. Thus, formally they resembled a hub-and-spoke structure without a rim. On the one hand, this structure allowed the rulers to keep local populations distinct from each other, prevent collective action among them and thus, the spread of rebellion. On the other hand, the firewalls among the subject communities constrained the coercive and extractive capacity of the central elite. In composite states, the central state had to rely on indirect rule by local magnates. Thus, the network structure of composite states produced a distinct pattern of collective action and collective mobilization. In this regard, Nexon claims that the realist assumption of states as primary sites for collective action cannot be taken for granted. The study of early modern states demonstrates that the scope conditions for states-under-anarchy model shows considerable variation. In contrast to realism, constructivism assumes that collective action is norm-governed. Nexon, however, criticizes constructivist emphasis on the uniqueness of norms. The focus on particular norms and principles of different states systems makes it difficult to generalize about formal properties of structures. Thus, constructivism is not able to explain very similar behavioral patterns common to many societies and states over time.[81]

In contrast to prevailing approaches in international relations, which define structures by their categorical attributes, Nexon's relationism characterizes structures by patterns of transactions themselves. For relationists the 'stuff of social reality – of action no less than structure, and their intersection in history – lies in relations.' Thus, relationism uses the concepts of social ties (routine transactions with imputed meanings by actors), categories (generalized roles providing collective identification), and networks (patterns of social ties with varying properties of density and distribution of social interactions).[82] In this context, composite states, states with indirect rule, can be classified into two ideal-types: federations and empires. In federations the center and each periphery are connected by uniform contracts. In contrast, empires are characterized by heterogeneous contracting, meaning the terms of incorporation between the center and each periphery involve different rights and privileges, and indirect rule.

In this regard, both the Holy Roman Empire and early modern dynastic agglomerations such as France and England approached the imperial model of indirect rule through heterogeneous contracting.

Under these circumstances, the logic of early modern international relations differed from the realist conception of international relations: first, statecraft was led by the principle of dynastic reason rather than national interest; second, the heterogeneous nature of dynastic composite states made transnational politics much more significant. In this context, the Reformations had a significant effect in the transformation of the early modern state system into the modern one: The confessional division of Latin Europe set important limits to the future development of dynastic-empire building. The Reformations also contributed to the rise of conceptual innovations such as sovereignty, reason of state etc. Finally, the territorialization of confessions paved the way for the emergence of nationalism and the nation-state.[83]

The transformative effect of the Reformations can only be explained by analyzing the network structure of the early modern state. Central authorities could employ divide-and-rule strategies to keep grievances local and build firewalls to prevent the spread of rebellion. Two mechanisms would undermine divide-and-rule strategies: increasing peripheral connectivity and simultaneous resistance. For several reasons, both mechanisms were triggered by early modern developments. Moreover, the structural features of divide-and-rule strategies were also exposing central authorities to cross-pressures from peripheral segments. The more segmented the structure and the more heterogeneous the relations are, the higher will be the cross-pressure on central authorities. The inability to manage this cross-pressure would lead to – what realists called – strategic overextension. To minimize cross-pressure the composite states would employ multivocal or polyvalent discourses signaling different identities and values to different subject communities. The lack of communication between the segments made this polyvalent discourse possible. Indirect rule through intermediaries cut government costs and provided the central authority with a possible scapegoat during rebellions. However, it also yielded significant principal-agent problems, inefficiencies in taxation and problems in the implementation of central policies. Nexon emphasizes that in pre-Reformation Europe resistance could be legitimated by customary right, dynastic claim or republican principles. The Protestant Reformations destabilized the divide-and-rule strategies by increasing communication among peripheral segments, raising cross-pressure on central authorities and reduced the chances for polyvalent legitimation.[84]

Daniel Nexon's account is a theoretically and historically sophisticated approach to the question of early modern international change. He makes a convincing case for the argument that social and international structures are co-constitutive.[85] As the next chapter argues, this insight is crucial for a mutual dialogue between historical sociology and international relations. However, this book will concentrate on two important aspects of change, which have not been specifically dealt with by Nexon: the dynamics of path dependency of self-reinforcing institutions and the formal properties of legitimating discourses. While institutionalist economics contributes to the understanding of path dependency, Habermas's approach to the evolution of the life-world distinguishes between formal and metaphysical qualities of world-views.

Even though Nexon does a superb job in applying network theory to explain the effect of the Reformations on international relations and in going beyond the ontological debate between realists and constructivists, the scope of his work is confined to the European experience. In this respect, why the Sunni-Shia rivalry between the Ottomans and the Safavids and the ensuing Anatolian rebellions did not create similar effects in the Middle East remains a very important question. The comparison of the Habsburgs and the Ottomans will be vital for theoretical refinement in the network approach to international change.[86]

Thus, the comparison of the Habsburgs and the Ottomans yields important insights for international relations theory and historical sociology. In this context, this study conceptualizes early modern state-formation as the product of a crisis of the state on both the domestic and inter-state levels. Hence, the rise of the territorial state and the emergence of the modern international system, based on the recognition of mutual political boundaries, are two aspects of the same transformation process. The solutions to the crisis of the late-medieval polity are devised and implemented by state elites, which try to balance the requirements of the system with the state's need for legitimacy.

Outline of the Chapters

The next chapter will review the state formation literature on empires and absolutist states. It will delineate the major characteristics of the two state forms in the fields of administration, taxation, conduct of foreign affairs and political legitimation and the institutional indications of transformation in each. Thus, the chapter assesses a diverse body of historical sociological research to demonstrate how its empirical and conceptual findings are relevant for the theory of international change.

Chapter three proposes to improve the historical-sociological research agenda by introducing two problems: the impact of past institutions on institutional change and the role of world-views in preventing or initiating change. The chapter initially introduces Avner Greif's approach to institutional change incorporating the role of cultural beliefs and path dependence in the pace and direction of institutional change. It also identifies an exclusive focus on institutional rationalization as the historical-sociological literature's main weakness and asserts that political legitimation needs to be taken into account as well. Thus, the chapter re-formulates Jürgen Habermas's theory of communicative action to yield a theory of state formation, which combines both the aspects of bureaucratization and legitimation in the emergence of the modern state.

Chapter four compares the respective legal traditions of the Holy Roman and the Ottoman Empires in two major aspects: legal institutions and legal discourse. It argues that Islamic law proved less suitable for modern state formation due to its lack of the concept of legal personality. However, the reason for this does not lie in an inherent quality of Islamic law but rather in the institutional framework and the legitimating principle of the Ottoman Empire, which prevented the development of Islamic law in this respect. Similarly, the forces behind secularization of public authority and the disenchantment of law in Europe should be sought in the institutional structure of the state and the legitimating discourse of natural law rather than in the inherent and essential characteristics of Latin Christendom.

Chapters five and six examine the argument developed in chapters three and four by investigating the transformation in the Holy Roman and Ottoman Empires in four fields: administration, taxation, the conduct of foreign affairs and legitimation. Chapter five investigates the rise of the territorial states in the Holy Roman Empire. The reform process in the fifteenth and sixteenth centuries was constrained by the legacy of medieval institutions and the confessional crisis in the sixteenth century. Administration and taxation were dependent on the princes of the empire. Imperial foreign affairs were conducted by multiple organs and parties. With the Peace of Augsburg in 1555 and the Peace of Westphalia in 1648, the empire became territorially demarcated and the princes within the empire began the consolidation of their own territorial authority. Focusing on the Habsburg hereditary domains, the chapter demonstrates how the end of imperial claims enabled the Habsburgs to establish their territorial state.

Chapter six examines the transition in the Ottoman Empire. Compared to the Habsburgs, the Ottomans were not bound by any prior institutional arrangements. Thus, they built strong central imperial organs in administration, taxation and the conduct of foreign policy. However, these strong imperial institutions also made change harder in the eighteenth century after the closure of the imperial frontier. Systemic pressures, such as the change in warfare technology and the rise of modern diplomacy, led the Ottoman elites to reforms which had important social consequences. However, as long as the Ottoman Empire maintained its traditional world-view, the decision-making process remained crippled by political fragmentation.

By studying the reform processes in the Holy Roman and Ottoman Empires, this book emphasizes that institutions facilitate the translation of material and ideational resources into power. Thus, the pre-existing institutions and the underlying legitimating discourses determined the way the two empires responded to the survival imperatives of the state system and thereby the outcome of their state formation. In this respect, this book does not formulate another system theory but focuses rather on how states react to systemic pressures. Historical evidence suggests that different states respond differently to survival imperatives. This book outlines the structural conditions that enable and restrain states' adaptation to survival imperatives.

By focusing on the institutional constraints of power in international relations, this book explains historical change of the state system. Although it argues that every state has to fulfill certain functions (such as administration, taxation, foreign policy and legitimacy), it emphasizes that the institutional mechanisms fulfilling these functions vary over time and across cultures. In this respect, this study relativizes the concept of the state and examines the impact of the changes in the organizational principles of states in their conduct of foreign policy and their power in the state system.

Relying on historical sociology, this book demonstrates that the preconditions of a successful foreign policy (including both warfare and diplomacy) for medieval empires were fundamentally different from the territorial states of the seventeenth century. In medieval empires the organizational principle was universal suzerainty over all other states, while the modern state rests on the organizational principle of sovereignty, which recognizes other states as having equal status. The transformation of the empire to the territorial sovereign state is conditioned by the states' capability to learn within the given imperial organizational principle or to change its organizational principle.

2

FROM EMPIRES TO ABSOLUTIST STATES: POLITICAL CHANGE IN EARLY MODERN EUROPE

A major task for a theory of international change is to demonstrate how the rationale for pre-modern states was different from that of modern states and how this difference translated into international politics. The theory should explain how and why the powerful imperial dynasties, Habsburgs and Ottomans, lost their pre-eminence to smaller yet stronger absolutist monarchies. In other words, it should trace the early modern transition from empires that claimed universal suzerainty to absolutist monarchies that recognized the sovereignty of other states. In this regard, international relations theory should first integrate the significant empirical findings and theoretical concepts of the sociology of state formation pertaining to the emergence, maintenance and transformation of pre-modern states. The review of this literature first needs to provide definitions for the different kinds of states in early modern Europe: aristocratic empires and absolutist states, and illustrate why absolutist states were better equipped to compete in the state system than empires. Second, it should delineate what the transition from empire to absolutist state entailed.

Empire-states

Most studies lump together pre-modern and modern states from different historical periods in a single concept of empire – Athenian, Roman, Mongolian, Inca, Russian, Ottoman, Habsburg and colonial empires of the nineteenth and the twentieth centuries.[1] The definitions in these studies depict the empire as a multiethnic state stretching over vast areas. Generally, an empire denotes 'a large, composite, multiethnic polity formed by conquest by a strong center (metropole), and characterized by some form of indirect rule of the subordinate parts.[2] This definition demonstrates that an empire rules over several communities as opposed to the nation-state's claim to represent the nation as a single community. The peripheries are connected to the imperial center separately; they do not form a single community.

Michael Doyle argues that the functioning of empires is similar to domestic politics in some ways and to international politics in others. His comparison along five dimensions reveals that the characteristics of empires contradict the characteristics of both the modern state and the modern state system.[3] Like modern states empires were ruled by a single sovereign, but they looked like a state system since they were far less socially integrated than modern states.[4] Compared to international hegemons, empires could control both domestic and foreign policy. The range of imperial power was wider and weightier than the international power but narrower and less weighty than the domestic power of modern states. Finally, as distinct from temporary occupations, empires lasted at least for a generation.[5] Doyle's argument highlights the advantage of territorial states over empires; since the subject populations in empires did not constitute a unified political community, communities under imperial rule had less sense of identification with the empire. In contrast, the closed territorial boundaries of absolutist states contributed to the creation of meaningful political identifications. In order to analyze how these characteristics of empires influenced their adaptation to the early modern state system, one also needs to distinguish between medieval and modern empires. The latter had a core nation-state equipped with modern political, ideological and economic technologies and institutions.

Immanuel Wallerstein's work sheds light on the distinction between medieval and colonial empires and the transition problems in the former. Medieval empires were inclusive polities that put limits on the exploitation of the surplus of other economies and increased the costs of economic extraction due to a cumbersome political structure. In contrast, the modern world-system is based on a world-economy comprising multiple sovereign states.[6] Empires could not act as entrepreneurs in the world-economy, since they pretended to be a universal polity ruling the whole world. Thus, they could not act like territorial states which as entrepreneurs enriched their economy by exploiting other economies.[7] In this respect, European monarchies in the late Middle Ages had different *raisons d'état* than empires. Increasingly, they aimed at the creation of a national society.[8] The emergence of absolutist states was related to changes in international market roles that determined class alliances within.⁹ These territorially bounded states were much better equipped to compete in the modern world-system and build colonial empires. Wallerstein's analysis reveals the importance of the distinction between empires with universal suzerainty and absolutist states with mutually recognized sovereignty. The success of absolutist states depended on their standing in the world-economy. The pretensions of empires to universal suzerainty made them less competitive in comparison to absolutist states.¹⁰

Shmuel Eisenstadt and John Kautsky's works complement Wallerstein by providing important insights into the internal mechanisms of imperial political authority. Eisenstadt makes an important distinction between modern polities and 'historical bureaucratic empires,' which analytically and historically stand between traditional and modern political systems.¹¹ Eisenstadt compares polities according to four criteria: the differentiation of political activities from other social roles; the differentiation of political groups from other social groups; the differentiation of political goals from other cultural and economic goals; and the type of legitimation.¹² Historic bureaucratic empires exhibited a relatively high level of societal differentiation and a political elite with wider aims and perceptions of political authority.¹³ Accordingly, a limited level of non-ascriptive political participation distinguished empires from patrimonial or feudal systems, where ascriptive social groups (aristocracy, kinship, etc.) dominated the political, sphere.¹⁴ Empires had more free resources, i.e. resources not embedded in ascriptive groups and social sectors and committed to use in such sectors,¹⁵ compared to tribal, patrimonial and city state regimes. Rulers were interested in the generation of 'generalized power,' i.e. freeing resources from traditional or ascriptive aristocratic, rural, or urban groups and in the development of free groups. However, the availability of free resources to the ruler was limited in two aspects: first, along with more differentiated political goals, there existed traditional and undifferentiated activities; second, rulers were also constrained by political legitimation couched in traditional terms. The success of the ruler was dependent on maintaining a balance between free resources and ascriptive settings.¹⁶ The increasing dependence of rulers on non-ascriptive groups, the contradiction between the ruler's promotion of free resources and traditional legitimacy, the pressure of foreign policy and interstate competition, and the emergence of autonomous strata with their own political demands constituted the main reasons for change in bureaucratic empires. Change might be both in the direction of pre-bureaucratic polities or more differentiated polities.¹⁷ Thus, the bureaucratization and centralization of political authority made empires more powerful than the societies under their control.

Although Eisenstadt's work provides a useful theoretical framework to study the emergence, maintenance and change of political authority and administrative capacity in pre-modern states, it does not distinguish between empires legitimized as universal suzerains and absolutist monarchies legitimized as territorially demarcated sovereign states. Hence, it neglects the crisis that originated from the discrepancy of imperial universal suzerainty with equally sovereign states as dominant units in the state system. The effective control of the ruler and bureaucratization were much more advanced in the territorially bounded sovereign state than in the universally suzerain empire. Moreover, universal suzerainty was one of the major elements of the traditional legitimacy of empires. Thus, the transition from empire to a territorially demarcated state made further bureaucratization possible and increased the state's chances in inter-state competition.

In contrast to Eisenstadt, John Kautsky criticizes a strict distinction between feudal empires (government by the prince and the barons) and centralized bureaucratic empires (government by the prince and his servants). Kautsky argues that in practice the difference between the two forms of empire is only a matter of degree and not a matter of kind. Both types can be defined as 'aristocratic empires' in which the low level of communications and transportation technologies made local aristocracies autonomous to some extent. There are no essential differences between the bureaucrats of Eisenstadt's bureaucratic empires and the aristocrats of Kautsky's aristocratic empires. According to Kautsky, first, bureaucratic officials in bureaucratic empires had the same function as aristocrats in all aristocratic empires. Second, bureaucrats, similar to aristocrats, were recruited from a narrow stratum. Third, they usually passed on their privileges to their offspring. Lastly, government in bureaucratic empires was as uninterested in the daily lives of the population as aristocratic government.[18] Thus, Kautsky provides support for comparing the Holy Roman Empire, the paradigmatic feudal state, and the Ottoman Empire, a highly bureaucratized and centralized state since they can both be subsumed under aristocratic empires.

According to Kautsky, the main functions of government in agrarian economies, in which aristocrats lived off peasants, were taxation and warfare. Since the entire surplus produced by peasants was extracted by the aristocracy, there was no investment in the improvement of production. Neither the aristocracy nor the peasants had an incentive for such improvements, since aristocrats could more easily increase their income by adding more people or lands to their domains and peasants would gain nothing from the increase in productivity. Change in these societies came through commercialization that marked the beginning of modernization.[19] Since merchants were an important source of taxation and credit for rulers, aristocratic empires had to encourage trade to a certain extent. Commercialization occurred when growing wealth transformed merchants into political actors. In this regard, commercialization did not mean the domination of the economy by trade but that the aristocracy no longer governed alone and only according to aristocratic values.[20]

An important aspect of aristocratic empires was the absence of class conflict due to immense class differences. The cleavage between the two classes was so deep that conflict could not cross it. Thus, an aristocratic empire was not a society, but a collection of agrarian societies independent of each other but linked to a common aristocracy through exploitation. Politics took place not between classes but inside classes.[21] Since the empire consisted of multiple societies, individuals in general were very dimly aware of the overarching aristocratic empire. Peasants had their own government in their villages.[22] Thus, empires did not have the same mobilization capability as the territorially demarcated state. They could not provide meaningful identities with which their entire population could identify.

Recent studies of empires using network analysis also emphasize the diminished opportunities for peripheral collective action against the imperial center. Scholars applying network analysis to the study of empires, such as Daniel Nexon and Karen Barkey, focus on the formal properties of the network structure of empires: a hub-and-spoke network without a rim.[23] In this structure, the imperial center uses its structural position of brokerage to rule over diverse communities. Karen Barkey argues that, because of this structure, the empire as a whole could not be highly and continuously mobilized. In order to maintain their rule, empires had to satisfy three conditions: employing a supranational ideology or an imperial culture; managing multiethnic diversity through toleration, forced conversion, and assimilation; using divide-and-rule strategies to prevent collective action of local intermediaries, while integrating them vertically in an imperial hierarchy. But while the segmented nature of imperial polities decreased their capacity for mobilization, it also made them flexible. Imperial institutions could strike separate deals with different communities, institute organizations and maintain imperial ideologies that integrated these diverse communities. As long as imperial institutions maintained flexibility, empires could rule for centuries. Flexibility was achieved by the constant segmenting and integrating of diverse communities through mobile markers of difference.[24]

Barkey's explanation of Ottoman transformation is slightly different from Nexon's explanation of Habsburg transformation in two important respects. First, Barkey demonstrates how Ottoman state formation had a different trajectory than European state formation despite a similar network structure. Differences in these trajectories were intimately linked with available collective action strategies beyond mere religious differences. Second, Nexon's account emphasizes the composite state as a common ideal-type shared both by empires and absolutist states, but does not distinguish between the two.[25] Indeed, with respect to the network structure both state types looked similar. France, the paradigmatic model of absolutism, in the sixteenth century resembled more a 'polyglot empire' than a 'proto-nation state.'[26] But, as Nexon also notes, compared to Habsburg Spain or the Holy Roman Empire, France was more 'integrated.'[27] Moreover, the reason why Huguenots did not attempt to secede from the French monarchy was the unattractiveness of secession to most participants in the Civil War from a comparatively centralized and modernized state. Under these circumstances, the weakening of the French monarchy strengthened sovereign-territorial impulses in France.[28] Nexon's analysis focuses on how royal dynasties responded to the Protestant Reformations. However, as Barkey's analysis reveals, a study of social and political institutions is crucial to explain differences in state formation trajectories.

Barkey criticizes the Eurocentric bias in the literature of state formation, in which state centralization and bureaucratization went hand in hand with peasant rebellion. The Ottoman state avoided the conflict in European state formation by co-opting and integrating traditional and new social elements affected by centralization.[29] The trajectories of European and Ottoman states appear to move in opposite directions: while most European states moved from an indirect mode of governance through landed nobility to direct rule through royal appointees, the Ottoman state developed from direct rule through centrally appointed officials to indirect rule through local notables.[30] Barkey argues that while in most European states state formation was stimulated by international warfare, taxation and co-optation of capital and landed interests, in the Ottoman Empire state formation was an outcome of negotiations and wars with bandits or mercenaries under the pressure of international warfare. The difference can be explained by the social structure and the particular style of the Ottoman state, which combined patrimonial rule with a brokerage style of bargaining.[31]

By the end of the sixteenth century, the Ottoman state had already built an empire with a bureaucratic administration ruling over territories with diverse communities under local power holders. These regional elites were barred from the right of autonomous organizations. In the absence of corporate bodies the state manipulated non-state actors. The combination of a patrimonial and bureaucratic state drew on Middle Eastern tradition and constituted the political culture of the Ottoman Empire embodied in the well-known circle of equity.[32] In contrast to European landed nobility, Ottoman administration was based on a military class which owed its privileged status to the sultan rather than to hereditary right. Thus, the military class lacked autonomy and the absence of corporate bodies implied that the acquisition of political power was possible solely through endowment by the sultan. The sultan bestowed land as prebends or fiefs to cavalrymen and governors. The land legally belonged to the state but was controlled by the military class. The governor-general sat at the top of a provincial military hierarchy. The central government put a check on the governor-general by appointing two additional bureaucrats: a financial officer and a judge. Moreover, all these officials were shuffled regularly from one location to another to prevent them from establishing connections with the locals. Similar to elites, subject populations also lacked corporate bodies. Isolated religious, ethnic, occupational and village communities were incorporated into a vertical hierarchy. In this respect, the most important characteristic of Ottoman society was the absence of civil society with corporate bodies which gave a certain autonomy to social actors in Latin Europe.[33]

The seventeenth-century economic and technological changes in Europe challenged the Ottoman state on the international level. While the strength and infallibility of Ottoman society were put in question, changes and crises in Europe reverberated throughout the Ottoman lands. Demographic, economic and political changes led to a crisis in Ottoman society, to which the state responded by rearranging its institutions to maintain surplus extraction from subject populations. However, the initial political institutions led to a different outcome in the Ottoman Empire than in Latin Europe.[34]

A brief review of the literature on empires reveals major weaknesses of medieval empires, which were facing the rivalry of absolutist states in the sixteenth century. Medieval empires lacked direct control over a unified political community which identified with the state, thereby proving an important weakness in the competition with absolutist states. The function of political discourse was to ensure collective action among the imperial ruling elite rather than to forge a single political community out of the multiple societies under imperial rule.

Empires were less efficient in economic exploitation because they had a costly political structure which extracted resources under their control. In contrast, the absolutist state extracted resources by means of international markets. Domestically, empires were restricted by traditional legitimacy and ascriptive groups that formed the basis of their rule. Central bureaucracies tended to gain independence from the rulers and to follow their own logic. The concept of commercialization captures the tendency of free resources to become forces independent of the ruler and even challenge the rule of the aristocracy. Hence, empires, due to their comparative disadvantages, were less competitive than absolutist states.

The basic insight of the literature on empires is that these entities were fundamentally different – with regard to both organization and ideology – from today's nation-states. A neo-realist analysis of material capabilities cannot explain how large empires, such as the Ottoman and Holy Roman Empires, lost their competitiveness against a tiny insular state such as England. Moreover, the empires had a different modality inherent to the claim of universal suzerainty which was incompatible with the modality of the modern state system. Wendt's constructivist systems theory fails to recognize that imperial states incorporated various identities and cannot be identified with a single identity such as a national identity. Imperial ideologies were characterized by syncretism, which molded various traditions into a cosmopolitan imperial culture.

Most importantly, the literature on empires demonstrates that the unitary actor model of both Waltz and Wendt cannot be sustained for the study of empires. The emergence and maintenance of empires was predicated on the enhancement of the administrative capabilities of an imperial ruling class. Given the level of technology of these agrarian societies, the state had to depend on local magnates who were in charge of administration and taxation. Political power was divided between the central state and the local magnates. The centralization of the state was limited by the degree to which new resources were put under the direct command of the central state apparatus. The organizational framework of the empires significantly constrained the autonomy of the state and its foreign policy making. Lacking the competencies of the modern state, the empires had to establish rules and institutions to secure the collective action of local magnates. In the face of increasing competition against territorial absolutist states with far more centralized institutions, reforms in the empires were dependent on the pre-existing imperial institutions that had once helped the central state to create incentives for collective action. Institutional path dependence explains why medieval empires acted differently under survival imperatives than what Waltz's and Wendt's models predict. However, we need to illustrate first why the early modern territorial state won the competition against aristocratic empires.

Absolutist States

The study of the emergence of the modern state system is essential to understanding that the autonomous territorial state, taken for granted both by Waltz and Wendt, is a product of historical conditions. The literature on the origins of the absolutist state reveals the extent of social and political transformations that yielded the early modern state and the state system. As the review here demonstrates, the absolutist state marked an unprecedented level of centralization of political authority which manifested itself in three main domains: administration, taxation and foreign policy. In all these domains the state managed to achieve and sustain a stable coordination of the ruling class. This political and social coordination was the foundation for the emergence of the early modern state as a unitary actor in world politics. Thenceforth, the state would claim exclusive authority in domestic as well as foreign policy.

According to Perry Anderson, the absolutist state was a precursor of the modern state. In the sixteenth century, the centralized monarchies in France, England and Spain broke with the pyramidal, parcellized sovereignty of medieval social formations, with their estates and liege-systems.[35] Absolutism was a reaction of the feudal aristocracy to commercialization; the transformation of the serf into a wage laborer could be prevented by the displacement of politico-legal coercion upwards to a centralized state. With the help of Roman law, the sovereignty of the state was established in more absolute terms and the fief system was turned into an allodial regime – an absolute, inalienable property regime. While transforming feudal ownership into private property, the absolutist state also used the sale of offices as a means of centralization and control over the tax-exempt aristocracy.[36]

The emergence of the absolutist state also transformed the state system. Since the absolutist state was still aristocratic in character, the calling of aristocrats, i.e. war-making, remained the political rationale of the absolutist state. The absolutist ideology, mercantilism, was based on a zero-sum model of international politics. Although the dominant class remained the same, absolutist states formed a far more unified and centralized state structure that also transformed the state system and led to the creation of the first modern international institutions. As feudal pyramids were contracted into territorial monarchies, they created a formalized interstate system with resident embassies and permanent chancelleries for foreign relations. Modern diplomacy was another institutional innovation in the service of absolutism.[37] Moreover, the enhancement of political power in the absolutist state created systemic pressures on rival states. Under increasing survival imperatives, absolutism was soon transplanted into Eastern Europe as well, albeit in circumstances that offered fewer free resources for rulers.[38]

Like Anderson, Anthony Giddens also regards the absolutist state as the progenitor of modern development in Europe. The emergence of the absolutist state marked the reception of Roman law, the distinction between private and public law, the obliteration of the public authority of estates, the dissolution of feudal forms of land ownership, the commodification of land and products, the creation of a legally free labor force, the monopolization of issuing money, the detachment of money from the bullion value and the development of fiduciary money, the universal taxation of the population, (the development of) internal pacification, state surveillance and social disciplining (in institutions such as schools, hospitals, asylums, orphanages).[39] Thus, although the absolutist state based on a class-divided society was quite different from the nation-state based on a capitalist, industrial society, it created the centralized sovereign state and the state system. The enhanced surveillance and disciplining capacity of the absolutist state was essential for the later nation-building project. In this respect, absolutist sovereignty also paved the way for modern citizenship.[40]

The major difference between the absolutist state and earlier state forms – such as city-states, feudal states and empires – was its relation to other states. In Giddens' words, in 'feudal Europe, boundaries were mere frontiers, chronically disputed and nebulously administered. "Diplomacy" existed, but it was of the traditional type. In other words, it consisted mostly of attempts to buy off other groups by the offering of goods and rewards, or to exact tribute that would be a recognition of dependency.'[41] In contrast, the new state system was predicated on the mutual recognition of the sovereignty of states. The innovation of absolutism was congress diplomacy, which extended state surveillance into the state system and thus created what came to be known as international relations.[42] The emergence of absolutism involved the restructuring of both the external and internal frontiers of the state. It demarcated the domestic from the interstate realm, the inside from the outside, and laid down the basic framework of international politics. Three advances in military technology influenced the development of the absolutist state and became its basic arsenal: the technological change in land-based warfare, military discipline and naval power.[43]

Technological changes in warfare such as artillery and the use of firearms made feudal warfare obsolete. As warfare intensified between centralizing states, maintaining permanent armies became inevitable. The emergence of permanent armies meant the dissolution of the feudal structure in the countryside. If the aristocracy were to maintain its function as a warrior class, it had to move to the political center where permanent armies were lodged. The emergence of permanent armies also required the enhancement of the administrative power of the state within the armed forces, i.e. the accentuation of military discipline. Similarly, changes in the technology and organization of naval power made possible unprecedented levels of sea-borne expansions. Thus, the state system through warfare and diplomacy influenced the emergence and diffusion of the absolutist state.

How inter-state competition and warfare influenced early modern state formation constitutes the main concern of historical sociology, in which the fiscal-military model of the Max Weber-Otto Hintze tradition is the prevailing approach.[44] Weber emphasizes that, '[t]he bureaucratic tendency has chiefly been influenced by needs arising from the creation of standing armies as determined by power politics and by the development of public finance connected with the military establishment.'[45] The thesis of military revolution confirms the Weberian argument. First formulated by Michael Roberts, the military revolution between 1560 and 1660 denotes four changes in the art of war: tactical changes based on the introduction of muskets and arrows replacing the lance and the pike; the growth of army size; the adoption of more complex strategies and the increasing impact of war on society. Similar changes in history are known to have led to significant international changes. Radical change in the practice of warfare, for instance, led to the emergence of a unified Chinese empire between 246 and 221 BC.[46] In Europe, however, the military revolution of the seventeenth century had the opposite effect: it consolidated the political fragmentation of the state system. In contrast to the empires of the East, in Europe the fragmented state system sparked an arms race facilitating market forces, stimulating competition and the emergence of economies of scale. Thus, the European states system created strong incentives for innovation, while Oriental empires lacked similar drives.[47] The fragmented state system also had important consequences for domestic regimes. Weber's immediate successor, Otto Hintze observes that large world empires correlate with despotic constitutions, while the plurality of states correlates with freer constitutions. In Europe, the plurality of sovereign states, which recognized each other's authority despite conflicts among them, not only created international law but influenced constitutional law as well. Combined with the conflict between the state and the church, political pluralism in the state system led to the emergence of estate assemblies. The pluralistic nature of the European state system also accounts for the transition from the corporate state (*Ständestaat*) to the absolutist state.[48]

In the Weberian tradition, Charles Tilly asserts that states always emerge in a system of states because they emerge out of competition for control of territory and population.[49] He explains the development of cities and states in terms of two variables: capital and coercion.[50] Using this analytical framework, Tilly distinguishes three types of state in European history since 990: tribute-taking empires; systems of fragmented sovereignty like city-states and urban federations; and national states. Empires emerged under conditions of low accumulation but high concentration of coercion. They usually depended on a large military apparatus oriented towards extraction of tribute, but left local administration to local power-holders. Systems of fragmented sovereignty were distinguished by high accumulation but low concentration of coercion. National states had medium levels of concentration with medium levels of accumulation. They always operated in a system of states. Rulers in all three types of state had to grapple with some common problems but in different ways. They had to distribute coercion unevenly in their domains, usually more concentrated in the center and at the frontiers. The larger the state and the greater the discrepancy between the distribution of coercion and capital, the stronger were the incentives against centralization. This constituted the main obstacle to empires in their rivalry with absolutist states. From the seventeenth century on, the capitalized coercion model proved more effective in interstate competition and became the model for other states. But before this convergence, all three paths led to different state forms.[51]

Similarly, Michael Mann asserts that three forces influenced early modern state formation: costs of warfare, inflation and the increase in the role of the state as the coordinator of the ruling class. Only the third is the distinguishing characteristic of the early modern state. But, at this stage, the state as a coordinator, is still not an organic state for the population to identify with. The power of the state is limited mainly to military and taxation functions; it coordinates the elites mainly for these two purposes.[52]

Mann focuses on the effects of the military revolution, which not only increased the costs of warfare but also transformed them into permanent public expenses. Inflation and growing costs of warfare led to the expropriation of church property, the debasement of coinage, the sale of crown lands, and public borrowing but, most importantly, the introduction of peacetime taxation. These changes within the early modern states also transformed the European state system and created systemic pressures on other states. Europe was to become a multi-state system, in which the main actors were more or less centralized territorial states with similar conceptions of state interests and formal diplomacy. Thus, the military revolution reduced the survival chances of the feudal states, city-states and city-leagues in the state system.[53] An important insight of Mann's analysis is the need for elite cooperation. Given the low level of technology, it was hard to assess where landed wealth was, even in the presence of standing armies. Under these circumstances, the central state needed the cooperation of the landed nobility. This dependence of the king on the landed nobility eventually led to an organic class-nation with the court or the court/parliament as the political center.[54]

The role of the absolutist state in coordinating collective action constitutes the focus of Norbert Elias's work. In absolutist states, the monarch's court was transformed into an institution which provided collective action and allocated resources. Court etiquette provided both the distancing of the king from the rest of the nobility and a means of domination. Political competition among the aristocracy was regulated through the rules of etiquette, conspicuous consumption and royal grants of income and title.[55] The aristocracy was forced to live in the court and cut its ties with the countryside. Conspicuous consumption meant that the nobility constantly lived at the edge of bankruptcy. Thus, absolutism created a court nobility dependent on the crown. The analysis of court society reveals the achievement of absolutism in facilitating collective action of the nobility. The bureaucratization and centralization of the state depended on the court as the institutionalization of collective action.

Fiscal unification was an important achievement of the absolutist court that enabled the constitution of the state as a unitary actor. Jean-Laurent Rosenthal explains this in a model in which the economy is divided into two sectors: one controlled by the elite (elite sector) and another controlled by the crown (royal sector). The elite and the crown share the fiscal burden of war-making. The spoils of war are distributed among the king and the elite according to the extent of their fiscal control over the economy. Thus, where the elite has more control over fiscal authority, profitable war-making becomes desirable for the elite.[56] Rosenthal also introduces ideological rewards (national, religious glory, etc.) of war as a determining factor in the decision to start a war. The ideological rewards are 'pure public rewards' or 'fixed rewards', which do not depend on the distribution of fiscal power. If fixed rewards are sufficiently large, then the elite and the crown will tend to unify taxation in the hands of the sector (elite or crown) which controls most of the economy. If the elite and the crown have approximately the same degree of control, they will struggle with each other and prevent fiscal unification.[57] Through fiscal unification and centralized financial institutions, the absolutist states could pool far more free resources than the empires which had much looser connections with their peripheries. The empires ruled over vast areas, but they could not translate the resources in these areas directly into political and military power.

Some studies also emphasize the ideological dimension of early modern state formation. In this context, Philip Gorski's recent work argues that 'state capacity is a function, not only of administrative rationalization, but of the strength of the social infrastructure and the rationality of sociopolitical ethics. The more extensive the infrastructure and the more rational the ethic, the stronger the state will be.'[58] Gorski asserts that Calvinism led to a new mode of statecraft which he dubs the disciplinary revolution. In his words, 'discipline increases state power insofar as it increases overall levels of administrative efficiency and social order because a more orderly society is cheaper to govern and a more efficient administration is cheaper to run.'[59] Gorski does not focus merely on absolutist states but also on republican states such as the Dutch United Provinces. Thus, he emphasizes the independent effect of the Protestant Reformations on early modern European states. In this regard, the territorial sovereign state was far more effective in social disciplining than the aristocratic empire in which the ruling class had no direct political relation to the tax-paying peasants. Daniel Nexon, however, wonders whether the effect of the Reformations is overstated. Reformations might have indeed served as catalysts of state formation which in fact was a product of military and economic change.[60] In Nexon's view rather than creating the sovereign-territorial state, the Reformations stimulated the formation of trans-state and trans-regional political movements based on religious identities which transformed the hub-and-spoke network structure of composite states. Nexon argues that a focus on the sovereign-territorial state is misleading and conceals how composite states have been much more prevalent even in the modern era. He argues that the problem lies with the ideal-type of sovereign-territorial state. Nexon asserts:

> Human history has never seen a sovereign-territorial state system of the kind that international-relations theorists take as a baseline for their debates. The kind of system described, for example, in structural-realist theory is an ideal type, not an exhaustive description of real political relations in international politics.[61]

Nexon's critique, however, does not amount to a critique of the construction of ideal-types as a methodology. Instead, he constructs ideal-types of formal properties of relational structures.[62] His idea-typification of early modern European states along two formal lines – form of rule and contracting – is an important step in the conceptualization of state forms. Thus, this conceptualization reveals how much early modern dynastic agglomerations such as England and France shared common characteristics of composite states with medieval empires.[63] Indeed, in terms of the composite nature of the state the French and the English monarchies had much in common with the Holy Roman and Ottoman Empires. However, the subtle differences were important enough to lead to different institutional trajectories. Unfortunately, Nexon does not dwell on the question of absolutism, a state form fervently debated in the historiography of early modern Europe. In order to improve historical-sociological concepts, Nexon's ideal-types need to be related to the historiographical debates on absolutism. In this regard, absolutism can be conceptualized as direct rule through heterogeneous contracting (what Nexon calls class-divided states).[64] Thus, the transition from empires to absolutist states involves the switch from indirect to direct rule.

Transition

Studies of the absolutist state might disagree on the causes of its emergence. However, they all agree that the absolutist state marked an unprecedented level of state centralization, autonomy from ascriptive settings and ability to coordinate collective action. In the administrative field it unified the legal system, relying mostly on Roman law. In the financial field it unified the fiscal system through new financial institutions such as central banks. In the field of foreign and military politics it introduced permanent armies under regular training, resident embassies and foreign offices specialized in the conduct of foreign policy. In all these fields the absolutist state generated more power and mobilized more resources than its predecessors – including the aristocratic empires of the Middle Ages. The review of the literature on the emergence of the absolutist state gives important reasons to go beyond state-centric analyses in international relations. If war-making and international competition put pressure on states to pursue more or less the same goals, historically the domestic social structure determines the form of the state and thus its capabilities in the state system. In contrast to Waltz and Wendt, this review illustrates that the autonomy of the modern state cannot be taken for granted when one is trying to theorize about systems change. The historical sociological literature of the absolutist state contributes to international relations by highlighting the political, social and economic conditions of the most basic unit of the international system, the modern state.

	From	To	Indications of transition
Administration	Multiple communities separately connected to a political center through peripheral governments (Indirect rule, heterogeneous contract)	Multiple communities within territorial boundaries directly connected to a political center (Direct rule, heterogeneous contract)	Unified, central administration, court society, social disciplining and coordination
Taxation	State only interested in taxation	State interested in commercialization	Fiscal unification, financial institutions, civil code
Conduct of Foreign Affairs	Universal suzerainty	Territorially bounded sovereignty	Military revolution and congress diplomacy
Political Legitimation	Legitimation by universalist religious discourse	Legitimation by *raison d'état*	Political thought based on state reason and natural law

Table 2.1: The transition from empire to absolutist state

The ideal-typical method constitutes an important topic for the study of international change as well as comparative political study. As Table 2.1 demonstrates, conceptualizing change in political science and historical sociology usually involves the description of the characteristics of some idealized state forms in a trajectory of stages. In the domain of administration, empires were ruled through powerful local magnates. Compared to absolutist states, imperial governments were much less interested in, and much less capable of, regulating the daily lives of their subject populations. Moreover, empires were marked by multiple communities that were subjected to their own customs and laws. In contrast, the absolutist state defined the population within its territorial boundaries as one single political community. Contrary to imperial suzerainty, territoriality was much more capable of creating mass political identification. The main advantage of the absolutist state was the territoriality of its political authority. Within its political boundaries the absolutist state coordinated the collective action of the nobility in the court and carried out political centralization and social disciplining. Lacking the territoriality of the absolutist state, the organizational principles of empires were the main obstacle in their competition with the state system.

In the domain of taxation, empires were interested only in the concentration of extraction in the imperial center, while absolutist states aimed at increasing their wealth through economic and fiscal policies. Whereas empires acted as universal entities, absolutist states could define their territories as economic units. Thus, the latter devised mercantilist policies to increase their share of world trade and domestic productivity. They introduced universal civil laws that created the legal infrastructure of early modern capitalism. The main result of these changes for state formation was fiscal unification and the emergence of financial institutions that increased the ability of the state to pool more resources for public projects (including war-making). Fiscal unification in turn contributed to the political centralization of the absolutist state. In contrast, empires experienced difficulties in mobilizing the enormous resources under their direct control. Without fiscal consolidation, empires increasingly failed to make accurate estimations and were significantly less able to endure prolonged warfare.

In the domain of foreign policy, empires claimed universal suzerainty over all other states, while absolutist states recognized other states as equal sovereigns. The territoriality of the absolutist state made it easier to establish reciprocal resident diplomacy with other states. Empires, with their pretensions of universal superiority, were unwilling to establish resident embassies. They preferred to maintain relations mainly through the embassies of other states in their capitals. The universalist ideology was also reflected in the conduct of foreign policy which was not differentiated from domestic politics. Empires regarded the world in terms of a continuum of political power from the imperial center of the universe to the peripheries – direct subjects, vassals and tributaries and barbarians. In contrast, absolutist states regarded the state system in terms of balance of power. They rationalized their foreign policy by centralizing decision-making in specialized bureaus and councils. The centralization of administration and fiscal unification also increased the capacity of the state in foreign policy making by enabling the state to organize and budget its activities more accurately.

The domain of political legitimacy was crucial for the transition, since reform in all three domains had to be justified politically. The universal suzerainty of empires was based on religious dogmas and the idea of a universal religious community. Since political legitimation was based on religion, politics was – to some extent – evaluated with regard to religious teachings. The absolutist state, by basing its authority on territoriality, managed to divorce political legitimation from the universal aspirations of religion. Absolutism was based on the theory of divine right, but increasingly political theory became autonomous, independent from theology and individual ethics. Thus, it provided the legitimating discourse of the absolutist state based on state interest. The autonomy of politics was legitimized by early modern doctrines of natural law that provided the basic discourse for both state formation and international law.

This scheme might seem too caricaturized, especially to historians of the period. Historian James Collins claims that the concept of 'absolute monarchy is a myth, promulgated by the royal government and legitimized by historians.'[65] Admittedly, the French state became stronger, more centralized, gathered more information, expanded outside of its traditional scope and enlarged its administration to involve not only the nobility but also lawyers, merchants and even farmers and artisans. Despite these changes, however, the state still retained many of its traditional features. According to Collins, the French king tried to combine a society of orders consisting of unequal social corporate actors such as the Church, the nobility, the towns and the guilds, and a society of classes which was composed of equal individuals. This early modern state was involved in mainly three areas: judiciary, warfare and taxation.[66] Although Collins disputes the absolute authority of the French king, he describes the growth and centralization of the judicial and financial institutions in the late sixteenth and seventeenth centuries. Indeed, no monarch enjoyed absolute power; royal authority was based on a coalition of social forces. The position of the monarch was always precarious. Tim Blanning points out:

> Of the last nine kings of France, two were assassinated (Henry III in 1589 and Henry IV in 1610), one was executed (Louis XVI in 1793), one died in prison (Louis XVII in 1795), one was exiled (Louis XVIII in 1815) and two fled (Charles IX in 1830, Louis Phillippe in 1848). The long period separating these two outbursts of regicidal activity was less placid than might appear. Louis XIII fought three wars against his Protestant subjects and had to surmount a major conspiracy led by his brother, Gaston, duc d'Orléans. His son, Louis XIV, never forgot

the night of 9–10 February 1651, when he was obliged to feign sleep in the Palais-Royal, as a mob of rebellious Parisians forced their way into his room to see for themselves that he was still in the capital and still their hostage.[67]

Absolutist monarchy served as the coordinator of collective action among the ruling elite, as the hub of the network. However, as the trajectory of the English monarchy illustrates, the coordination of the elite could also be facilitated under a model which came to be known as constitutional monarchy. Perry Anderson claims that the Norman and Angevin dynasties created the strongest monarchy in the West, which eventually became the weakest and the most short-lived absolutist state. A unified parliament was the creation of a unified monarchy.[68] It was not the existence of estate assemblies that actually marks the different trajectory of English political development from the continent. The English landowning class was unusually civilian and commercial. The consequence of this fact was a smaller bureaucracy, a limited fiscality and no permanent army.[69] Being an insular kingdom, the English monarchy never had to build a mass army like its European counterparts. These characteristics enabled the defeat of English absolutism by the bourgeois revolution. John Brewer also confirms the early centralization in England:

> As early as the thirteenth century feudal suzerainty in England had come to resemble royal sovereignty. The royal courts handled almost all important legal cases, the royal writ ran throughout the land, the monarch had established one of the most sophisticated financial systems in Europe centred on the royal exchequer, and the crown exacted taxes from the entire realm.[70]

Although the same degree of centralization was not the case for the British state (since Ireland, Scotland and Wales had considerable autonomy), the English state emerged much earlier compared to the French state. As the latter added new provinces, it evolved into a mosaic state. In contrast to the English parliament, which represented the entire community of the realm, the French estates-general never achieved the prowess of the provincial estates. Another important difference from continental state formation was also the decline of the English as a European military force between the end of the Hundred Years War (1453) and the second Hundred Years War (1689). Thus, England did not take a major part in the military revolution of the sixteenth and seventeenth centuries. For much of the period the

English state did not maintain a standing army. Observers like Lewis Namier and Otto Hintze emphasized that insular geography and naval power made a standing army a matter of choice rather than a necessity and thus prevented the emergence of absolutism in England. The equation of standing army with absolutism and navy with constitutional monarchy is however misleading. The English navy did not establish its naval hegemony until the mid and late seventeenth century. Moreover, the greatest naval build-ups occurred under the more autocratic regimes of Henry VIII and Cromwell. However, an invasion across the Channel was very costly and of little strategic value both for the French and the English. Thus, while the English state remained militarily inactive on the continent, it forged a British political union by conquest, annexation and assimilation, although English centralization was not to be repeated in the British context. An important upshot of English absence from continental warfare, however, was the light fiscal load for the state. While in continental Europe fiscal burdens urged the monarchs to sell state offices, in England, venality was much more limited. All contemporary monarchs and bureaucrats were aware of the financial liabilities created by the sale of offices in the long run. However, unlike English monarchs, continental monarchs needed the extra income to finance their wars. Thus, when the English military-fiscal state emerged in the late seventeenth century, it was much stronger than its continental counterparts. By that time England had already created a national judiciary and fiscal system maintaining high tax rates without much resistance.[71]

This brief discussion of French and English monarchies illustrates that the concept of the absolutist state is contested by various historians for various reasons. However, this study agrees with Tim Blanning, who suggests that 'in practice and theory, at the level of both perception and reality, absolute monarchy was an identifiable phenomenon. What it most certainly was not was omnicompetent or totalitarian.'[72]

In this regard, absolutism is used in a context-dependent fashion to delineate a historical trend in European history. Indeed, constructing ideal-types always involves more than just generalization. It also entails emphasizing the important aspects of a phenomenon for analysis. One important caveat is not to take these ideal-types as self-evident assumptions.[73] Methodologically, this is possible by combining individualizing, hermeneutic methods with systematic analysis of social structures and processes.[74] One can make a theory of international change more context-sensitive by taking the effect of past institutions and ideas on decision making at a given moment. In this regard, the following chapter will review how the conceptualization of social change by Avner Greif and Jürgen Habermas can contribute to the analysis of early modern state transformation and international change.

3
INSTITUTIONS AND WORLD-VIEWS

The late sixteenth- and early seventeenth-century state system put enormous pressure on all European states. However, how states responded to the survival imperatives of the system depended on two important factors: past institutions and legitimating discourses. Both factors influenced the formulation and implementation of reform as well as the direction and pace of institutional change. In this context, Avner Greif emphasizes that institutional change is determined by both exogenous factors (such as survival imperatives) but also by endogenous factors (such as existing state organs and value systems). Greif's analysis provides a useful model to understand institutional change and points out the role of belief systems in bringing about change. In this context, Jürgen Habermas's discussion on world-views presents an important guide to understanding when, how and why belief systems generate or suffocate critical and innovative thought. Both authors offer important insights into how imperial elites of the seventeenth-century Ottoman and Holy Roman Empires dealt with a changing international environment.

Institutional Change and Path Dependence

If military and economic changes put systemic pressures on all early modern states in Europe, including the Ottomans, how can one explain the different trajectories of state formation? Why was reform harder to formulate and implement in some states? Why would some inefficient institutions persist? The persistence of suboptimal institutions and endogenous institutional change constitute the core of Avner Greif's recent work. Greif starts with the concept of institutions as equilibria and defines transactions as his unit of analysis. Institutions provide micro-foundations of behavior and aggregate individual decisions. An important corollary of his conceptualization is the implication that past institutions lead societies towards different trajectories.[1]

A common definition of institutions in economics and international relations, for example, is based on the reduction of transaction costs. Greif emphasizes the centrality of intertransactional linkages to institutions. Institutionalized beliefs link one transaction to another transaction in specific ways and through specific means.[2] Thus, he defines an institution as 'a system of rules, beliefs, norms and organizations that together generate a regularity of (social) behavior.'[3] Rules make normative behavior explicit, disseminating a common cognitive system, and coordination and information, while beliefs and norms motivate individuals to follow the rules. Organizations make and disseminate these rules, reproduce the beliefs and norms motivating individual behavior and shape the set of feasible behavioral beliefs. Greif criticizes the neo-institutional approach for taking beliefs and norms as exogenous to the analysis. Rather than assuming that people simply follow rules, Greif points out the need to understand why people follow some rules rather than others.[4]

Greif argues that one needs to overcome the separation between two prevalent approaches to the study of institutions in the social sciences: the agency perspective defining institutions as reflections of the interests and intentions of their creators, and the structural perspective emphasizing how institutions influence people's preferences and behavior. While the former approach focuses on the micro-level, the latter prefers the macro-level of analysis. In Greif's view both approaches capture a different side of reality: institutions are both man-made and exogenous to individuals. Greif's definitions distinguish three aspects of institutions: their social, man-made character, their externality to individuals, and their generation of behavioral regularities. These aspects cannot be assumed *a priori* but need analytical and empirical examination.[5]

Human action is social to the extent that it is linked with the action of others. Therefore, the central focus in the study of institutions is transaction. A transaction denotes 'an action taken when an entity, such as a commodity, social attitude, emotion, opinion, or information, is transferred from one social unit to another.'[6] Greif distinguishes between central and auxiliary transactions. Central transactions are transactions in which an institution generates behavior. Auxiliary transactions facilitate the generation of beliefs about behavior in another transaction. When two trading partners sign a legal contract, the economic transaction constitutes the central transaction and the legal transaction constitutes the auxiliary transaction. Actions in auxiliary transactions generate institutional elements such as rules, norms and organizations. Organizations link a central transaction with an auxiliary transaction. In order to link an economic transaction to a legal transaction, a court system must exist to induce a belief in the legal sanctioning of behavior. With respect to the central transaction, organizations are institutional elements – components of institutions – influencing individual motivation. However, organizations can also be viewed as institutions in their own right with respect to their members' behavior. The courts system is an institutional component in the context of signing a trade contract, but it is an institution in the context of the behavior of judges, lawyers, attorneys, plaintiffs, defendants, etc.[7]

Drawing on game theory Greif claims that the only beliefs to be common knowledge are those regarding self-enforcing or equilibrium behavior. However, since there are usually multiple equilibria in social situations, just the knowledge of the structure of the situation and rationality is not enough to choose a particular path of action. Socially articulated and disseminated rules provide actors with cognitive, coordinative and informational guides of behavior. Based on these guides individuals form beliefs about the situation and what to expect from others. Common knowledge is very important since it enables different individuals to attribute the same meaning to a situation or action. Social pacts, customary rules, traditions, constitutions and laws embody rules that specify the meanings of actions and sanctions associated with their transgression. When each individual responds to a situation based on these rules and his/her private information, institutions aggregate private information and knowledge. When an institution generates behavior, each individual finds it optimal to follow the rules. Thus, game theory evaluates the logical consistency of an institution by associating institutionalized rules with the set of admissible beliefs and behavior that are self-enforcing.[8]

Game theory can explain the persistence of an institution when institutions generate behavior motivated by beliefs embodied in institutionalized rules. In such a framework, change can only be induced by exogenous changes making the current behavior no more self-enforcing. When institutions are conceptualized as equilibrium phenomena, explaining endogenous change becomes difficult since no individual has an incentive to change the rules. In order to refine this framework, Greif introduces two concepts: quasi-parameters and institutional reinforcement. Game theory distinguishes between the parameters and variables of a game. Parameters (number of players, payoff structure, time discount factors, risk preferences, wealth, etc.) are exogenous to the game and their change implies a new equilibrium.

Variables are endogenously determined outcomes of the game. Greif argues that some aspects of the game can be treated as exogenous and parametric in the short run, but as endogenous and variable in the long run. If self-enforcing outcomes influence the values of a parameter in the long run, i.e. lead to long-term behavioral change, then these parameters need to be re-defined as quasi-parameters. If the behavior through the changes in quasi-parameters increases the range of parameter values in which the institution is self-enforcing, then an institution is self-reinforcing. If an institution is self-reinforcing, more individuals in more situations will behave in accordance with the rules of the institutions. In such cases even exogenous changes may not induce institutional change. In contrast, a self-enforcing institution can be self-undermining if changes in quasi-parameters cause the behavior to be self-enforcing in a smaller set of situations. If changes in quasi-parameters are unobservable, learning will be slow and it will take time for self-undermining to lead to a behavioral change. When institutional changes could not be foreseen *ex ante*, but past behavior is perceived as suboptimal *ex post*, the change will be sudden and institutional change can be described as punctuated equilibria. If the changes in quasi-parameters are observed and understood, institutional change will be intentional and gradual.[9]

Greif points out that past institutional elements influence the direction of institutional change. There is an asymmetry between past institutional elements and technologically feasible alternatives. Past institutional elements constitute part of individual memories, cognitive models, and preferences, and thus become default options in new situations by providing individuals with cognitive, informational, coordinative, and normative guidelines. Moreover, the creation of new institutional elements induces bargaining, coordination, search, and learning costs. Because organizations are both institutions and institutional elements, they do not stop being self-enforcing even though the institution which they are part of is no longer self-enforcing. Organizations also usually defend their interests by leading institutional change. Institutional change is characterized by institutional refinement, with environmental, coordination and inclusive effects. Institutional refinement is the attempt to reinforce rather than create new institutions. Greif argues that wholesale institutional change is only possible during times of crisis in which past institutions are perceived as deficient. He chooses Ottoman military reform as an example of such radical change in which Western army structure was selected as the role model. Past institutions have an environmental effect on new institutions since they are exogenously given. Existing institutions also have a coordination effect on new institutions by serving as focal points in new situations. Finally, the inclusion effect reflects how past institutional elements are included in new institutions. These effects of past institutions indicate that institutions form institutional complexes in which one institution supports another. Institutions within a complex reinforce each other and increase the cost of institutional change, which is less likely to occur but more likely to be comprehensive when it does occur. The concept of path dependence emphasizes how past institutions influence institutional change and evolutionary trajectories.[10]

Path dependence explains how institutions can persist even if they become suboptimal. It denotes that once a path is taken relevant actors adjust their strategies to the prevailing pattern. Once introduced, institutions develop their own logic, stabilize actor expectations and contribute to the maintenance of particular strategies and behavior. Two concepts of institutional analysis provide useful insights into institutional change: institutional layering, the creation of new institutional arrangements on top of existing institutions, and institutional conversion, the redirection of institutions from their original goals to new ones.[11]

In this regard, the comparative study of the evolution of political institutions, designed to induce collective action for taxation, war-making, foreign policy conduct and legitimation in the Holy Roman and Ottoman Empires, yields important results for the study of early modern state formation. The initial institutions in the two empires deeply influenced political outcomes in the seventeenth and eighteenth centuries. The Holy Roman Empire was characterized by a weak royal court and monarch, strong representative assemblies, and the lack of a political capital, centralized bureaucracy or fiscal policy. Weak imperial institutions enabled the Habsburgs, as well as other German princes, to establish their territorial absolutist states. In contrast, the Ottoman Empire had a strong court, centralized bureaucracy and treasury and no representative assembly. Strong imperial institutions prevented the transformation of the Ottoman state into a territorial absolutist monarchy until the nineteenth century. Thus, the two cases provide a critical pair to study the effects of path dependency and collective action in the adaptability of states to a changing inter-state environment.

Greif's model emphasizes the importance of the change in cultural beliefs and public discourse for institutional change. In this vein, Timur Kuran's theory of preference falsification predicts that a community might be attached to a status quo even if none of its members intends to sustain the status quo as such. Recent history certainly shapes expectations and choices, but, more importantly, the incumbent equilibrium has the capacity to reshape expectations of public opinion. Indeed, individual actors may refrain from expressing their demand for change in order to avoid punishments. When inefficiency is maintained by preference falsification, actors pursuing their interests may end up reproducing the inefficiency on the aggregate level. Thus, inefficiency is not caused by the inability of the actors to follow their self-interest, but rather by their proficiency in maximizing it.[12] In this regard, this insight of new institutionalism connects well with Habermas's discussion of the rationalization of world-views. What kind of belief systems and what kind of sociological conditions are conducive to the emergence of self-critical and self-reflexive world-views capable of generative innovative thought and reform?

Rationalization of the Life-world and Institutional Change

Rationality and Legitimacy of Institutional Change

Similar to Greif, Jürgen Habermas is also concerned with combining an agent perspective with a system perspective. He also emphasizes the critical point at which changes in fundamental institutional elements (quasi-parameters) lead to institutional reinforcement or self-undermining. His classification of the crisis tendencies in the modern state is helpful for conceptualizing the dynamics of institutional change. According to Habermas, not every systemic pressure leads to crisis. Crisis occurs when social actors feel that their identities are threatened and the ground for social consensus is shaken. In this sense, 'the crisis situations have the form of a disintegration of social institutions.'[13] But crises do not always occur when the members of a society simply say they do. They are caused by the steering problems of social systems that are influential in the consciousness of individuals.[14]

The concept of crisis captures the extent of the problems faced by imperial rulers in the seventeenth century, when the survival imperatives of the state system threatened the organizational principles of medieval empires. What state-centric theories of international relations miss is the fact that the capability of the imperial ruling elite to solve the crisis depended on their collective learning capacity, which was limited by the organizational principles of the state. Organizational principles 'delimit the capacity of the society to learn without losing its identity.'[15] They lay down learning mechanisms, determine the scope of variation for identity-securing meanings systems, and set down the institutional limits to the possible increase in steering capacity. The basic organizational principles of empires were their rule over multiple communities, exclusive focus on taxation, and universal suzerainty justified by religion. These principles were changed in an absolutist state: rule over an agglomeration of communities defined by territorial boundaries, interest in increasing productivity and commercialization, and territorially bounded sovereignty, recognizing other states as equals. As absolutist states increased their political capacity in the seventeenth-century state system, survival imperatives initiated a crisis for empires that could not be solved within the possible range of social change defined by imperial organizational principles.

The prevalent Weberian approaches in historical sociology, which conceptualize early modern state formation only in terms of instrumental rationality, cannot appreciate the limits on reforms set by organizational principles. According to this approach, competition against other states and domestic power holders increases the instrumental rationality of the state. Such a conception neglects the ideological aspects of the emergence of the absolutist state. In his studies on economic rationality, Weber points out how the change in moral values brought on by Calvinism paved the way for economic rationality. Nevertheless, in his studies of state formation he narrows down his definition of rationality and explains the development of political, bureaucratic rationality solely as a response to military rivalry. However, a change in dominant moral values and legitimating discourses was also necessary for instrumental rationality to become dominant in the political domain. Machiavellian separation of state interest and personal virtue could find fertile ground only in the legitimating principles of the territorial state. In this regard, state formation in the fields of administration, taxation and military and foreign policy had to be justified by political discourse. As we will see in the case studies, the inability to legitimize reforms can effectively block them. Thus, following Jürgen Habermas, the study of state formation needs to account for the legitimacy and justification of bureaucratization.[16] In this regard, the transition of empires claiming universal suzerainty to absolutist states claiming territorially bounded sovereignty reveals a legitimation crisis faced by the monarch and the ruling class. Despite their enormous resources, the imperial dynasties faced two problems in their competition with other states: first, the institutional reorganization of political authority over vast and diverse territories; second, the shifting of the legitimation basis of the polity from universal suzerainty to absolutist sovereignty, which recognizes other states as equals.

The solutions to this crisis were conceived and implemented by the imperial ruling elite, which tried to balance the requirements of the state system with the state's need for legitimacy. Habermas's discussion of rationality and legitimation crises offers a useful conceptualization of these problems. The political system is fed by the input of mass loyalty and produces output in the form of administrative decisions. Output crises occur in the form of a rationality crisis, in which the state cannot render survival imperatives of the state system compatible with its organization of administration, taxation and conduct of foreign policy. Input crises occur in the form of a legitimation crisis, in which the state cannot maintain the level of loyalty for the implementation of reforms in order to increase competitiveness in the state system.[17] The systemic pressure on empires unleashed both a rationality crisis regarding the conduct of state affairs (involving administration, taxation and foreign affairs) and a legitimation crisis regarding the discrepancy of imperial suzerainty with the principle of territorial sovereignty. The specific historical form that the Holy Roman and Ottoman Empires took in the seventeenth and eighteenth centuries was contingent upon the particular solution devised by their respective ruling elites to strike a balance between solving the rationality and legitimation crises. Bureaucratization and rationalization of administration, taxation and the conduct of foreign affairs could proceed only when the organizational and legitimating principles provided an adequate motivational framework.

The capability for institutional reform was intimately linked with the law-making capability of the state. Law has a dual function for the state: First, it is an organizational tool; the state decrees its orders, institutionalizes its practices, and organizes itself through law. Second, law embodies values that cannot be controlled by the state. This relative autonomy of the values procures legitimacy for political authority.[18] Law is the mechanism by which society sanctions deviant behavior.[19] Legal institutions stabilize behavioral expectations and social interaction. They also embody moral values legitimated by legal discourses.[20] The ability of imperial elites to introduce reforms relied on the existing legal institutions and the legal discourse legitimizing these reforms. Since the transition from empire to absolutist state required a drastic change in the organizational principles of the state, reforms of imperial organizational principles would be regarded as deviant behavior as long as legitimating values remained unchanged. Thus, the reform capacity of imperial elites was determined largely by the law-making capability of the state. A major advantage of the absolutist state was its monopoly over law-making and its capacity to promulgate new codifications and regulations.[21] This increase in the law-making capacity of the absolutist state was a product not only of bureaucratization but also of a change in normative structures.

Rationalization of Life-World and Law: Discourse and State Formation

What kind of legal institutions and discourses can induce institutional stagnation and rigidity? Habermas's answer to this question rests on the concept of life-world (*Lebenswelt*). The life-world stores the interpretations of previous generations and thus, constitutes a conservative counterbalance against the risks of dissent. Daily social communication entails a process of reaching an understanding in which actors either accept or refute the validity claims raised by another. The life-world provides the common knowledge or what Greif would call internalized beliefs against which certain behavioral beliefs could be validated or denied. Historically, different world-views varied in their potential for rational action.

Habermas's concept of rationalization departs from a narrow Weberian conception defining rationality. According to Habermas, the rationality of life-forms cannot be measured solely by only looking at the cognitive adequacy of the underlying world-views, i.e. the coherence and the truth of possible propositions, but also the efficiency of action plans.[22] In this context, Habermas approaches human learning not solely from a cognitive-instrumental aspect, but also from moral-practical and expressive aspects. He relies on Piaget's concept of learning, which distinguishes the stages of cognitive development not by new contents but by structurally described levels of learning capability. Habermas suggests that similar conceptualization of learning might be applied to world-views.[23] In this regard, cognitive development is predicated upon the decentralization of an egocentric world understanding. A reflexive and critical attitude towards a certain world-view can only develop as far as the cognitive, moral and expressive references to the world are differentiated. As long as the world-view remains sociocentric it does not allow a differentiation between existing facts, valid norms and expressible subjective experiences. The linguistic world-view is reified and cannot be penetrated as a criticizable interpretive system.[24] Habermas distinguishes between closed and open world-views. Closed world-views secure social identity by inhibiting interpretative alternatives. Legitimacy is procured at the expense of individual participation and reflection. These world-views curtail the individual's readiness to learn and ability to criticize.[25] They do not allow any differentiation between the validity claims pertaining to existing facts, social norms and subjective experiences.

A reflexive and critical attitude against a world-view can develop only as far as cognitive, moral and expressive validity claims are differentiated. The rationalization of the life-world is facilitated only through the decentralization of the world-view, in which objective, social and subjective value spheres follow their own logic. These value spheres provide the basic concepts with which individuals interpret the world.[26] Objective advances in each sphere become possible only when science, morality, and art are differentiated into autonomous spheres of values, each under autonomous validity claims – truth, normative rightness, and authenticity or beauty.[27] Thus, rationalization in a single value sphere can be measured by value-enhancement with respect to the corresponding validity claim. Subjecting a scientific theory to normative validity claims (like the Inquisition's condemnation of Galileo Galilei's heliocentric explanation of the universe) for example, can constitute a significant block on the development of the scientific value sphere. The transition from traditional to modern world-view is backed by the rationalization of the life-world, which involves the transition from a normatively prescribed consensus to a communicatively reached understanding.[28]

In this respect, the real difference between modern and pre-modern world-views does not lie on the level of logical operations and is not determined by the cognitive development of individuals. The rationality of world-views is not measured against the yardstick of logical and semantic features, but by the basic concepts with which individuals interpret the world.[29] Traditional life-forms are expressed in particular and overlapping group identities which are maintained by particular traditions. In modern societies these life-forms lose their totalizing powers and become subject to the universalism of morality and law.[30] The differentiation of culture, society and personality is accompanied by a differentiation of form and content at those levels. At the cultural level, identity-securing (*identitätsverbürgende*) traditions depart from their contexts and are replaced by formal elements like world concepts, communication assumptions, argumentation processes, abstract values etc. At the societal level, general principles are derived out of particular contexts. Principles of legal order and morality become less related to particular life-forms. At the level of personality, cognitive structures are freed from contexts of cultural knowledge.[31]

However, if the decentralization of the life-world means that all three value spheres (objective, subjective and social) become autonomous and follow their own logic, what re-establishes the unity of the modern life-world? What procures legitimacy and rationally motivates the individual in modern society? For Habermas, the formal procedure of argumentative redemption (*Einlösung*) of validity claims secures the unity of rationality and thereby, the unity of the life-world. Validity claims are distinguished from empirical claims through the presupposition that they can be made good by means of arguments. Only and only arguments and reasons can unfold the power of rational motivation.[32]

Rationalization of the world-view is essential for the rationalization of the legal system and law-making. Habermas suggests that the disenchantment of the religious world-view and the decentralization of the life-world are preconditions for the transformation of sacral legal concepts by principally free and equal members of a legal community.[33] In conceptualizing legal evolution and its connection to morality Habermas relies on L.Kohlberg's stages of moral consciousness (see Table 3.1).[34]

Stages of moral consciousness	Basic socio-cognitive concepts	Ethics	Types of law
Pre-conventional	Particular behavioral expectations	Magical ethics	Revealed law
Conventional	Norm	Ethics of the law	Traditional law
Post-conventional	Principle	Ethics of conviction and Ethics of responsibility	Formal law

Table 3.1: Stages of moral and legal development according to Habermas

At the pre-conventional stage an action is only evaluated with regard to its consequences, at the conventional stage with regard to its conformity to or violation of norms, while at the post-conventional stage norms themselves are evaluated under the light of principles. Higher stages of moral development indicate higher levels of differentiation between law and ethics. At the stage of principally-led (*prinzipiengeleitet*) or post-conventional moral consciousness, morality is deinstitutionalized, so that it is anchored only in the personality system as internal behavior control. Simultaneously, law becomes an externally imposed force. Modern compulsory law (*Zwangsrecht*) is sanctioned by the state and disconnected from the customary (*sittlich*) motives of the legal community and is an institution predicated upon abstract legal obedience.[35] Thus, while morality becomes an autonomous private sphere accessible only to the individual, law becomes an autonomous public sphere with an inherent logic independent from morality.[36]

Jürgen Habermas and Klaus Eder suggest that in social evolution, higher levels of integration cannot be established until the founding of legal institutions which incorporate higher levels of moral consciousness. As long as the kinship system is embodied as a total institution, as in tribal societies, there is no place for jurisdiction.[37] In archaic societies interactions are determined solely by the roles of kinship. In status societies, where the place of the family within society becomes more important than one's own place within the family, the concept of status becomes central. Status order is determined by participation in political power and position in the production process. The nucleus of political power is the royal office of the judge, which is predicated on the legitimacy of the legal order.[38]

Conventional moral consciousness was formed in such status or class-divided societies. Only the consciousness of traditionally anchored and morally obligating norms enables a transformation of factual power into normative power. Only the availability of legitimate power enables the political enforcement of legal norms. Only forcible law can be used for the organization of state power. Thus, religiously embedded morality, legally legitimized power and legally organized administration are co-constitutive.[39] Traditional law emerges first in the transition to conventional legal and moral discourse, which judges action in the light of given legal norms. These judgments are of course still particularistic and not based on universalistic legal principles. This is accomplished by early modern natural law. In its initial stage, natural law of course still holds to the idea of the givenness of legal principles. Only when this idea is first shaken and these principles themselves become reflexive, can law become positive in the strict sense.[40] The rationalization of the life-world makes it increasingly harder to legitimate a law that is legislated by a ruler by referring to tradition and custom.[41] In the modern legal system, post-conventional morality and law are differentiated and laws can be criticized. These post-conventional concepts of law and morality were first developed in the form of rational natural law (*Vernunftsrecht*). The natural law model for the justification of legal norms is an uncoerced agreement (*ungezwungene Vereinbarung*), in which the participants meet each other as free and equal contractual parties. Modern law needs an autonomous justification independent of sheer tradition, so that, in Weber's terms, traditional consensus is replaced by rational consensus.[42]

The notion of legal evolution drawn above can be criticized in several aspects. Susan Reynolds criticizes the presentist notion that modern society is superior in rationality to medieval society. She argues:

> We have our superstitions and rituals too, which we take for granted or explain away. 'Primitive people may, like us, operate on several

levels of belief and reasoning; you do not have to believe that God intervenes directly in an ordeal in order to accept its result any more than you have to believe in the invariable fairness and rationality of juries in order to accept theirs.[43]

In a different vein, Seyla Benhabib points out the gendered nature of the autonomous individual taken as a model of mature moral agency by Jean Piaget and Lawrence Kohlberg. She draws on Carol Gilligan who questions whether moral principles can be deduced merely from procedural and formal qualities of moral laws. In this respect, Gilligan's feminist critique converges with neo-Aristotelian and neo-Hegelian critics of neo-Kantian formalism arguing that moral judgments of justice and good government (i.e. legitimacy) cannot be divorced from cultural values. Piaget, Kohlberg and Habermas define morality only by issues of justice leaving out questions of altruism and care for others. But, in every society morality does not only regulate human conflict but also collective action. As Benhabib emphasizes, however, the definition of the moral domain can be expanded without dropping a commitment to the discursive procedure for the validation of moral norms.[44] There are differences between justifications based on belief in the regenerative capacity of ritual, belief in the appropriateness of a decision to a myth or a religious precept and belief in the legality of a decision. The difference of discursive justification is not so much in the metaphysical content of the beliefs, but in the formal-pragmatic, communicative presuppositions of justifications.

Finally, what is the heuristic value of the concepts of stages for understanding social and political development? Stephen Toulmin suggests stages should be a 'descriptive convenience' rather than 'the basis for the discovery of "laws" or "mechanisms" of development.'[45] Toulmin argues that a healthy balance between a deductive and inductive method can be struck to make such a conceptualization useful. If one accepts epistemology as an *a priori* subject, one can start with an ideal-type of the modern state (commonly the Weberian state) independent of and logically prior to empirical studies. Thus, by analyzing the logical prerequisites of political development one can define a standard historical sequence defining the normal and necessary stages. In this research design, the task of empirical study is to specify the sociological conditions enhancing or limiting a state's development. Toulmin suggests that this approach can be maintained only as an initial step, but cannot be maintained throughout for the analysis not to lapse into Cartesian oversimplification. In contrast, if one invokes an empiricist epistemology, the evolution of the state is studied without any preconception by reporting the appearance of capacities, institutions and policies with the passage of time. There is nothing necessary nor normative about the historical sequence. One cannot talk about a successful or an unsuccessful state formation. This approach, however, neglects the environment within which state formation takes place. In order to avoid this, the researcher must maintain a dialectical link between particular conceptual and particular empirical questions. Thus, conceptual analyses should lead to empirical questions, whose answers should lead to a refinement of concepts and the formulation of new empirical questions.[46] In this context, Toulmin's critique of Piaget for neglecting the social aspects of child development can be also instructive for Habermas's conceptualization of moral and legal development.[47] Rationalization of the world-view in a society should be thought of as a process shaped by its past institutions and its experience in relations with other societies.

Overview of the Argument

Habermas's attempt to link the rationalization of law to the development of moral concepts and interpretive frameworks has important consequences for state formation that have not yet been explored. The state's ability to implement institutional reform is not only constrained by material resources or their institutional organization, but also by the rigidity of the underlying moral structure. Medieval aristocratic empires like the Holy Roman and Ottoman Empires were legitimized with reference to the universalism of world religions. The legislative power of these empires was constrained by the rigidity of their prevalent world-view, since law-making derived its legitimacy from sacral law and imperial custom and not only from state interest. The fact that their legitimating imperial discourses were far removed from the realities of international politics – the empires were never universally suzerain – reflects the unity of the objective, subjective and social value spheres. Subjective experience and objective reality were subjugated to the normative precepts of Christianity and Islam. Under these circumstances, it was increasingly difficult for empires to implement reform in order to compete with the absolutist states of the sixteenth century. The imperial government's authority was constrained by sacral law as the legitimating discourse, as well as the existing institutions embodied in customary law. In contrast, absolutist states shifted their legitimation basis to natural law, which gave the rulers an opportunity to displace sacral law and custom. In absolutism, the church was not the representation of a universal ecumene, but a tool of state formation.

Habermas's discussion of rationalization of the life-world illustrates the importance of world-views for institutional reform. The concept of sovereignty, as the indivisible and inalienable rule over a territory, had to be legitimated by recourse to the nature of the relationship between the ruler and the subjects, i.e. the social contract. Thus, natural law became the legitimating discourse for both the early modern state (in the field of public law) and the state system (in the field of international law). The emergence and impact of natural law, however, was conditioned by existing institutions and discourses. In other words, legal institutions and legal discourse played an important role in state formation and the adaptability of states to their international environment.

4

LEGAL EVOLUTION AND STATE FORMATION: A COMPARISON OF ROMAN LAW AND ISLAMIC LAW

Neo-realist and constructivist approaches in international relations have neglected the role of law in enhancing the capacity of the state in the international system. Yet without the proper legal infrastructure it is impossible for the state to act as the unitary autonomous actor that underpins the theories of both Kenneth Waltz and Alexander Wendt. This chapter compares the legal traditions in the Holy Roman and Ottoman Empires and asks whether Roman law was better equipped for institutional reform than Islamic law. I investigate this question in two domains: legal institutions and legal discourse. Early modern state formation in Europe was marked by the emergence of the state as a legal person and the emergence of natural law as the legitimating discourse. These institutional and discursive changes in Europe were possible thanks to the decline of the idea of a universally suzerain empire. In contrast, the absence of such changes in the Ottoman state is explained by the persistence of the claim of a universally suzerain empire.

The first section explains how the development of legal personality in Roman law helped the state to achieve the legislative autonomy necessary to introduce legal codification. It then discusses the consequences of the lack of legal personality in Islamic law. It demonstrates that the autonomy of the state, a fundamental assumption for Waltz and Wendt, required a legal framework allowing the state to act as a unitary actor. The second section compares the organization and legal traditions of Latin Christianity and Sunni Islam, with their respective implications for state-formation in the Ottoman and Holy Roman Empires. It demonstrates that the historical variation of political systems within Christianity and Islam cannot be explained merely by reference to religious doctrines, but needs to take into account the organizational principles and their embodiments, political institutions. The last section examines the conditions surrounding the emergence of natural law in Europe and its absence in the Ottoman Empire. It asserts that modern natural law cannot be conceived as a Judeo-Christian tradition handed down from the Ancient Stoics to European humanists. Natural law is conceptualized as the legitimating discourse of the territorial state in Europe.

Legal Institutions

The concept of the state as a legal person proved essential for the enhancement of state autonomy, the regulation of social interaction and the secularization of political authority. The state as a corporate body or, in Alexander Wendt's terms, the 'corporate identity of the state,' represents the constitution of a legal community under a single law within a bounded territory. In a law-making state, the will of the sovereign rather than God's will becomes the sole source of law. Law functions as an instrument for the state to organize itself, to reach its political, social and economic goals, to legitimize its activities and, finally, to forge a legal community constituting the subjects of the state. The relation between divinity and the ruler is replaced by the relation between the territory and the state. Thus, the development of legal personality has important implications for the modern state system.

Legal Personality and State Formation

The concept of legal personality separate from real persons is a distinctive product of European legal development. Legal personality allows a collective group to act as a unitary actor in the legal system, to regulate its own affairs, to issue its own by-laws, to have representation against third parties and to keep its existence and its assets separate from the existence and assets of its individual members. As such, legal personality is an important element in the legal infrastructure of various modern organizations such as states, business ventures and international and transnational organizations.

Legal personality provides the modern state with the concept or the capability of legal rights and duties.[1] These legal capabilities cannot be reduced to the state's members, constitution, powers, or purposes. They belong to the state as an independent entity.[2] Legal capacity enables the state to muster more resources and coordinate individual and collective interests by providing legal regulation. Legal personality also generates an objective system of subjective rights for the subjects leading to their identification with the legal community sharing the same legal system. Thus, by acquiring legal personality the state also establishes more direct and more homogenous relations with the subject population. As such, legal personality increases a state's capability for collective action by providing a more efficient institutional framework and by increasing the probability of individual identification with a larger legal community.

Historically, these aspects of a modern legal personality first emerged in Europe with the corporation. The corporation (*universitas*) is a group of people which has a legal personality distinct from the persons comprising the group and which does not perish when its members die or change. The debt owed by the corporation is not collected from the members individually but collectively.[3] As Timur Kuran emphasizes, limited liability for members of a partnership, i.e. owner shielding, is a common element of most forms of business partnerships or religious endowments. The distinct quality of the corporation is the liability for the corporation itself, i.e. entity shielding.[4] In this regard, the development of the business corporation reveals the strengths of legal personality as an administrative technology. The development of joint-stock companies in the form of corporations paralleled the development of depersonalized government. In order to illustrate how legal personality can enhance the capabilities of the state, a comparison from business law is useful.[5] In Islamic law, the absence of the concept of corporation led to economic inefficiency since Muslim business partnerships tended to be relatively purpose-specific and short-lived. European business corporations, on the other hand, could pool enormous amounts of capital through entity shielding. Even when the shares of the corporation were divided among many, the corporation would continue to exist.[6]

Analogous to business partnerships, legal personality also helped states to pool more resources, mobilize and discipline their populations, make more credible commitments and finally undermine the actions of those entities which had no legal personality.[7] States with legal personality could offer entity shielding and make more credible commitments both domestically and internationally. As a corporate body, the state could be conceived as independent from the person of the ruler. It became an entity outliving the ruler and the sole bearer of liability for its actions.[8] Thus, over time, those states without legal personality could enter domestic and international contracts only with very high transaction costs. However, the emergence of the state as a legal person was not only influential in the conduct of state affairs but more broadly in the conduct of social interaction. The concept of the state as an independent body led to a separation of public and private legal spheres. Private law endowed the subjects of a state with inalienable rights and provided the basic legal infrastructure for the market thereby leading to the rationalization of the economy. The legal protection of private economic activity not only enhanced the tax base of the state but also its opportunities to borrow money for its public projects (including public works as well as war-making).

In addition to its role in enhancing the organizational capacity of the state, legal personality also increased the chances of individual identification with the state.[9] In the traditional society of the Middle Ages these identities were defined by guilds, cities, villages and the church, while feudal kingdoms were conceived as communes of the realm. In contrast, the state as a legal person provided a dominant identity for all the members of the legal community. In contrast to the commune of the realm, territorial monarchies provided an objective system of subjective rights to all subjects and gradually eliminated local and social privileges and customs.[10] Thus, legal personality and the concept of the corporation in Europe provided the modern state with both an efficient administrative technology and an effective identification. The next section will discuss how and why legal personality emerged in Latin Europe and not in Eastern Europe or the Middle East.

The Origins of the Concept of Legal Personality

When and why did the concept of legal personality emerge? Legal historians usually trace its origins to the concept of the corporation in classical Roman law.[11] The Eastern Roman Emperor Constantine (*circa* 272–337) established the church as a *corpus*.[12] According to the Digest of Justinian (part of the *Corpus Iuris Civilis* promulgated between 529 and 534), the notion of the corporation is based on the model of the ancient Roman state (*ad exemplum rei publicae*).[13] Despite the affinity of the medieval concept of corporation with the corporation of classical Roman law, the European concept of corporation was not inherent in classical Roman law but emerged from the interpretation of Roman law in the twelfth and thirteenth centuries after the decline of the authority of the Holy Roman Empire and the Gregorian reform of the Roman Catholic Church. According to Otto Hintze, the emergence of the corporation in Latin Europe was made possible by the political fragmentation of the state system.[14] The medieval interpretation based on the study of Roman law became the predominant mode of conceptualizing the state until the mid-seventeenth century when new ideas of natural law mutated European legal thinking once more.[15]

Despite its origins in Roman civil law, the term *corpus* was used in an ecclesiological rather than legal sense throughout the Ancient and Middle Ages. Saint Paul referred to the whole church as the body of Christ, composed of faithful believers (*universitas fidelium*). Every Christian was reborn through baptism as a member of the *corpus Christi* and, accepting the law given by God, was transformed into a believer (*fidelis*).[16] The concept of legal personality and corporation was derived from Roman law only around 1200 by scholars of canon law in Latin Europe.[17] Prior to that, and similar to Islamic law, collectivities in Europe had no legal personality. As in Islamic law, these collectivities were represented by real persons such as abbots, mayors, syndics and reeves.[18]

What gave impetus to the emergence of the concept of legal personality? The work of legal historian Harold Berman provides support for Otto Hintze's argument that the emergence of corporations is related to the fragmentation of the state system in Europe and the antagonism between church and empire. The reforms of Pope Gregory VII (1075–1122) established the Roman Catholic Church as a corporate body with its own hierarchy, rules, and ecclesiastical courts. One of the major aims of the reforms was to assert control over ecclesiastical properties, especially lands owned by the Church. The reforms of the Papacy emulated those of the Abbey of Cluny founded in 910 by the Count of Auvergne in today's France. For the first time, the Cluniac reform established a hierarchy of monasteries which had previously been part of a loose federation. Its aim was to save the monastery from the interference of lay rulers – feudal lords and kings but especially the emperor. The Gregorian reform adopted Cluniac principles to organize the Roman Catholic Church[19] in order to assert its authority against the authority of the emperor and other feudal lords.[20]

The decline of a universally suzerain empire in Latin Europe made it possible for the Roman Catholic Church to assert its spiritual authority and its institutional autonomy from secular rulers. This led to the emergence of the legal concept of corporation and thus legal personality as legal technology. Throughout the Middle Ages, the corporation theory of the *Corpus Iuris Civilis* became the predominant model.[21] By the mid-seventeenth century, however, this model became increasingly obsolete to explain the growing public law in the Holy Roman Empire. The constitutional reality of the empire stood in stark contrast to the imperial model of Justinian. The challenge of absolutism to this model can be observed in the reception of Bodin's theory of sovereignty in the empire. While Roman civil law became a conservative force defending the corporate autonomy of municipalities, natural law provided the legitimating discourse for the early modern state by predicating the absolute authority of the state on the absolute will of the individual.[22] Thus, while the corporation theory of Roman law enabled the conceptualization of the state as a person with rights and obligations, it was natural law that combined this theory with the political theory of sovereignty. In this regard, a closer look at the emergence of natural law is essential to understand the institutional and discursive changes that accompanied the rise of the early modern state.

Indeed, religion played an important role in the evolution of legal traditions, which were legitimized by reference to religion. Thus, before proceeding to the study of early modern natural law, it is useful to compare the organizational and discursive traditions of Sunni Islam and Latin Christianity to delineate their role in the Holy Roman and Ottoman Empires. As the next section demonstrates, the divergence of Islam and Latin Christendom in the organization of religion and law can be explained in part by the presence or absence of a universally suzerain empire rather than solely by theological orientations.

Religion and the Rationality of Legal Traditions

Organization of Religion: the Papacy and the Caliphate

The fundamental difference between the organization of religion in Latin Europe and in Eastern Europe and the Middle East can be explained by the decline of imperial authority in the former and the persistence of imperial institutions in the latter. Although theological differences certainly made an impact on legal development in an age in which religion provided the main source of political legitimation, there is considerable variation in the organization of religion in both Christianity and Islam. This variation within religions and across time can be explained by variation in organizational principles and institutions.

The history of early Christianity in Western Europe and in the Eastern Roman Empire illustrates that Christianity as a religion did not mandate a strict division of secular and temporal authority. The codification of Emperor Justinian (529–534), which became the basis for the revival of Roman law in Europe, gave the emperor ultimate authority in religious matters. As the living law (*lex animata*), the emperor was the protector of the *oikumene*, including both the *imperium* and the *sacerdotium*. The *Novellae*, the compilation of Justinian's decrees, stipulated that God had given the emperor leadership of all nations in the Orient and Occident and appointed him as the guide of all divine things.[23] Early Christian councils were convened by imperial decrees. Ecclesiastical officers counted as public officers and were subject to the code of the imperial civil service. Hence, the separation between state and church did not originate from Roman law that conceptualized the emperor as the lord of the world (*dominus mundi*). The Roman form of government came to be known as caesaropapism which denotes the combination of secular government with, or its superiority to, the spiritual authority of the church.[24]

Early medieval Western Europe retained the ancient Roman caesaropapist system. In 794, Charlemagne summoned a universal church council where he made changes in ecclesiastical law and theological doctrine. In 813, he himself crowned his son. Moreover, of the twenty-five popes who held office in the century before 1059, twenty-one were directly appointed by the emperors and five were dismissed by emperors. Only in 1059 did a Roman council assert the right of the Roman cardinals to elect the pope. Most church property belonged to secular rulers such as emperors, kings and feudal lords. Clerical concubinage (nicolaism) was widespread and provided the clerics with connections to lucrative benefices (ecclesiastical offices). The Roman bishop was *primus inter pares* rather than being at the top of a hierarchy. He was revered as the deputy of St. Peter but only in the twelfth century did he start using the title, 'deputy of Christ' which, until then had been a title of the emperor.[25] Thus, in the early Middle Ages Western European Christianity resembled Eastern Orthodox Christianity; it was neither concerned with reform nor aspired to ecclesiastical unity and hierarchical organization.[26]

The distinction between state and church followed the decline of imperial authority in Western Europe. As the authority of the Eastern Roman government in Constantinople over the Italian peninsula waned, the Roman church supported the idea of the Carolingian Empire as an alternative. However, radical change occurred in 1075 when Pope Gregory VII issued a document entitled *Dictatus Papae* (Dictates of the Pope), in which he asserted the supremacy of the Pope over the whole church and the emperor. The Pope announced the Dictates to Emperor Henry IV, which resulted in the controversy known as the Investiture Struggle. In the end, neither party could actualize their initial claims, but the Gregorian reform changed Europe in a substantial way.[27] It not only established the Roman church as an independent corporate body, but also separated the realm of secular government from that of spiritual government and successfully undermined caesaropapism. It constituted a major break with Saint Augustine (354–430), who considered both the church and the secular government as part of the earthly world. The Gregorian reform continued to condemn secular governments but asserted that, under the tutelage of the Pope, there was hope for change and improvement.[28]

The decline of a universally suzerain empire prepared the conditions for the separation of church and state in Latin Christendom. Despite the weakness of the Western Empire there was no institutional separation between secular and spiritual authority until the Gregorian reform. The reform itself was the product of the struggle between the pope and the emperor. The papacy, the winning party in the struggle, institutionalized the separation between church and state and created a corporate body that served as a model for secular governments throughout Europe. The territorial monarchies in Europe, supported by the papacy, used the corporate model to establish their own authority and assert their sovereignty against the empire. In contrast, in the Byzantine sphere of influence, in the Russian and Ottoman states for example, caesaropapism survived both ideologically and institutionally.

A prevalent argument claims that the lack of separation between church and state in Islam originates from Muslim theological orientations. For example, historian Bernard Lewis emphasizes that the word for religion in Islam is the Arabic word *din*, which, as in other Semitic languages such as Hebrew, means law. In contrast, the word *religio* derives from Latin antiquity and signifies cult and ritual. Moreover, in Islam there is no equivalent to the Church, no synods, councils, hierarchies or priesthood. The caliph as the head of the Muslim community is simultaneously the head of state.[29] The biblical maxim 'render therefore unto Caesar the things which are Caesar's and unto God the things that are God's' does not have a counterpart in Islam.[30] According to historian Patricia Crone, the Islamic fusion of political and religious community is a consequence of the initial conditions in which Islam was born. While early Christians had dual membership as citizens of the empire and believers of the church, Islam had no such bifurcation. Muslims as believers and citizens were members of the community of believers (*umma*). Thus, Muslims came to regard the prophets as founders of states. In Crone's view, this divergence led Muslims to think that questions of truth and power were intimately linked, while for Christians cognitive and moral truths and political power belonged to different spheres.[31]

However, such an assessment draws an essentialist picture of Islam and Christianity as unchanging entities. As Michel Foucault would remind us, questions of truth and power are always closely linked. In this regard, Foucault complained that even in modern writing and speaking the Greek wise man, the Jewish prophet and the Roman lawmaker provide the model.[32] The belief in prophets as state founders may be widespread, but this did not prevent a prominent Muslim thinker such as Ibn Khaldun to argue that most people had founded governments without receiving prophets.[33] Moreover, the fusion of political and religious functions in the person of the caliph was not peculiar to Islam. The conceptualization of the ruler with full powers followed the Hellenistic concept of kings.[34] Thus, the persistence of caesaropapism in Eastern Europe and the Middle East can be explained by ideological and institutional factors rather than by the inherent characteristics of Islamic law.

In Islam, the institution of the caliphate (*khalīfa*) emerged immediately following the death of the Prophet in 632. With the spread of Islam over and beyond the Arabian peninsula, the caliphate became a central office of the Islamic state. In contrast to the Roman Church, the caliphate was never a law-making institution; it issued decrees solely on fiscal and administrative matters. Despite the famous suggestion of Persian scholar Abdullah Ibn al-Muqaffaʿ to the caliph al-Mansur to establish a uniform legal code, the juristic/theological schools operated independently from the caliphate. Moreover, as the grand-emirates and sultanates emerged in the tenth century, the caliph's power to intervene in their affairs was effectively curtailed. The distinction between the caliph and the *amīr* did not correspond to a strict division between spiritual and temporal matters. While the caliphs tried to intervene in political matters, the *amīrs* used their powers to settle religious issues. Thus, although the *amīrs* recognized the caliph as their titular lord, they were in practice independent in matters of both secular and spiritual authority. Moreover, the Abbasid caliph in Baghdad was not the only one claiming legitimacy. From the tenth century on, the establishment of the Fatimid imamate led to the emergence of rival caliphs in western Muslim lands.

Historian Marshall Hodgson points out that, after the demise of the Abbasid High Caliphate in 945, the Islamic community was divided among several governors and generals who represented only fragments of the old caliphate. They did not bring new political ideas.[35] Two important Muslim medieval states, the Shiʿi Fatimids and the Sunni Seljuks, had an imperial vision but failed in their attempts to re-establish a universal Muslim empire. Thus, until the consolidation of the Ottoman Empire in the sixteenth century, the Muslim region, like Latin Europe, was politically fragmented. The crucial difference between the two regions was that there was no transnational corporation in the Muslim community such as the Roman church in Europe. The Muslim jurists who articulated the main theological and legal doctrines were not part of a formal organization; they were a distinct community autonomous from the authority of both the caliph and the *amīrs*. The authority of the jurists was based on the validity of their arguments.³⁶ In the absence of a central state the juristic/scholarly community was the main transmitter of Islamic traditions. For centuries after the decline of the high caliphate Islamic societies were governed by various dynasties. These dynasties shifted frequently as did political boundaries. Under these circumstances, the subjecthood of ordinary Muslims or jurists to a certain state could be at best transitory. The main identification was the transnational Muslim community, the *umma*. According to Hodgson, this divergence between the transitory characteristic of the state and the enduring characteristic of the community led to a split between the military rule of the *amīrs* and civil institutions.³⁷ The divide between military rule and civil institutions was one of the main causes of the failure of Muslims to establish territorial states. Hodgson emphasizes that Muslims 'never succeeded in creating a national political structure rooted in the land; nor did they discover a political idea that would make up for this by way of a special combination of interests.'³⁸ In Europe, changes in the ruling dynasties were also a frequent phenomenon. However, the incoming dynasties had to deal with the demands of the local estates for the continuation of their privileges that were attached to certain land. The absence of territorial corporations in Islam made territorialization of political authority impossible.

Hodgson argues that the major cause of divergence between Islam and Christianity with regard to corporations lies in their cultural patterns. Islam emphasized personal moral responsibility and thus produced a contractualistic pattern of social organization. Islamic contractualism defined status not by ascription but by achievement. It maintained an atomistic approach to social relations by imputing responsibility to all individuals for the maintenance of moral standards. Thus, it led to what Hodgson calls occasionalism that allowed more leeway for improvisation as new situations emerged. Ultimate legitimacy did not lie in the autonomous office but in egalitarian contractual responsibilities. In contrast, Latin Christendom was organized according to corporatism. Occidental corporatism secured social legitimation by reference to autonomous corporate offices regardless of the persons occupying them. The offices constituted a closed and fixed structure of hierarchical and mutual relations. This cultural pattern led to a legitimism that separated personal morality from autonomous office.³⁹ Thus, the Arabic term *dawla*, which became the standard designation for the concept of the state in the modern Middle East, originally denoted the 'turn of fortune' and more specifically, 'the era in which a particular dynasty held sway rather than governmental institutions.'⁴⁰ The impersonal conception of the state emerged in Europe in the sixteenth century and was adopted later by Middle Easterners.

Hodgson emphasizes that neither Islamic nor Latin Christian norms of social organization can be derived directly from religious orientations though they were not totally unrelated. Islamic contractualism was a product of the mercantile-oriented communal tradition of the Nile-to-Oxus region. Islamic moralism, with the emphasis on personal responsibility, made the contractualist pattern predominant in Muslim lands. The unitary contractualism of Islam and the hierarchical corporatism of Latin Christendom are indeed related to the cultural values of the two religious traditions. However, the divergence cannot be reduced solely to the cultural differences between Islam and Christianity. The corporations of the Middle Ages did not naturally derive from the Christian faith. Such an argument would not only disregard Christian societies without the corporate structure but also fail to explain the timing of the emergence of the corporate structure in the eleventh century. In the eleventh century, the decline of the empire and the emergence of European kingdoms created an opportunity for the papacy to introduce a new political idea which became a model for other territorial states in Europe. In contrast, the Muslim emirates, following the decline of the Abbasid caliphate, did not bring new political ideas. This might be due to the fact that, in contrast to Europe, the heartlands of Islam were permanently under pressure from military incursions by Turkic nomads who were constantly migrating and exploiting urban and agrarian settlements. The emirates based on the social network of pastoralist tribes never became territorial states. Although the empire had in practice collapsed, there was nothing new to replace it.[41]

Following the conquest of Egypt in the early sixteenth century, the Ottomans claimed to be the legitimate caliphs, thereby ending the caliph-*amir* duality prevalent since the time of the Seljuks (1037–1153).[42] In empire-building, however, the Ottomans relied heavily on Byzantine and Roman practices.[43] An effective symbiosis of theocratic legitimation and law-making was the product of Ottoman imperial state formation. The Ottomans established a hierarchy of jurists with the office of the grand müfti (*şeyhülislam*) at the top. They centralized the appointment of judges (*kadıs*) in their Imperial Council. They also declared the Hanefi school, one of the four Sunni schools of law, as the primary legal theory to be applied in the courts of the empire.[44] Most importantly, although Ottoman sultans used their legislative powers in fiscal and administrative matters – sometimes even contrary to basic Islamic rules – in matters of civil law they did not change the Sunni Hanefi doctrine.[45] Using religion as legitimating discourse for their empire, the Ottoman sultans indeed fused religious and political leadership in their hands. However, such a strong ceasaropapist regime needs to be explained by the peculiarities of the Ottoman Empire rather than the inherent characteristics of Islam. The Ottoman state made a fine distinction between Islam as an institution facilitating the administration of the empire, and Islam as a system of meanings establishing the community of the faithful and providing guidelines for the conduct of everyday lives. Although the two were connected in the office of the judge (*kadi*), they were still separate fields.[46]

The major institutional difference between Islam and Latin Christianity after the Gregorian reform was the organization of the papacy as a transnational corporate body. The conditions for the incorporation of the Roman Church were created by the decline of imperial authority. The Gregorian reform also stimulated the revival of Roman law and the creation of canon law. In contrast, despite the decline of the Muslim Empire after the tenth century, successive dynasties retained the imperial vision and no territorial state emerged in the Muslim world. Under these circumstances, Muslim states were characterized, not by the separation of religion and state, but by the separation of Islamic civil law worked out by autonomous scholars from administrative law promulgated by state bureaucracy. However, when the Ottomans built the last great Muslim empire, they managed to incorporate both Islamic law and administrative law in the same state structure. In the next section, we will observe that the development of legal traditions in Europe and the Muslim world – despite the similarities of intellectual problems and solutions – diverged, mainly due to these institutional differences.

The Rationality of Legal Traditions

An important argument regarding the comparison of Western and Islamic legal traditions suggests that Roman law, which became the basis of continental European legal systems, had inherently formal qualities.[47] Did the emergence of the state as a legal person and the separation of state and church derive from these inherent qualities of Roman law? The works of Weber and Habermas are particularly relevant for answering this question.

In Weber's view there are two aspects to the rationality of law.[48] The first is generalization; that is, the reduction of reasons guiding the decision in a single case to one or more principles, i.e. legal propositions. Legal propositions are abstract norms that determine the legal consequences of a certain factual situation. Basic tools for generalization are casuistry and analogy. The second aspect of legal rationality is systematization, i.e. the logical integration of legal propositions to a system of rules.[49] Weber suggests that rationality is inherent in the formal qualities of law. Any reference to moral values, which he dubs substantivization (*Materialisierung*) and moralization (*Moralisierung*) of law, destroys legal rationality.[50] Habermas argues that, in contrast to his studies of economic ethics, Weber disregards the role of moral values in legal development.[51] Weber neglects the principle of justification and focuses merely on the principle of enactment (*Satzungsprinzip*). Thus, in explaining the positivation of the legal order he merely focuses on who is making the laws but not how the laws are justified. In contrast, Habermas emphasizes that the positivation and rationalization of law needs to be analyzed with regard to changes in legitimation values.[52] Therefore, the comparative study of Western and Islamic legal traditions has to take the legitimation of law into account.

Both Roman and Islamic law underwent a rationalization process in which they became not only a system of action but also part of a cultural transmission articulated by specialized intellectual elites. However, the positivation of law occurred only in the Western legal tradition. Weber's comparison of the methods of Islamic law to English common law leads him eventually to explain Islamic legal development in institutional terms rather than in terms of the intellectual orientations of Islamic jurisprudence. Weber ultimately concludes that the instability of *kadi*-justice and the inflexibility of the *shari'a* are products of patrimonial government, i.e. Islamic prebendial feudalism.[53]

Jurisprudence along with legal institutions also had a big impact on the rationalization of Roman law. However, Weber seems to put too much emphasis on the logical systematization of law by doctors of Roman law. Casuistry played as much a central role in the intellectual rationalization of Western legal tradition as it did in Islamic law. In their account of casuistry, Jonsen and Toulmin assert that

> the need to consider the whole corpus of law as a 'system' sprang not from any theoretical taste for the abstract rigor and necessity of mathematics but from the practical needs of men who sought to teach effective ways of dealing with concrete problems of law and justice. The general concepts and principles in terms of which medieval scholars restated the implicit content of Roman law were thus taxonomic rather than geometrical. They organized the detailed holdings and edicts embodied in the classical texts substantively – in terms appropriate to any particular subject matter – not formally, as 'theorems' deduced from universal and invariable 'axioms.'[54]

Medieval Roman law was casuistic and untheoretical. Preference for the geometrical method (systematization) over casuistry (generalization) became predominant much later, in the sixteenth century, especially with Pascal's quest for mathematical certainty in moral matters and his attack on moral laxism.[55] The motive for geometrical certainty lay in the political crisis of the sixteenth and seventeenth centuries caused by religious strife rather than in the inherent intellectual characteristics of Roman law.[56] Until then both Roman and Islamic jurisprudence had depended on casuistry and analogy. In this respect, the difference between the development of Islamic and Roman jurisprudence cannot be explained by the inherent rationality of the latter. The factors that facilitated or prevented rationalization and positivation of these legal systems are institutional.

Medieval Roman law was fundamentally different from Roman law of antiquity. Therefore, the main characteristics of modern Roman law should be sought, not in the inherent characteristics transmitted from antiquity, but in the jurisprudential practices and functions of law in medieval and early modern Europe. Moreover, the capacity of Roman law for generalization and systematization should not be taken as intrinsic but needs to be explained in terms of the specific intellectual and political context within which jurisprudence was operating. Thus, this section argues that the major difference between Roman and Islamic law was the medieval institutional context of each.

With the demise of the western part of the Roman Empire, Roman law disappeared in the west while it developed further in the Eastern Roman Empire. Emperor Justinian's appointment of a commission under the chairmanship of Tribonian in 527–528 was a milestone for the development of Roman law in late antiquity. The end product (534) consisted of three parts, the *Digest*, the *Code* and the *Novellae*, which were given the title *Corpus Iuris Civilis* by medieval scholars.[57] The emperor himself and his contemporaries had thought of each part as an independent whole and this was also reflected in teaching and transmission. The *Digest* contained extracts from the writings of classical Roman jurists. The *Code* consisted of formal imperial constitutions and rescripts dispatched by emperors to imperial officials. The *Novellae* was a systematization of supplementary legislation by Justinian. Finally, the *Institutiones* was issued by Justinian as the official textbook of Roman law.[58]

Justinian's legislation was formally applied for only a brief period in the Italian peninsula and did not dominate Italian legal practice.[59] With the advent of the Lombards, the Byzantine presence as well as Byzantine legal institutions in the peninsula began to wane.[60] Therefore, one needs to ask what spurred the revival of Roman law. It was caused by the Roman Church's opposition, first to the emperor in Constantinople, and then, to the emperor of the Holy Roman Empire. With Saint Jerome's translation of the Bible into Latin, important concepts of Roman law had already entered into Roman Catholic theology.[61] However, the papacy started to make use of Roman law as an organizational tool in its competition with Constantinople and supported the emergence of a western emperor in 800. Greater efforts toward legalization and institutionalization of the church occurred during the Gregorian Reform and the Investiture Struggle.[62] Both processes gave the church its corporate structure based on concepts derived from Roman law.

There was nothing inherent in Roman law that commanded the jurisprudential developments in Latin Europe. Justinian's codification aimed at restricting legal interpretation and legal teaching and prohibited any deviations from the official text-book *Institutiones*. The emperor also prohibited philosophical teaching in the neoplatonist Academy in Athens in 529. Some pagan philosophers migrated to Zoroastrian Persia and even established a school in Harran (Carrhae) which survived into the Islamic period. In Alexandria more tolerant relations between pagans and Christians contributed to the survival of Neoplatonism there.[63] This intellectual heritage was taken over by Islamic philosophy and legal scholarship. Thus, the revival of Roman law in the eleventh and twelfth centuries did not proceed from an inherent tendency for generalization and systematization. Rather, it was the huge gap between the original texts of antiquity and medieval European social practices that led to the emergence of jurisprudence focusing on interpretation.

The first systematizers of jurisprudence were the glossators in the eleventh and twelfth centuries in present day's Italy, France and Germany, whose lectures consisted of reading the *Corpus Iuris Civilis* and explaining it by means of glosses between the lines.[64] The accumulation of these glosses over time created a new body of literature focusing on the taxonomy of general topics as well as the treatment of special topics.[65] In the first half of the thirteenth century the glossatorial school was replaced by the postglossators (also known as commentators or conciliators), who dominated jurisprudence up to the sixteenth century.[66] Postglossators produced a new theory, arguing that Roman law (along with canon law) had to be taken as a common system of justice for all parts of Europe.[67] They also argued that the empire was divine, but that the emperor received his duty from the people (*imperium a Deo, sed imperator a populo*). Italian lawyer Bartolus de Sassoferrato (1313–1357) developed these ideas further by elaborating the concept of sovereignty based on conciliarism that reflected the prevailing corporatism. In the fourteenth and fifteenth centuries, conciliarism asserted that spiritual authority rested in the Roman Church as a corporate body represented by the church council and not merely by the pope. However, the Great Schism of 1378, during which three pontiffs claimed to be the true pope, led to the assertion of papal absolutism in the Council of Constance of 1414. Still, conciliarism was preserved in secular political thought.[68] The teachings of Bartolus prevailed in the universities until the emergence of the humanist school in the sixteenth century. Although conciliarism was eventually condemned by the Fifth Lateran Council (1512–1517), it continued to exert enormous influence on the development of European political theory as well as on political institutions, especially on the Imperial Estates of the Holy Roman Empire.[69]

As noted earlier, the Roman Church was a major force behind the revival of Roman law. Building on Roman jurisprudence, canon law emerged as the first modern legal system in Europe. Major methodological inventions were made by scholars of canon law since the church operated according to Roman law (*ecclesia vivit iure Romano*).[70] Canon law was a product of the monarchic functions of the papacy. From the ninth century onwards, the proprietary church system led to legal particularism: each bishop issued his own decretals, since he could be appointed by the landowner who endowed the local church. Thus, there emerged a need for reconciling the controversies between contradictory decrees. Around 1140, Gratian, a canon lawyer from Bologna, introduced the dialectical method – also known as the scholastic method – as a means of resolving contradicting decrees, which later provided the legal solution to the Investiture Struggle.[71]

In the fourteenth century, humanists such as Francesco Petrarch (1304–1374) and Giovanni Boccaccio (1313–1375) criticized the scholastic interpretive methods, which aimed at achieving uniformity by using deduction. In the fifteenth century, philologist Lorenzo Valla (1407–1457) developed the claims of early humanists. According to these humanists, scholastics lacked the philological and cultural knowledge of antiquity. Humanists were not interested in the original meanings of terms but in the nature and concepts of Roman legal texts and their application to various cases. Early humanism raised an attack on the sanctity of both the transmitted texts and the interpretive tradition. A second wave of humanism in the sixteenth century went beyond the early humanists by not only criticizing the scholastics but also by arranging legal rules according to broader principles. The new humanist legal science did not start with texts or glosses but with legal principles and concepts. In this regard, the humanists of the sixteenth century combined the syntheses of scholastic jurisprudence with the new humanist methods of the fifteenth century.[72]

This brief overview of western legal tradition demonstrates that major developments in Roman and canon law occurred in the eleventh and twelfth centuries during the competition between the Roman Church and the emperor. In the process, the Roman Church established itself as a transnational and global corporation and subjected all its members and assets to a single hierarchy. For their part, secular princes emulated the reforms of the church and established themselves as rulers of territorial bodies. The development of Islamic law took place in a different institutional setting that led to a different trajectory of legal evolution.

We have already seen that the Muslim organization of religion was substantively different from that of Latin Christendom. There was no priesthood, no formal religious organization, and, therefore, no formal division between spiritual and secular authority. When the first Muslim juristic circles emerged, the caliphate was already in place with its administrative, military and criminal regulations.[73] Therefore, the development of Islamic law took a different course from that of Roman and canon law. Although Muslim jurists had to grapple with more or less the same intellectual problems as their European colleagues, the institutional context within which they operated was radically different.

Major developments in Islamic law took place before the revival of Roman law in Europe. Divine legislation came to an end with the death of the Prophet Muhammed at a time when the Islamic community was about to expand beyond the Arabian Peninsula. By then, the Muslim community had inherited a legal order composed of Islamic natural law (*ius naturale*) and Arabian common law (*ius gentium*).[74] Compared to Christianity, Islam became an official religion early on and therefore had to develop a new sacred law, since it would not adopt the Mosaic law of the Bible.[75] The expansion of the state and the religion beyond the Arabian Peninsula made the enactment of new laws imperative. Thus, quite early in the history of Islam, the caliphs, who succeeded the Prophet as leaders of the community, had to resort to personal opinion (*ra'y*) in order to complement divine legislation and customary law.[76] However, over time *ra'y* came to be considered illegitimate as the source of religion, the Koran and the Sunna became textualized, and *'ilm*, the knowledge of both sources, came to be regarded as the sole basis for legislation.[77] Whereas *ra'y* could lead to legislation by man, *'ilm* would ensure the accordance of legislation with theological sources. This, of course, corresponded to the emergence of Muslim jurists and Islamic legal schools that proposed ways of determining the law on the basis of the divine sources.

In the eighth century, Abu Hanifa (699–768) became one of the most renowned and revered among Iraqi jurists by suggesting the use of analogy (*qiyas*) as a source of law. He argued that, instead of personal opinion (*ra'y*), one should choose the least harmful local traditions. This method became known as *istihsan*. However, Abu Hanifa's method was later criticized, since it allowed later Hanefi jurists to use casuistry (*al-hiyal al-shar'iyya*) to evade the law.[78] As an alternative, Malik ibn Anas (718–796?) from Medina proposed *ijma'* (consensus) as a legal method. Basing consensus on the custom in Medina, he accused the Hanefis of diverging from the *Sunna* of the Prophet. He also suggested a method of forming legal opinion on the ground of public good, which is called *istislah*. *Ijma'* was accepted by Iraqi jurists with reservations since consensus could also lead to legislation by men, thus it became a term denoting the consensus of the community of legal theorists.[79]

Muhammad Ibn Idris al-Shafi'i (767–820), founder of another legal school, aimed at a synthesis of the traditionalists and the rationalists by offering a rigorous method of interpretation of authoritative texts. His essay *al-Risala* was, 'an attempt at synthesizing the disciplined exercise of human reasoning and the complete assimilation of revelation as the basis of law.'[80] In Shafi'i's work analogy (*qiyas*) and legal reasoning (*ijtihad*) emerged as basic concepts in legal theory. Analyzing the various types of *qiyas*, legal historian Wael Hallaq points out that, rather than being mere analogy, this method was grounded in logic. However, the legal theorists' main interest was not in the analysis of logical structure but rather in 'the substantive relationship that exists between a linguistic proposition in the original texts and the new case or problem confronting the believer.' Thus, 'their concern revolved exclusively around the degree to which the *ratio legis* (*'illa*) made itself manifest in the original texts, and its applicability, or lack thereof, to a new case at hand.'[81]

This brief review of Islamic legal theory clearly contradicts the depiction of Islamic law as arbitrary and exclusively oriented towards substantive-rationality. The validity of jurists' claims was warranted, not merely by their personal status, but by the intrinsic quality of their argumentation. Muslim scholars believed that valid reasoning was neutral. It could be used for good or evil purposes.[82] Thus, the method of legal reasoning was – to some extent – different from the substance of law. This distinction illustrates that Muslim jurists resorted to procedural rationality of argumentation in order to substantiate their claims.[83] Like their European counterparts, Muslim jurists did not regard generalization as a goal in and of itself. Islamic law was grounded in sacred foundational texts and this textualism both limited and justified,[84] therefore Muslim scholars abstained from unwarranted generalizations. Analogy had to be grounded in the texts and yield a rule that is on the same level of particularity as the original rule. Analogists would of course search for general rules but these would not constitute a rule in their own right; they would merely guide jurists in the formulation of a concrete rule. Therefore, every jurisprudential effort would begin as a response to a particular question.[85] As a result, the rationalization of Islamic law was constrained by its textualism.

The first four centuries of Islam attest to the development of a common lexicon and grammar of Islamic law. The expansion of Islam to Syria, Iraq, Iran, and Northern Africa necessitated the emergence of a legal theory that could not be developed within the legal language of tribal Arabia. What western scholarship erroneously dubbed as the 'closing of the gates of *ijtihad*' was in fact a summation of this process. In the fourth century of Islam, only four schools, Hanefite, Malikite, Shafi'ite and Hanbelite, were recognized as orthodox, and departing from them was regarded as innovation (*bid'a*). Khadduri claims that this ushered in a process in which imitation (*taqlid*) gradually prevailed over legal reasoning (*ijtihad*).[86]

However, as Hallaq demonstrates this did not lead to the end of *ijtihad*. Even after the controversy broke out regarding *ijtihad* and *mujtahid*s (jurists engaging in legal reasoning) at the beginning of the twelfth century, a consensus among parties to the debate was impossible to reach during the following centuries.[87] As early as the eighth century, when Ibn al-Muqaffa' suggested to Caliph al-Mansur (754–775) that he promulgate a formal codification in order put an end to legal pluralism, the caliph refused his proposal.[88] However, Muslim jurists never became a closed circle since there was no official agency – like the Roman Church – to confer upon individuals the status of *mujtahid*.[89] In this regard, Muslims accepted fallibilism and probabilism which allowed for the diversity of Sunni legal schools. In this context, Islamic law was as 'an extreme case of jurists' law' in which the authority of jurists was based on the social and academic prestige they enjoyed. However, this authority was not legislative but declarative; ultimate authority belonged only to God.[90]

The jurisprudential development in Latin Europe and the Middle East exhibits significant similarities. Legal historian Bernard Weiss claims that, compared to Roman jurists, Muslim scholars were more bound to sacred texts.[91] However, as noted in the previous section, Roman law also enjoyed some degree of sanctity that came under humanist attack in the sixteenth century. The next section will demonstrate how Roman law retained this sanctity even for the new humanists by providing precepts of natural law.

Thus, although one can argue that Muslim law represented an extreme case of jurists' law and textualism, the difference between Islamic and Roman law is only a matter of degree, therefore the emergence of natural law in Europe and its lack in Islamic law needs to be explained by institutional rather than by intellectual factors. Intellectually the jurists in both traditions had to deal with similar problems of interpretation of given authoritative texts. The emergence of the law-making state marked the generation of new legal texts and thus radically changed European jurisprudence and legal philosophy.

Weiss also provides evidence for the importance of political institutions in explaining the difference between Christian and Muslim legal development. Muslims created their own state and the mission of Islam was to replace old states with a new kind of polity. On the other hand, for three centuries, Christianity existed in a polity that was not its own creation. When Christianity prevailed politically in the fourth century, it took over the political institutions and laws of the Roman Empire. Thus, Roman law became the law of Christianity, but it was not Christian law. It never attained the sacredness of Islamic law. As a result, Christians resorted to natural law as the legitimating discourse.[92] Although Weiss's argument reveals the importance of political institutions for the origins of Islamic and Christian legal traditions, his claims about natural law do not take the medieval and early modern European political institutions into account.

In contrast, this chapter demonstrates how major developments in the Western European legal tradition (the articulation of the concept of legal personality, its application to state administration, its implications for public, private and international law, the emergence of a systematic legal science and natural law as a legitimating discourse) were consequences of the waning of imperial authority. The history of Roman and Islamic jurisprudence reveals that generations of legal scholars interpreted the materials handed down from previous generations differently under different political contexts. The Roman concept of legal personality found a radically different application in the hands of the popes, who were challenging the authority of the emperors. Unintentionally, however, the Roman church provided a model for other territorial monarchies, which first challenged the superiority of the emperor, and ultimately the superiority of the pope. The modern sovereign state required a new legitimating discourse that derived political authority neither from the emperor defined as the sole source of law in *Corpus Iuris Civilis* nor from the spiritual authority of the pope, but from an inherent bond between the subjects within a territory and the ruler; this was known as the social contract and was the achievement of natural law.

Legal Discourse: Natural Law and State Formation

Modern Natural Law and the Legitimation of the Modern State

In order to understand the origins and implications of natural law, it is essential to complement the analysis of legal institutions and the jurisprudential development in both legal traditions with the study of discourse that legitimizes law-making.[93] The evolution of legal systems reveals the significance of legitimating discourses for law-making. In pre-modern societies the ultimate basis for social values is sacral law and custom. Pre-modern legal systems are composed of three legal traditions:[94] First, the legal system is integrated through sacral law worked out by theologians and jurists. Second, the ruler enacts regulatory laws to achieve political goals. Third, the majority of the population lives its daily life according to customary law, which goes back to legal transmissions from tribal societies. The emergence of the modern territorial state is marked by increasing law-making based on the ruler's will at the expense of sacral law and custom.

There are two preconditions for regulatory law to emerge: first, there must be a differentiation of society and the state so that the law can acquire a public character; second, the customary rules of local ascriptive communities are replaced by positive rules defining the rights and obligations universally for all members of the political community within the state's territory.[95] However, pre-modern regulatory law lacks the universality that sacral law claims since it is limited to rare situations where there is a clear distinction between state and society.[96] The positivation of law means the emergence of a unified legal system, in which law shrinks to the dimension of bureaucratic instrumentality. The political power of the ruler is freed from sacral law and becomes truly sovereign. Now it has to fill the gap left by sacral law with positive legislation. Historically, this has been the task of natural law.[97]

All natural law theories establish a duality of legal existence between natural law and positive law and make the former a yardstick against which the latter can be measured. The distinction between natural law and positive law corresponds to the distinction between that which ought to be and that which is.[98] However, modern natural law is distinct from pre-modern natural law traditions in its foundation on reason rather than divine will.[99] Modern natural law provides an extralegal basis for positive law and replaces custom; but it differs greatly from custom in the generality of its formulation. Whereas custom remains a local rule, modern natural law – like sacral law – has a universal appeal. Modern natural law provides two important formal qualities of the modern legal system: universality and equality.[100]

Type of Law	Source of law	
Sacral Law	*Sacred texts worked out by theologians and jurists*	
Ruler's Law	Legislated by the ruler in accordance with **political will**	Rational natural law
Customary Law	*Dates back to tribal traditions*	

Figure 4.1: Positivation and the emergence of modern natural law

According to Jürgen Habermas, rational natural law is predicated on principles of procedural rationality. The basic model of modern natural law is the principle concept of bourgeois private law: the contract generalized as social contract to morally justify political power on the basis of subjective rights. Thus, moral rules are conceptualized as the reasoned consensus of sovereign individuals.[101] The *differentia specifica* of modern natural law is the structure of argumentation which becomes the fundamental legitimating discourse for positive legislation.[102] In this regard, the justification of political and legal arguments was dependent on the institutional structure of the Holy Roman and Ottoman Empires. The following chapters will focus more closely on the institutional dynamics of political legitimation. However, before proceeding to the institutional analysis, a brief snapshot of the legal system of the Holy Roman and Ottoman Empires in the sixteenth and seventeenth centuries is necessary to understand how they were influenced by the Roman Catholic and Muslim Sunni traditions and how they in turn molded those traditions.

Law and Legitimacy in the Holy Roman Empire

The Holy Roman Empire in the sixteenth century was an electoral monarchy in which the emperor and the territorial princes and cities ruled collectively. Due to the interregna and the absence of emperors, who were occupied with expeditions in Italy, public peace in the empire came to depend increasingly on the Imperial Estates, territorial entities with exclusive authority and autonomy.[103] The medieval German legal order was marked by the reception of Roman law, the introduction of canon law by the church and the persistence of customary law.[104] The revival of Roman law, with its focus on political will as the source of law, strengthened and enhanced the law-making capacities of the rulers. Still, both canon law and customary law complemented the jurisdiction of the ruler. The late fifteenth and early sixteenth centuries witnessed the emergence of new constitutional norms and institutions in the Holy Roman Empire. Civil law dominated public law until the mid-seventeenth century. From the late sixteenth century on, public law distanced itself from the categories of civil law and invoked the concepts, primarily the concept of sovereignty, developed by political theory. This legal foundation of the state was formulated by natural law doctrine.[105] In a nutshell, the problem for German public law scholars was the relationship between imperial authority and territorial authority. If the empire was to be defined as a state, it had to be invested with sovereignty. Simultaneously the territorial sovereignty of the Imperial Estates had to be recognized as a constitutional fact. If territorial sovereignty was analogous to imperial sovereignty, however, then Territorial Estates could claim the same rights as Imperial Estates. But an absolutist state formation was taking place at the level of Imperial Estates, increasingly excluding Territorial Estates from political authority.[106] Thus, natural law theory provided important responses to the political questions of the day by integrating legal doctrine with political theory.

In this regard, the Reformation in Germany had far reaching consequences for the secularization of political authority and the positivation of law. The German princes asserted their right to establish the Lutheran faith and thus to be the supreme rulers in their territories both against the emperor and the pope. In this process, the princes extended their jurisdiction not only to laymen but also to the clergy and created integrated legal systems and unitary secular states.[107] The immediate protection of Martin Luther (1483–1546) by the German princes cannot be explained by their religious convictions but by their defense of their territorial rights against the emperor and the pope.[108] Luther's theories gave the princes a legitimating discourse for the consolidation of their territorial authority. Luther defended the abolition of ecclesiastical jurisdiction arguing that the church is not a law-making institution but an invisible community of believers each of whom is personally responsible to God.[109] Luther's close associate and colleague Philip Melanchton (1497–1560) developed a radically new theory of natural law. He argued that God had implanted *a priori* logical and moral concepts – called elements of knowledge (*notitiae*) – that constitute the premises rather than the objects of rational inquiry. These concepts cannot be proved or disproved but are part of human nature. Thus, unlike early scholastic and humanistic approaches, Protestant legal science derived legal principles not from authoritative texts but from inborn reason and conscience and illustrated them by interrelated legal rules found in a variety of legal sources. Following the humanists, the Protestants denied the scholastic belief in the sanctity of Roman and canon law and refused the authority of traditional interpretation. In order to expose divine wisdom in the texts, one had to introduce principles implanted in humans by God. In this regard, the new Protestant approach raised questions not only of legal theory but more importantly of legal legitimacy.[110] Protestant legal science met the needs of the new territorial state in Germany. The unification of all jurisdiction under the authority of a single prince required a legal science that started with the systematization of legal principles underlying the whole legal body rather than the scholastic and humanistic approaches that started by systematizing the rules contained in authoritative texts. Protestant jurisprudence emphasized the legislative character of law, i.e. the will of the ruler as the source of law. It made a distinction between the source of legal rules and the purpose they served. Thus both schools of modern jurisprudence, positivism and natural law, were articulated by the Protestant approach.[111] This provides crucial evidence for the argument that natural law was essential for legitimating the positivation of law.

Legal historian Harold Berman points out that – contrary to Weber's claims – the Reformation did not foster an individualistic morality. Both Lutheranism and Calvinism were strongly communitarian. It was communitarianism not individualism that facilitated the emergence of capitalism in Europe. Weber was mistaken in regarding the capitalist spirit as a consequence of the individual psychology of Protestantism. The Reformation's influence on capitalism was institutional rather than psychological. The Protestant communitarian approach, with its emphasis on 'close-knit covenanted God-centered communities', gave birth to inventions such as joint stock companies, trusts, etc. In Berman's words, it was 'not Calvinist soteriology [a branch of theology dealing with salvation], but Calvinist ecclesiology [theological doctrine relating to the church]' that fostered the spirit of capitalism.[112] In this respect, the real difference between the legal traditions of Islam and Latin Christianity was mainly institutional. Like Muslim jurisprudence, European jurisprudence was textualist and legitimized ultimately by reference to sacral law rather than solely by the ruler's will. Thus, the main breakthrough in European legal science developed as a consequence of the decentralization of political authority in the Holy Roman Empire. According to Lutherans, political rulers, the princes of the empire, were guardians of the Decalogue (Ten Commandments). The principle of *cuius regio eius religio* adopted in the Peace of Augsburg (1555) and confirmed in the Peace of Westphalia (1648) was derived from the responsibility of rulers as guardians of the Decalogue.[113] The new territorial state was legitimized, not by reference to a universal ecumene, but to modern natural law.[114] Without the dissolution of imperial authority this transition would not have been possible – as the history of the Ottoman Empire demonstrates.

Law and Legitimacy in the Ottoman Empire

Unlike the Habsburgs, the Ottoman dynasty at its inception was not bound by an institutional framework. In contrast to the Holy Roman Empire, the Ottoman Empire was ruled by a hereditary dynasty with a central bureaucracy and a spatially fixed capital. A powerful land-owning nobility and representative institutions, such as the Imperial and Territorial Diets, were legally absent in the Ottoman Empire. In the sixteenth century the Ottoman emirate had transformed itself into an empire with territories in Europe, Asia and Africa. The Ottoman sultans based their claim to universal suzerainty on their role as leaders of the holy war (*gaza*).[115] However, the initial Ottoman central institutions made it harder for the empire to transform itself into a territorial state as part of a system of equal sovereign states. In other words, the closure of the imperial frontier led to a rationality crisis of the empire which could not be solved within the existing organizational principles. The institutions which had initially contributed to the success of the Ottoman polity in the fifteenth and sixteenth centuries proved inflexible and less efficient in the seventeenth and eighteenth centuries.

The legal structure of the Ottoman Empire was based on Sunni *shari'a*, local custom and sultanic legislation called *kanun*. In the field of civil law, the Ottoman legal system was based on the Sunni legal theory, *fiqh*.[116] However, most areas of public law lay beyond the *shari'a* and were subject to customary law and sultanic enactment.[117] Although there is disagreement on the extent to which the Ottoman state depended on religious or secular law, both sides of the controversy agree that the legislative power of the ruler is recognized by Islamic religious law.[118] It is true that sultanic legislative authority was rather limited in civil law due to the legal norms in the *fiqh* books and the autonomy of Sunni legal schools.[119] The consensus (*ijma'*) of the great legal scholars (*mujtahid*s) constituted the main legal dogma in civil law.[120] However, the autonomy of the legal scholars should not be idealized. Ottoman bureaucracy had its own language and operated autonomously from Sunni legal theory. Moreover, the Ottoman Empire centralized the appointment of scholars to colleges on an unprecedented level in Islamic history.[121] Compared to European political fragmentation, Ottoman domination over the entire Mediterranean basin made it harder for dissident scholars to find jobs and evade prosecution.[122]

Ottoman public law was predominantly grounded in customary law, which was partly codified by the sultan in provincial *kanuns*.[123] *Kanun*s were neither developed by jurists nor by judges. They were not a product of *ijtihad* but the will of the sultan, and the judges had to enforce them as much they had to enforce the *shari'a*.[124] Most significantly, the *kanun*s regulated the distribution of the newly conquered military fiefs to the members of the provincial cavalry (*sipahi*). Historians have detected a decline in the *kanun* and an assertion of the *shari'a* after the sixteenth century.[125] This tendency is reflected by a decree of Sultan Mustafa II in 1696, which prohibited the use of the word *kanun* and proclaimed the *shari'a* as the sole legal source of the empire.[126] However, this should not be interpreted as the decline of the secular character of the empire or a victory of the religious establishment.[127] Rather, it represents the decline of the Ottoman fief system, taxation and provincial administration. With the end of imperial expansion to Europe, the Ottoman sultan and the imperial government lost their legitimacy as the distributors of booty from the holy war. Changes in warfare technology in Europe increased the need of the government for cash and a larger army using gunfire. The decline of the Ottoman fief-holding cavalry had far-reaching social and political consequences. The social actors who benefited from this transformation emerged as new political actors. While old political institutions became dysfunctional, the sultans relied increasingly on *ad hoc* compromises with the new actors which were sanctioned by the religious-legal establishment. Thus, the state compensated for the legitimacy deficit by depending more and more on sacral law. The pre-existing imperial institutions based on the fief system made it impossible for the empire to replace the legitimating discourse of custom and sacral law with natural law based on state interest.

Summary

This chapter has investigated the historical origins of the legal institutions and the legal discourse that characterized the early modern state. It argued that both modern legal institutions and modern legal discourse were products of the decline of universal empire and the institutionalization of political fragmentation in Latin Europe. All major legal developments in Latin Europe (the Gregorian Reformation, the Investiture Struggle, the conciliar movement and the emergence of estates, and the Lutheran Reformation) occurred in the context of challenges to the authority of the emperor, the sole source of law according to Roman law. This argument was presented on two levels: legal institutions and legal discourse.

Institutionally, the modern state is a legal person that promulgates laws according to its own political will. As such, legal personality as an administrative technology is a prerequisite for the emergence of the sovereign state. Moreover, legal personality conceptualizes all subjects of the state as parts of a single body and establishes a legal community. In other words, it provides an important component of political identification in the modern state. Explaining the development of the modern state requires a focus on the emergence of legal personality and natural law that cannot be explained merely by reference to religion and jurisprudence, but rather by focusing on institutional development. The impact of religion and jurisprudence on law can also be explained by the evolution of political institutions in the transition from empire to territorial state.

Discursively, the modern state required a new legal and political discourse that could justify the monopolization of law-making by the central state apparatus (legal positivation and legal unification). Historically, natural law served this function. The second part of the chapter discussed how the decline of a universal empire and the emergence of the territorial state facilitated the emergence of natural law. Having now established the historical links between the legal institutions and the legal discourse of the modern state and the decline of the empires, the next step in the analysis is to focus more closely on the challenges that the territorial state and the modern state system raised for the Holy Roman and Ottoman Empires.

5

STATE FORMATION IN THE HOLY ROMAN EMPIRE

This chapter examines the transformation of the Holy Roman Empire and the emergence of the territorial state in Germany in four domains: administration, taxation, conduct of foreign affairs and political legitimation. It illustrates how the emergence of the territorial state in Europe challenged the rationality and legitimacy of a universal empire in these four main functions. The challenges to the empire will be examined at two important turning points, which are not only significant for the history of the empire but also for the history of international politics: the Peace of Augsburg in 1555 and the Peace of Westphalia in 1648. International relations conventionally takes these events as the starting point for the modern international system. However, the discipline usually pays no attention to the fact that both arrangements were primarily constitutional assemblies of the Holy Roman Empire. The fact that the constitutional documents of the Holy Roman Empire are simultaneously recognized as the founding documents of the modern international system substantiates my claim that the study of the transition of medieval empires into absolutist states is essential to understanding the emergence of the modern states system.

In this context, this chapter illustrates how the survival imperatives of the state system led neither to the emergence of a centralized state as they did in other European states such as France and England nor to the dissolution of the empire. Thus, the persistence of the corporate state in Germany constitutes an anomaly for both neo-realism and Weberian historical sociology which assume that systemic pressures cause the centralization of power. Constructivism can explain this anomaly partly by emphasizing the persistence of collective ideas. However, the Holy Roman Empire also poses problems for constructivism. How can constructivism explain the fragmented nature of the empire despite the emergence of a German identity in the fifteenth and sixteenth centuries? How can one explain the timing of territorialization in Germany? And most importantly how can one explain the predominance of certain ideas over other ideas? This chapter explains these questions by institutional path dependency and the persistence of legitimating principles. Following Habermas it argues that the modern reforms building the territorial state could not be introduced without changes in the legitimating principles.

The Holy Roman Empire

The institutional framework of the Holy Roman Empire in the sixteenth century was the product of a long evolution of the medieval German political system. Germany in the ninth and tenth centuries consisted of duchies ruled by dukes of equal status, one of whom was elected emperor. Still, the medieval empire combined both electoral and dynastic principles for regulating succession. Emperors were chosen from dynasties; the Carolingians were succeeded by the Ottonians, then by the Salians and finally by the powerful Staufens who ruled the Empire until 1254.[1] After the Staufen reign, the empire went through an era of interregnum, in which three dynasties – Wittelbachs, Luxembourgs, and Habsburgs – competed for the imperial crown. In the fifteenth century, the Habsburgs managed to obtain the imperial crown and became the imperial dynasty until the dissolution of the empire.

The Habsburgs were originally from Alemannic Switzerland where they owned allodial land that was held as absolute property and not as a fief.[2] The first Habsburg to be elected to the imperial crown was Rudolph I (1273–91). Upon the extinction of the Babenbergs, the ruling house of Austria, Rudolf acquired Styria and Austria by force in 1278 and granted them as fiefs to his sons.[3] Thanks to a privilege granted earlier by Emperor Frederick, Austria had a peculiar place in the empire; though part of the empire, it was not an imperial fief but in practice an independent duchy. Austria was turned into inheritable land and raised to the rank of a duchy. No imperial laws could be put into effect without the duke's authorization. In the fourteenth century the Habsburgs continued to enhance their autonomy and territorial authority.[4]

The absence of a strong dynasty in the Holy Roman Empire in the thirteenth and fourteenth centuries had important consequences for its future development. First, German emperors had far less centralized royal power compared to their counterparts in England or France. However, during the political chaos following the end of the Staufen reign, the Imperial Estates, entities with exclusive authority and autonomy in a territory of the empire and representation and voting rights in the Imperial Diet, enhanced their power. In the fifteenth century, they were divided into three colleges: the electors, the Imperial Princes and the Cities. When the Habsburgs became the imperial dynasty,[5] the estates had already established their territorial authority. Second, the election of the emperor became formally regulated by the Golden Bull of 1356, a decree promulgated by Emperor Charles IV in the Imperial Diet of Nürnberg outlining the constitutional principles. The Bull also gave lay electors the right to hereditary succession through primogeniture in their own domains.[6] The formalization of imperial elections gave the empire its constitutional form that set the fundamental institutional framework of imperial politics.

In addition to relations between the Imperial Estates and the emperor, the German rule of succession also had an impact on Habsburg administration and prevented the consolidation of their territories. German tradition rejected the seniority rule in succession and gave younger sons (cadets) duties as regents. The Habsburgs developed a regency system in which members of the dynasty ruled Habsburg domains under the head of the family. While the system became an important tool for preserving the unity of the dynastic domains, it also curtailed the centralization of these domains and preserved local autonomy.[7]

Thus, the Middle Ages created two important path-dependencies which would influence state formation from the fifteenth century on: elective monarchy and territorial authority of the princes. Like most medieval states, the empire was defined by a network of personal associations between the overlords and vassals rather than by territory. In the fifteenth century, countries like France and England were developing from a feudal state (*Lehenstaat*) into a territorial state, in which political authority became centralized within demarcated boundaries. In contrast, the empire evolved into a corporate state (*Ständestaat*), in which personal feudal rights were transformed into territorial rights. The central jurisdictional, fiscal and executive imperial institutions created in the late fifteenth century were grafted onto this corporate structure and ended up consolidating the territorialization of political authority. While the emperor and the imperial institutions became more dependent on ascriptive groups, the empire became less and less an actor in the state system. How can one explain the failure of central state formation? Why did the empire not emulate France and England? If the empire was too weak and the Imperial Estates too strong, how can we explain the survival of the empire into the nineteenth century? How can one explain the parcellization of political authority in a country in which German identity became increasingly predominant?

Administration

The administrative structure of the empire in the sixteenth century was to a large extent dependent on ascriptive groups. In the fifteenth century internal and external security problems stimulated a reform movement that created important central organs. These new organs were, nevertheless, grafted onto existing institutions. The central decision-making organ, the Imperial Diet (*Reichstag*) grew out of the assemblies (*curia*) held at the emperor's court and the electoral meetings during the great interregnum (1254–1273). It operated according to the conciliar principle of consensus of the affected parties and mutual obligations.[8] The diet consisted of three colleges, the oldest of which was the college of electors (*Kurfürstenrat*) established in 1273 and confirmed in the Golden Bull of 1356. Most state offices were assigned to certain hereditary titles.[9] The second curia of the Imperial Diet was the college of imperial princes (*Reichsfürsten*), which emerged in 1480 from the princes and counts trying to defend their rights against the increasing authority of the electors.[10] The third curia consisted of some eighty free and imperial cities.[11]

Imperial jurisdiction and executive organs in the fifteenth and sixteenth centuries were also dependent on ascriptive groups. While one high court, the Imperial Aulic Council (*Reichshofrat*), operated under the control of the emperor, the other court, the ImperialChamber Court (*Reichskammergericht*) was under the influence of the princes. The Imperial Regiment (*Reichsregiment*), a standing committee of select princes created as an executive organ, was short lived.[12] In addition to lawmaking, jurisdiction and the executive, the empire also lacked an imperial court society as an institution facilitating elite coordination. The imperial court did not develop into a central institution turning landed nobility into court nobility and regulating the competition among them. Instead, it relied on a network of personal vassalage ties to the emperor. It had to travel in order to function as the administrative center. As the court became less mobile and the emperor less often present, the territorial princes became more autonomous and the emperor more interested in dynastic rather than imperial politics.[13]

Due to their dependence on the Imperial Estates, the emperors were unable to centralize political authority even under the duress of interstate competition. Charles V's failure to create a unified universal monarchy reveals that – given the technological level of the age – the imperial organizational principles would not allow the construction of a centralized universal state. Under Charles V, who regarded the affairs of the empire as part of his larger universalist project, imperial offices became increasingly dysfunctional. Charles V's Imperial Chancery consisted of officers who came from different parts of his realms. They were not well-equipped to handle the affairs of the empire partly due their insufficient command of German.[14] Still, Charles tried to coordinate the policies of his individual domains through his chancellor Mercurino de Gattinara (1465–1530), who was bestowed with the powers of the official imperial chancellor, the archbishop of Mainz.[15] Gattinara attempted to centralize and rationalize the administration of Charles's domains by establishing the chancery as the central organ, encouraging the geographical specialization of secretaries and integrating Spain, the Italian domains, the Netherlands and the Holy Roman Empire under a single administration. His proposal attests to the bureaucracy's awareness of systemic imperatives for centralization.[16] However, the chancery as a medieval institution proved inadequate for the centralization of imperial administration of diverse countries with different local customs and traditions. The nature of political rule and administration was predominantly personal.[17]

In contrast to the empire as a whole, early modern state formation was carried out within the Imperial Estates. The rise of the princely territorial state was facilitated by the introduction of Roman law that turned the estate-nobility (Territorial Estates) into a privileged corpus representing their own private interests. Thus, the prince came to represent the public good, the public authority and ultimately the whole territory, while the landed nobility was transformed into court nobility.[18] This process was further stimulated by the advent of the Lutheran Reformation which designated the territorial prince as head of the territorial church.[19] The emergence of the territorial church destroyed the universalism of the Roman Church and the empire which meant that the medieval justification of political authority as devolving from the emperor became untenable. The adoption of the principle of *cuius regio eius religio* in the Peace of Augsburg (1555) marked a milestone in this regard.[20]

Since the universal empire depended on the idea of a universal church,[21] Charles V accurately perceived the Reformation as a threat to his universal monarchy. Despite the emperor's decisive military victory over the Protestants in Germany in the Battle of Mühlberg in 1547, the institutional structure of the empire would not allow for a centralization of authority in the hands of the emperor.[22] Overall, his policies increased the fears of the Imperial Estates of succumbing to a Habsburg absolutist monarchy.²³ The backlash against Charles's centralization efforts led him to suffer a humiliating defeat in 1553 by an army of rebellious estates in alliance with France.²⁴ The conflict was finally settled in the Imperial Diet in Augsburg (1555), when Charles V abdicated the imperial throne.²⁵ Contrary to Charles's plan to alternate the imperial title between the Austrian and Spanish branches of the dynasty,²⁶ the opposition of the estates led to the division of the House of Habsburg in two: a senior branch ruling in Spain, and a junior branch keeping the hereditary lands and the imperial title.²⁷ Thus, the Peace of Augsburg represented the end of the Habsburg's project of universal monarchy, since both branches carried out state formation separately in their own domains.

After Augsburg, the Habsburgs focused more on state formation within their hereditary lands. Nevertheless, Habsburg Emperor Ferdinand II still made an attempt to suppress confessional diversity and the territorial authority of the Imperial Estates through his Counter-Reformation policies.²⁸ His failure, the ensuing Thirty Years War (1618–1648) and the Peace of Westphalia (1648), marked the end of the Holy Roman Empire as a monarchic *imperium*.²⁹ After Westphalia, the emperor himself joined the territorialization movement by uniting his own hereditary lands. The emergence of the Habsburg monarchy marked the definite end of the universalism of the empire.³⁰

The Peace of Westphalia as a fundamental law of the empire made important changes in its constitutional composition.³¹ Foreign powers such as France and Sweden became important players in imperial politics. In an age when territorial monarchies were consolidated in France, England and Spain, the domestic politics of the empire was becoming increasingly susceptible to foreign intervention. All the electors and other Imperial Estates acquired territorial rights *ius territoriale* or *ius territorii et superioritatis* as well as the right to build and join alliances. The estates were still not recognized as sovereign states however; indeed the right of alliance could not be used against the emperor or the empire.³² Neither the emperor nor the estates could be counted as sovereign or autonomous states by themselves; only the imperial state as a whole was a sovereign entity.³³

The Westphalian state system paved the way for eighteenth-century great power politics, in which two Imperial Estates – Austria and Prussia – became major actors. This chapter will focus on the constitution of the absolutist state in Austria since being the hereditary domain of the imperial dynasty, Austria best demonstrates the transition from empire to absolutist state. In previous centuries Austria acquired a special status within the empire through imperial privileges. Until 1804, however, no Austrian monarchy officially existed. Rather, the kingdoms of Bohemia, Hungary, the archduchy of Austria, the duchies of Styria, Carinthia, Carniola, and the county of Tyrol had a common sovereign. The first attempts to integrate these constituent entities into a single monarchy were made by Ferdinand I (1503–1564).[34]

For the first time, Ferdinand created a central government in all three domains: Bohemia, Hungary and Austria. The government consisted of an Aulic Council (*Hofrat*) as the high court of appeals, a Privy Council (*Geheimer Rat*), a Court Chancery for daily government business and a Chamber of Accounts. The Privy Council was a loose consultative assembly of court officials rather than a cabinet. It included not only Habsburg officials but also a vice-chancellor representing the archbishop of Mainz, the imperial arch-chancellor.[35] Since Habsburg administrative organs were susceptible to the intervention of ascriptive groups of the empire (like the imperial arch-chancellor) and individual Territorial Estates, their autonomy was highly limited.

The development of a separate Habsburg state increased the dissonance between the dynasty's territorial interests and its imperial roles. The Holy Roman Empire was comprised of a multitude of principalities that were outside the reach of the Habsburgs while some of the Habsburg domains were not part of the empire. The eighteenth-century reform movement reveals the problems that the Habsburg patrimonial conglomerate had to face in its transformation to an absolutist European monarchy.[36] The indivisibility and inalienability of the Habsburg dominium was ensured legally by the Pragmatic Sanction of 1713 that, anticipating a crisis of dynastic succession, confirmed and created a unified state – though still without a name.[37] The Austrian absolutist state emerged finally with the Theresian reform movement (1749).[38]

The first wave of reform separated the administrative and judicial functions of the government and transformed seigniorial rights into private property rights by distinguishing between public and private law.[39] Thus, Theresian reform effectively diminished the autonomy of the Territorial Estates and thus, marked the transition from the corporate state to the absolutist state.[40] The second wave of reforms was carried out by Wenzel Anton von Kaunitz-Rietberg, a career diplomat and the Court Chancellor of the Habsburg Empress Maria Theresa.[41] Kaunitz established the division between the judiciary and the executive as a theoretical principle: the sovereign should be kept from private litigations.[42] The legitimating basis for the new reform movement was provided by natural law that was embodied in the Theresian civil code. The civil code created a single universal legal community out of subjects who had been living under the separate jurisdictions of the Territorial Estates.

Thus, Kaunitz's reforms were crucial in rationalizing the Habsburg state in an absolutist fashion. The separation between private and public law, the privatization of property rights, and the emergence of bureaucrats with a distinct professional identity mark the cornerstones of change in the Habsburg polity. This transformation of the Habsburg state into an absolutist state required a reorientation of Habsburg policies from pursuing a universal empire to building a territorial state within demarcated political boundaries. The central organs of the empire proved unable to forge a unitary actor from the patchwork of Imperial Estates that had acquired important royal prerogatives in the Middle Ages. The Protestant Reformation further consolidated the territorial authority of the Estates and shattered the medieval idea of the empire based on a universal church. The Reformation and the Counter-Reformation finally enabled the Habsburgs – like other German princes – to create a single political community out of a myriad of loosely connected domains and thereby, to emerge as a unitary actor in the state system.

Taxation

For the emperor taxation was the major means to create generalized power. The royal wealth of a German king consisted of his family possessions (*Hausgut*) and the crown possessions belonging to the empire (*Krongut* or *Reichsgut*). The most important royal income from the empire consisted of the *ad hoc* taxes extracted from the towns: support for campaigns, threats of penalty, gifts for the recognition of royal honor at the time of coronation or a royal visit to the city.

The king's rights over villages, forests, farmsteads, mills and other real property especially in Southwestern Germany provided a more steady income compared to other parts of the empire. The peripatetic imperial court could stay on these properties called imperial districts (*Reichsbereiche*) free of charge. Other sources of royal income were imperial forests and abbeys, which hosted the king and his appointees. However, imperial assets as well as Staufen domains were usurped and wasted during the interregnum and the competition between the dynasties. Thus, in the fifteenth century the burden of maintaining the imperial court lay entirely on the family possessions of the emperor.[43] In the field of taxation, as in the field of administration, the emperors after the Staufen dynasty increasingly lost control of free resources and became more dependent on ascriptive groups.

The dependence on Imperial and Territorial Estates for financial resources was a major impediment to fiscal unification.

The role of the corporate state in preventing the fiscal unification of the Holy Roman Empire is illustrated by the reforms of the late fifteenth and early sixteenth centuries. In the fifteenth century, two new methods of imperial taxation were tried in order to fight the Hussite Wars (1420–1434). Imperial Diets (in 1422 and 1433–34) agreed to a monetary tax, which extracted 1 percent from territorial governments, 1 percent from individuals and more from Jews. Once the war was over the tax was removed. Although the system was suspended after the wars, the reform presented a model for a later project called the Common Penny (*Gemeiner Pfenning*). The second experiment in the fifteenth century was the drawing of an Imperial Matricular System (*Reichmatrikel*), which itemized taxpayers and the amount of taxes assigned to them. But when it was put to use in 1437 the tax could be enforced only through princely decrees, and thus it increased the autonomy of the Imperial Estates even more.[44]

The tax reforms of the fifteenth century clearly reveal that the Imperial Estates were aware of the need for a common purse for maintaining public peace and political order. However, the past institutional set-up of the empire prevented the centralization and monopolization of taxation. The collection and monitoring of these resources was not carried out by central agencies but by territorial princes who created their own fiscal bureaucracy and increased their capacity to tax their subjects. Thus, the reforms were implemented in a fashion that further re-enforced the corporate state and the territorialization of political authority.[45] The fact that the Imperial Estates both granted and collected taxes was a major impediment to the fiscal unification of the Holy Roman Empire.

Fiscal unification was also a problem within the Habsburg domains. Without fiscal consolidation and central administration Charles V's dominions were too fragmented to perform as a unitary actor. Financial projections often failed due to the lack of coordination. In 1531, for instance, Charles V met with his sister Mary, regent of the Netherlands, to plan income and expenditures for the following six years. In 1534, Mary sent her brother another calculation illustrating that the projections from two years earlier would at best cover four instead of six years even if one excluded the unplanned expenses between 1531 and 1534 of around 350,000 gulden. Mary tried to keep interest at a lower rate by borrowing from subsidy receivers rather than Antwerp bankers. Around 1535 it was clear to the emperor that the Low Countries could not finance their own defense, let alone that of other Habsburg domains. From the 1530s on

Charles had to send funds from Spain to Mary several times.⁴⁶

However, the transfer of funds from one domain to another was not always easy since the resources available to the Habsburgs were hardly independent of ascriptive groups. In the Kingdom of Naples, for example, Charles's Burgundian advisors tried to make resources more available as early as 1516 when Charles followed his late grandfather Ferdinand to the throne. The president of the Council of State and the grand chamberlain Guillaume de Croÿ, lord of Chièvres, sent the president of the Chamber of Accounts in Lille to Naples to register the revenues and expenses properly. The mission was met with resistance from local officials of the kingdom causing the accountant to go back to Spain to meet with Chièvres. When he returned, he brought new instructions for the kingdom to contribute 200,000 ducats for defense against the Ottomans and for the election of Charles as emperor. The accountant summoned the barons and cities for an assembly, which agreed to a gift of 300,000 ducats, stipulating that the money be spent within the borders of the kingdom. Thus, Charles had to resort to other sources to finance his imperial candidacy. This second mission, however, managed to extract some 276,000 ducats through the sale of domain cities and villages. This money was used to pay Charles's bankers in return for financial support for his candidacy.⁴⁷

The financial system of Charles V, like most European rulers of the time, was marked by poor budgeting, a mixture of private and public expenses and high levels of debt. Despite the enormous resources available to Charles, they still could not cover his political activities. Even in 1534, a year of peace for all the lands under Charles's rule, the budget projection indicated a deficit of 435,118 ducats. Charles's councilors acted without economic planning, and relied mostly on short-term credit. Indeed, there was no regular budget in any of the domains under Charles's rule. Even when he transplanted the Burgundian financial institution into Castile as the Council of the Estate (*Consejo de la Hacienda*), the supreme accountant (*contador*) had no means to control and monitor the whole financial system in the absence of fiscal unification. The plight of the financial system was more or less the same throughout Charles's other domains.⁴⁸ Under these circumstances rulers had three choices: reducing expenses, summoning the Territorial Estates for taxation, or borrowing at high interest rates against future revenues through short-term contracts with agents of large banking houses.⁴⁹

In 1491, Emperor Maximilian I (1508–1519) started the Habsburg collaboration with the banking house of Fugger by granting them concessions to the silver mines at Schwatz in the Tyrol in return for

120,000 florins annually. From the sale of a silver mark valued at 16 florins, 50 percent would go to the holder of the concession, 18 percent to the Emperor, and 32 percent to the producers. Similar contracts were made with other Augsburg financiers, like the houses of Herwart and Baumgartner, regarding the Tyrolean copper mines. These networks helped the Habsburgs with their imperial policies. For example, when Maximilian was trying to have his grandson Charles elected as the king of the Romans (the future emperor), the Fuggers contributed one million florins.[50]

Although the availability of public credit varied across Charles's domains, generally there were no long-term, amortizable annuity bonds secured with a fund for paying the amortization and interest charges.[51] Charles was very well connected to European financial networks, since most were located in his domains, especially in Antwerp, Italy and Upper Germany. However, he had no control over the banking houses. While the big Genoese houses, the Fugger and the Welser from Augsburg, supported the emperor, other houses in Augsburg and Nürnberg gave loans to his arch enemy, the French king.[52]

Starting in the 1520s, the revenues from the inflow of American precious metals exceeded the revenues from the Netherlands. Charles designated banking houses as tax-farmers in the New World.[53] However, the Spanish fiscal bureaucracy was not capable of providing reliable income estimates in order to budget the financial resources and expenses. This lack of control over the budget led to the state's bankruptcy in 1557. The imperial treasury survived, thanks to the creditors' fear of losing their principal. The worse the financial balance became the more secrecy prevailed over the financial administration. The real size of the debt was kept secret even from the members of the financial council, since this knowledge could turn into a dangerous weapon in their hands.[54]

Fragmentation of the Habsburg domains and the lack of budgetary control constrained the availability of generalized power. The agents of the dynasty could still find resources by alienating other sources of income either permanently or for long periods. However, in the long run these methods could not be maintained. Interstate competition in Europe required more steady and sustainable methods of taxation yielding more regular income. Finance lay at the center of war-making and the rationalization of foreign policy and defense.

Unlike the Ottoman armies, Habsburg armies had no resources reserved for their maintenance. They had to rely mostly on credit for free resources.[55] In the hereditary lands in Austria, wars with the Ottomans exhausted the resources of the dynasty. In the last year of the rule of Ferdinand I the

STATE FORMATION IN THE HOLY ROMAN EMPIRE   97

income from the Austrian, Bohemian and Hungarian domains totaled around 970,000 guldens, while the expenses oscillated between 1,365,000 and 1,900,000 guldens. In Bohemia as well as in Hungary, Ferdinand tried to reorganize the financial administration through the establishment and reform of the accounting chambers. In 1554, the expenses for Ferdinand's own court – including the salaries for the Privy Council, the Court and Chamber Councils, the Chancery personnel, chroniclers and Post Master totaled more than 100,000 gulden. At his death, Ferdinand left a debt around 2,984,757 guldens.[56]

The analysis of the financial network of the Habsburgs reveals that the emperors were dependent on ascriptive groups.[57] The resources of the New World gave Charles V far more free resources than any of his contemporaries. But the administration of this huge conglomerate of countries was far from being a unitary actor. As with administration, taxation in the medieval empire or the project of a Habsburg universal monarchy was incompatible with the fiscal unification of the territorial state that was taking place at the level of the Imperial Estates. In this regard, the Peace of Augsburg and the Peace of Westphalia brought new opportunities for territorial states. A major indicator of the rise of absolutism in Germany after Westphalia is the imperial resolution of 1654 which made the Territorial Estates and their subjects responsible for financing territorial defense.[58] The Habsburgs also joined other German princes in building territorial states. The construction of the Habsburg monarchy clearly illustrated the reorientation of the dynasty from a universalist/imperial to a territorial/absolutist vision.

In the aftermath of Westphalia, the Habsburg state had two main fiscal resources: the chamber income (*Camerale*) and extraordinary subsidies (*Contributionale*). Under the control of the paymaster of the court, the *Camerale* income that came mostly from the ruler's domain lands, indirect taxes, duties, tolls, monopolies, and mining, was spent on the princely household and administration, while the subsidies were monitored by the war-paymaster. Although both paymasters were part of the Court Chamber, the war-paymaster had to coordinate with the military authorities.[59] The Court Chamber (*Hofkammer*) was in charge of all the cameral income. Several provincial chambers worked under its supervision. However, since the cameral income proved increasingly insufficient, the monarchy had to rely on subsidies. The provincial estates and their bureaucracies remained in control of the apportionment and collection of subsidies. The main source of taxation throughout the domain was landed property. However, the burden of taxation on land differed in every province. In Bohemia the burden fell entirely on the peasants, since taxation of the nobility was rejected, while in Austria landowners were the original tax-payers, who passed this burden on to the peasants. Regardless of the distribution of the fiscal burden, the revenues of the provinces proved insufficient for the war-making of the nascent absolutist state.[60]

During the Thirty Years War the invention of the contribution tax provided the foundation for military financing. The contribution, first tried in Bohemia in the 1620s, was born out of concern for supplying an army that was retreating to the hereditary lands either due to defeat or winter retirement. In order to prevent the army from living off the land, the estates were to provide supplies and cash regularly. Billeted troops would be monitored by the estate commissaries and supplied in cash and kind. This emergency tax was routinized after the Thirty Years War and constituted the basic means of maintaining a standing army.[61]

The two front war in the 1680s, the Ottoman wars and the war with France, created a huge deficit for the Habsburg state and the contribution was unable to cover it. In 1697, a General Cashier (*Generalkriegskasse*) was established under the Court Chamber, which was to have branches in provincial capitals. The Cashier's main task was to distribute liquid military funds centrally. At the same time, a *Deputation des status publico-oeconomico-militaris* was founded, to prepare annual military budgets and send them to the Territorial Diets. It was also to organize other military activity such as recruitment in line with the demands of the army and the estates. However, despite these reforms, Habsburg foreign policy and the military remained dependent on extraordinary taxes. The Habsburg state lived on the brink of bankruptcy. In 1703, in the most intensive phase of the War of Spanish Succession, the death and bankruptcy of the principal creditor of the Court brought army supplies to a standstill.[62]

Thus, due to its fragmented nature and despite the reform efforts, the Habsburg corporate state was still far from the fiscal unification that had been far more advanced in France and England in the seventeenth century.[63] The reforms of Ferdinand I and Ferdinand II created central institutions that connected Vienna to the provincial capitals and the Territorial Estates. However, all these institutions were still governed to a great extent by local interests. They were not unified under an overarching system coordinating the finances. The fiscal policy of the state was short-sighted and focused mainly on *ad hoc* financing of war efforts. In this respect, the official ideology of the early absolutist state was mercantilism in its Central European form – cameralism, derived from the word chamber. As the name denotes, the main purpose of this approach was focused on increasing state revenue. It was characterized by social conservatism, bureaucratization and narrow fiscalism, which aimed exclusively at increasing the tax base and the revenues of the state. However, plans for economic development usually contradicted conservatism and fiscal imperatives.[64]

In 1740, at the start of the Wars of Austrian Succession, the finances of the monarchy were already strained. The early Theresian reforms led by the head of the court chancery Count Friedrich Wilhelm von Haugwitz (1700–1765) attributed the main problem to the Territorial Estates, the financial mismanagement and corruption, and the inaccurate estimates of the fiscal cadastres, registers of the quantity, value and ownership of real estates used in apportioning taxes. Haugwitz introduced the notion of regular taxation of seigniorial lands in peacetime. The basic challenge was seigniorial tax evasion either through placing the tax burden completely on the peasants or simply hiding assets by under-reporting. The Theresian cadastres still relied on seigniorial reports, which had to undergo inspection by state officials. Despite the reforms, the calculations of the state officials demonstrated that Haugwitz's reforms were far from adequate for financing war-making. These still had to be complemented by extraordinary taxes.[65]

In this context, Maria Theresa's reformist chancellor Kaunitz and his protégé Count Ludwig von Zinzendorf put forward an extensive reform project based on the English model. Accordingly, Zinzendorf proposed to restructure the financial system of the monarchy and manage public debt through bonds. Both Kaunitz and Zinzendorf opposed extraordinary taxes, such as inheritance tax, poll tax, free gifts (*don gratuity*) in kind and capital gains tax, arguing that these constituted infringements on the right of private property. The failure of these taxes and the end of the war in 1763 gave the reform party a chance to implement their proposals – albeit only partially. A new ministry, the Court of Audit, yielded the first overview of the finances of the whole monarchy. Zinzendorf suggested the establishment of a national credit system based principally on voluntary loans, the creation of a permanent Exchange and a National Bank under the joint guarantee of all the Estates. Moreover, the reformers were influenced by the eighteenth-century French political economists, the Physiocrats, with their emphasis on agricultural productivity. The reformers claimed that a short-sighted fiscal policy with excessive taxation and excessive tariff regulations was a major impediment to long-term economic development.[66]

Kaunitz and his protégé's reform projects clearly constituted a break with the traditional cameralism of early absolutism. Kaunitz argued that war-making was dependent on socio-economic endurance and therefore, defended the maintenance of a military of a size that did not prevent economic development. Taxes should be collected efficiently, be equal and proportionate to the real wealth of the subjects and should not reduce the standard of living. Extraordinary taxation was counterproductive since it overburdened the people and curtailed the incentive to produce. In this regard, Kaunitzian reforms were not limited to the fiscal field but envisioned a total restructuring of the economy and society. In his reports, Kaunitz underlined the improvement of agriculture, the creation of trade companies to stimulate domestic industry, and the removal of tariff regulations. In contrast to early Theresian cameralist policies of direct industrial subsidies and the granting of monopolies, Kaunitz defended the indirect involvement of the state in the economy. The state should be concerned with building infrastructure. Most of Kaunitz's proposals met severe resistance from the conservative party so that the final reforms bore the mark of compromise.[67]

The imperatives of the state system were driving the state not only to find resources for occasional warfare but also to establish a unified financial system. The debate between the conservatives and the reformists reveals that fiscal unification and innovation of financial institutions required larger social and political reforms: the abolition of the corporate state and of feudal land tenure, the advent and protection of private property, the creation of a single legal community with equal civil rights and the rise of the state as the only entity responsible for legislation and jurisdiction. In this regard, Theresian reform was crippled by the dependence of the Habsburg state on the Territorial Estates, which were still indispensible for legitimation. In this context, a groundbreaking project of absolutist reform was the codification of a civil code that established a direct relationship between the ruler and the subjects to the detriment of the estates.[68]

Analysis of the Habsburg financial system illustrates the challenges that the imperial framework faced in the late sixteenth century. Without an analysis of the pre-existing institutions one cannot explain the financial shortcomings of Charles V's rule. Despite the vast resources in his domains, the lack of centralization and autonomy of political institutions made it very difficult for Charles to mobilize these resources effectively. Fiscal reform was a survival mechanism for war-making and public peace. The reform movement in the Holy Roman Empire attests to the awareness of the need for financial reform. However, the major beneficiary of financial reforms was not the emperor but the Imperial Estates which used new taxes to consolidate their territorial authority. After the failure of a universal monarchy, the Habsburgs joined the rest of the German princes in building their territorial state. Taxation was a major aspect of this process. Once they had re-oriented their policies toward territorial rather than imperial goals, they succeeded in curtailing the political and fiscal authority of the

Territorial Estates and created an integrated hereditary domain with a central state.

Foreign Policy

Analysis of the Holy Roman Empire in the fields of administration and taxation demonstrates how the fragmentation of political authority among the Imperial Estates prevented the emergence of the empire as a unitary actor. This section will demonstrate how this institutional plight influenced the conduct of foreign policy. The inadequate state formation of the empire made it impossible to demarcate imperial domestic politics from interstate politics. While the Habsburg dynasty was pursuing goals beyond the boundaries of the empire,[69] the Imperial Estates were allying themselves with foreign powers to protect their rights against the threat of the transformation of the empire into a hereditary state under the Habsburgs.[70]

The struggles against the French Valois and the Ottomans constituted the defining challenges of Habsburg foreign policy.[71] Militarily, Charles V achieved victory several times against the French, but translating these victories into a universal monarchy was to prove impossible. After the French king, Francis I, was taken prisoner at the Battle of Pavia (1525), he had to sign the Madrid Agreement (1526) and recognize Habsburg rule over contested territories. However, following his release Francis declared the agreement void and united with the pope, Florence, Venice and the Duke of Milan (1526) against Habsburg rule in Naples and Milan.[72] Facing an Ottoman threat in the Habsburg hereditary lands, Charles presented himself as the defender of Christianity against the Ottomans and the heretics. Imperial propaganda charged the anti-Habsburg alliance with disturbing the unity of Christianity. The conflict lasted until the Peace of Cambrai (1529) between the Valois and the Habsburgs.[73] However, while Charles V strengthened his grip over Italy he destabilized the political order inside the empire.

The empire did not behave as a unitary actor in Charles's conflict with the French. Distinguishing between Habsburg dynastic interests and their own interests, the Imperial Estates did not participate in the emperor's war against the king of France. The Imperial Estates were opposed to the hegemonic projects of the emperor outside of Germany, since they feared that a strong foreign power base might give the emperor the opportunity to establish an absolutist monarchy in the empire.[74] Instead, the estates tried to arbitrate between the emperor and the French king.[75] Only one time, in the Diet of Augsburg in 1544, did the estates provide military support for the emperor against the French king in return for concessions to the Protestants.[76]

The empire was more involved in the struggle against the Ottomans. However, the Imperial Estates again left the burden of defense largely to the Habsburgs, whose territory was immediately threatened by Ottoman expansion. The Ottoman victory in Mohács (August 1526) and the death of the Hungarian king on the battlefield led to a direct confrontation between the Ottomans, who supported their protégé John Zápolya as the newly elected king, and the Habsburgs, who claimed the Hungarian crown for Charles's brother Ferdinand. Habsburg policy was conducted on two major fronts; Ferdinand was in charge of continental defense, while Charles pursued a maritime strategy in the Mediterranean. Confronting the Ottoman annexation of Belgrade (1521) and Buda (1526) and, finally, the siege of Vienna (1529), the Habsburgs tried to mobilize the empire against the Ottoman threat. Between 1522 and 1542 the Imperial Estates contributed militarily to the defense of the empire; after 1542 they offered only cash contributions.[77]

Ferdinand's finances demonstrate the institutional weakness of Habsburg defense against Ottoman attacks. When Ferdinand started his rule in the hereditary lands, most revenues had already been alienated by his grandfather, Maximilian. He had to rely on subsidies, extraordinary taxes from hereditary lands and contributions from the Imperial Estates. But even in his hereditary lands, Ferdinand found little willingness to increase contributions for defense. Since Territorial Diets (*Landtage*) deliberated over the contributions in their own sessions in the presence of their overlord, Ferdinand had to travel to at least a dozen cities. Still, the cash flow was usually very slow and could be increased only in an emergency.[78]

Ferdinand's appeal to the Imperial Estates or to his siblings reflected the fragmented nature of policy-making both in the empire and the Habsburg system. Instead of sending help to Ferdinand, Charles demanded troops to support him in Italy. The Spanish representative assembly (*Cortes*) in Valladolid refused to pay for Austrian defense. Almost half of the Spanish troops sent by Margaret from the Netherlands either deserted or attempted mutiny due to unpaid salaries. In 1528, the Imperial Diet, at which Ferdinand hoped to present his case for imperial support, was cancelled at the last moment by Charles without prior notice. After Ferdinand was able to convince his brother to hold another Diet, he sent to the estates projections of the cost of the war against the Ottomans. The estates, however, were very reluctant to give the Habsburgs the requested help due to their suspicion that the dynasty would use it for its own policies in Hungary, or against the Protestants. When they finally agreed to help, the sum was much lower than what Ferdinand had requested and was tied to the condition that it be used only for the defense of Germany against the Ottomans: the estates refused to pay for any offensive war. Duke Frederick of Palatine was elected supreme commander of the imperial army and Ferdinand agreed to pay his expenses. But even this was subject to negotiation. Frederick demanded 1,500 florins, while Ferdinand offered only 800 florins. Finally, they agreed on 1,000 florins. Despite Ferdinand's energetic diplomacy, imperial help was too slow when the Ottomans besieged Vienna. The siege was unsuccessful mainly due to the retreat of the Ottomans, who were probably not aware of Ferdinand's plight.[79]

The organizational inefficiency of the defense demonstrates the consequences of the lack of collective action and the dependency of the empire on ascriptive settings. The Imperial Estates were wary of giving the Habsburgs too many resources, and the confessional division within the empire exacerbated the collective action problem. The Peace of Augsburg in 1555 and the Peace of Westphalia in 1648 consolidated the political authority of the Imperial Estates, but also delegitimized the role of the Roman Catholic faith as the universalist ideological trust of the empire. Thus, Charles V was the last emperor who attempted to implement a hegemonic program in accordance with his traditional obligations to Christianity. His successors became German emperors and gave up imperial obligations towards Western Christendom and the pretension of political superiority.[80] Another consequence of the confessional crisis was the increasing intervention of other European states in the empire, obliterating its right to sovereign independence and non-intervention in domestic affairs. Westphalia gave the Imperial Estates the right of conducting their own foreign policy, but questions of war and peace would be decided by the emperor and the estates together.[81] Thus, the parcellization of authority inside the empire also curtailed its agency in the states system, since neither the Imperial Estates individually nor the emperor could act as sovereign.[82] The empire was legally sovereign until 1806; however, it could not perform as a unitary actor in the state system.

The problem of the sovereignty of the empire was reflected not only in warfare but also in the diplomatic representation of an empire that lacked its own diplomatic corps. Habsburg diplomats represented the emperor and the empire in foreign courts and diplomatic conferences. The German scholar Johann Jacob Moser asserted that the emperor had the right to dispatch diplomats but could not close deals without the confirmation of the estates. Nevertheless, imperial diplomats excluded the deputies of the estates whenever they could, in the Conference of Nijmegen (1677), in Rijswijk (1697) and in Utrecht (1713). The attempts of the estates to participate individually or as a group were prevented both by the emperor and by other European powers. Furthermore, despite the protestations of the Imperial Chancery, the Habsburg Court Chancery accredited imperial diplomats from Vienna to other capitals. Discrimination against the Brandenburg diplomats in Rijswijk provided a major incentive for the elector Frederick III to seek the royal title for Prussia, since European states only allowed the participation of kingdoms in diplomatic congresses.[83]

Until the mid-eighteenth century, Habsburg decision making was intertwined with the decision making procedures of the empire. This created significant problems for the Habsburgs since the divergence between the Habsburg and the empire's interests grew as political fragmentation increased. The Privy Council (*Geheimer Rat*) established by Ferdinand I in 1527 was an assembly working on both domestic and foreign affairs of the empire and the hereditary lands. Until the 1670s, it processed reports from the ambassadors and instructions to them. The most important court officials, the lord high chamberlain (*Obersthofmeister*), and the imperial vice-chancellor (*Reichsvizekanzler*) were permanent members of the council. After 1648, due to concerns of secrecy, smaller commissions working on individual problems came to be preferred over the increasingly enlarging council. Enlarging participation enhanced the legitimacy but decreased the efficiency of decision-making. In 1699 a smaller assembly, the Privy Conference (*Geheimer Konferenz*), was established to process incoming reports for the Austrian Court Chancery. Thus, after the emergence of the Privy Conference, the activity of the Privy Council was limited to the discussion of relatively insignificant dispatches to the Imperial Chancery. Soon the Privy Conference too became so crowded that the system of small commissions was reinstalled and in 1705 the Privy Conference was completely abolished. In 1709 a Permanent Privy Conference was founded, out of which a Privy or Narrower Conference was selected the same year.[84]

Thus, the bureaucratization of foreign policy was neither complete nor stable; foreign affairs were conducted by several organs in Vienna. The main problem for Habsburg foreign policy was the competition between the Imperial Chancery and the Austrian Court Chancery. From the time of its establishment in 1620, the Austrian Court Chancery gradually increased its influence in the foreign affairs of the empire. Especially during the office of anti-Habsburg arch-chancellors Schönbronn (1647–1673) and Metternich (1673–1675), the Imperial Chancery was excluded from consultations on secret state affairs.[85] Still, the Imperial Chancery claimed authority regarding matters involving the entire empire. Schönbronn maintained correspondence with diplomats in Moscow, Copenhagen, Stockholm and Rome. The Court Chancery took control of correspondence with these posts as late as the first half of the eighteenth century. In 1705, to correspond with foreign states, the Imperial Chancery's authority was transferred to the Austrian Court Chancery. From then on, the Imperial Chancery communicated only with other Imperial Estates.[86] Besides these competing chanceries, Ottoman affairs were exclusively under the authority of the Court War Council (*Hofkriegsrat*) until 1753. In addition to the tripartite conduct of foreign affairs by the Imperial Chancery, the Court Chancery and the Court War Council, the chanceries of territorial and provincial administration were also permitted to have diplomatic correspondence with foreign powers.[87]

The plurality of organs and the frequent change of organizational protocols and procedures of coordination produced an inefficient articulation of foreign policy. This lack of rationalization of foreign policy decision making can be explained by deficient state formation. The emperor, who was at the center of secret diplomacy, was still the major unifying element in this network of overlapping authorities.[88] The rationalization of foreign policy made it possible for the Habsburgs to define their interests and build their strategy more clearly. First, by establishing their own central institutions, the Habsburgs disentangled themselves from the constraints put on them by imperial politics. The institutionalization of foreign policy conduct in Austria reveals the increasing exclusion of old imperial offices from the decision making process. Thus, in Rijswijk (1697) and Utrecht (1713) it became apparent that the Habsburgs were negotiating from a great power perspective rather than an imperial perspective.[89]

In 1681 the failure of the Habsburg model of an imperial war constitution (*Reichskriegsverfassung*) and an imperial army (*Reichsheer*) based on the Imperial Diet led Vienna towards a final break with the idea of an imperial monarchy. Thus, in the course of the seventeenth century the Habsburgs became hereditary rulers in both Bohemia and Hungary,[90] while several Imperial Estates acquired royal titles and representation in European politics; the prince of Saxony received the Polish Crown in 1697, Prussia became a kingdom in 1701, the prince of Hessen-Kassel received the Swedish Crown in 1718, and the prince of Hanover the English Crown in 1714.[91] The turning point in German history however came in 1740 when the Habsburg Emperor Charles VI died without a male heir. King Frederick II of Prussia decided to use this moment as an opportunity to invade Silesia, a Habsburg territory. Against the efforts of the English king George II (who was also the prince of Hanover) to build an anti-Prussian alliance, Frederick allied himself with France and promised the Bavarian prince his support in the imperial elections. In January 1742 Charles Albrecht of Bavaria was elected emperor, and in July 1742 the Austrian archduchess Maria Theresa had to sign the Treaty of Berlin with Frederick, who thereby enlarged his territory threefold. The short reign of the Wittelbach Emperor Charles VII was protested by the Habsburgs, who did not even hand over the imperial archives.[92]

These changes in imperial politics led to a radical reorientation of Habsburg foreign policy, which was possible only with the detachment of the Habsburgs from the empire and their pursuit of an independent Habsburg politics in their hereditary domains.[93] The articulation of Habsburg state interests and foreign policy required institutional changes that transformed the Habsburg hereditary domains into a unitary actor in the states system in the seventeenth and eighteenth centuries. A clear indicator of this transformation was the famous Diplomatic Revolution of 1756 or the overturning of alliances (*le renversement des alliances*). Following Prussian aggression against the Habsburgs, Prince Kaunitz proposed, in the State Conference of 1749, that the centuries-old hostility towards France be reconsidered. Prussia, the elector of Brandenburg traditionally loyal to the Habsburg emperors, was the main enemy of Austria. All relationships with other states had to be regarded in accordance with this fundamental conflict. England, which had been traditionally considered as an Austrian natural ally due to its enmity to France, demonstrated its preference for Prussia during the Wars of Austrian Succession. A Russian attack on Prussia would ease the Austrian re-acquisition of Silesia. However, Russian aggression in the East would also start a conflict with Sweden, which was supported by the French. Thus, Kaunitz's immediate goal was to separate Prussia and France and neutralize the latter in case of Russian aggression. In the context of approaching imperial elections, Kaunitz invoked a rather passive policy in order not to push the French to the Prussian side. The revolutionary character of this plan lay in the fact that both Austria and Prussia were legally part of the Holy Roman Empire. In the past, to designate an Imperial Estate as the main enemy and define the grand strategy accordingly would be inconceivable for the Habsburgs as the heads of the empire. Moreover, imperial officials such as the arch-chancellor could intervene in the policy making process or make secret Habsburg plans public. In this regard, foreign policy making based on Austrian state interest was enabled by the detachment of the Habsburgs from the empire. Kaunitz argued that Austria should not put her security in danger for the vanity of a mere imperial title. These ideas guided the Treaty of Versailles in 1756 between Austria and

France which was a reaction to the Treaty of Westminster in 1755 between Prussia and England.[94]

For the next century, Germany would be characterized by the dualism between Prussia and Austria which emerged as the great powers of the late eighteenth and early nineteenth century. The rise of the absolutist state and the institutionalization of foreign policy in Austria required a political reorientation of the Habsburg dynasty which involved giving up the idea of universal monarchy and basing its legitimacy on the territorial sovereign state and the balance of power. The Diplomatic Revolution would have been unimaginable within the institutional framework of the Holy Roman Empire.

Legitimation

The history of the political institutions of the empire illustrates the inadequacy of the prevailing approach in historical sociology arguing that the survival imperatives of the state system lead to the concentration and accumulation of power in the hands of the king. In addition to institutions, the legitimating principles of political authority also contributed to the trajectory of state formation in the Holy Roman Empire. In the late sixteenth century, the rise of the territorial state was legitimated by the theory of sovereignty of the French publicist Jean Bodin (1529/30–1596). By defining the absolutist sovereign state as the only legitimate state, Bodin questioned the statehood of the empire. The diffusion of Bodin's theory and its influence on German political thought attests to the challenge of the territorial state to the empire in the field of political legitimation.

The analysis of administration, taxation and foreign policy reveals that the organizational principles of the Holy Roman Empire obstructed its transformation into a unified, centralized, territorial state. Even though the need for reform was felt as early as the fifteenth-century, the pre-existing institutional framework of the empire gave the Imperial Estates the opportunity to use imperial reforms for consolidating their territorial authority. However, the Imperial Estates were also dependent on the Territorial Estates. As Ferdinand's defense efforts demonstrate, the Habsburgs ruling over several territories had to negotiate with several Territorial Diets for financing the wars against the Ottomans. Moreover, in case of a breach of their rights, the Territorial Estates could file a complaint against their territorial lord in the higher imperial courts. In this regard, despite the weak royal authority of the emperor, the empire was held together by the principles of the corporate state. However, as chapter four illustrated, these organizational principles were changed radically by the advent of the Protestant Reformation which designated the territorial prince as the guardian of the Decalogue. This principle was confirmed by the Peace of Augsburg and allowed the territorial prince to forge a single political community with central political institutions. Thus, the emergence of absolutist states, such as Prussia and Austria, required a shift in the legitimating and organizational principles away from those derived from the idea of a universal Christian empire toward those derived from natural law. These changes are evident in German public law literature, which focused on the nature of sovereignty and the form of empire.

The medieval empire was based on the fiction of *translatio imperii* (transfer of rule).[95] Accordingly, the Holy Roman Empire was the continuation of the Roman Empire which, in the Book of Daniel, was prophesied to be the last human kingdom on earth.[96] The revival of the empire was dated to Christmas Day 800, when Charlemagne was crowned emperor by Pope Leo III.[97] Alternatives to the idea of a universal empire began surfacing as early as the eleventh and twelfth centuries during the Investiture Conflict between the pope and the emperor. According to historian Walter Ullmann, the Luxembourg Emperor Henry VII's attempt against King Robert of Naples was the last imperial endeavor to exercise the rights of the emperor to universal lordship. In accordance with *Corpus Iuris Civilis*, the emperor asserted that he was the lord of the world (*dominus mundi*) and charged Robert with *crimen laesae maiestatis* for inciting revolt in Lombardy and Tuscia. Robert ignored the summons to the imperial court and was convicted of treason in absentia. However, in 1314, Pope Clement V issued the bull *Pastoralis cura*, in which he formally repudiated the supremacy of the empire over other kingdoms.[98] The papal rejection of imperial suzerainty was a major blow to the universal suzerainty of the empire. However, the idea of a universal monarchy still carried significant weight until the seventeenth century.

The arguments for the universal monarchy in the sixteenth century were based on two distinct but closely related medieval traditions. The first tradition was based on the concept of the emperor in Roman law as the ruler of the world (*dominus mundi*) and the embodiment of law (*lex animata*) as the source of all law. According to Roman legal theory (known as *lex regia*) the Roman people had transferred their law-making rights to the emperor. The second tradition was embedded in the concept of a universal corporate church and regarded the emperor as the head of the body of all Christian princes. This theological argument rested on Pauline teachings as well as on the medieval theory of the two swords which represented the authority of the pope on the souls of Christians and the authority of the emperor on their bodies. The sixteenth-century variation on these medieval traditions also employed Aristotelian teachings to argue that the emperor and the universal empire represented the ordering of a plurality of polities into a single empire analogous to the ordering of all parts into a whole unity in nature.[99] Thus, although in practice Europe was ruled by a multiplicity of autonomous states, ideologically the idea of the universal empire continued to carry weight in the sixteenth century.

The idea of a universal empire was revived when Charles V was elected emperor in 1519.[100] The new emperor inherited large domains in the Netherlands, Austria, Spain, Italy and the Americas which gave him more resources than any of his predecessors.[101] The extraordinary powers and vast domains of Charles V made it possible to derive concrete actions from the idea of a universal monarchy and implement them against other rulers.[102] Interestingly in the sixteenth century, the concept of universal monarchy was used not only by the imperial publicists but also by their opponents. The resistance against Charles's empire did not resort to the principles of the individual sovereignty of states but, rather, to the argument about the depravity of the empire. Thus, both the imperial propaganda of Charles V as well as its opponents operated in the same universalistic world-view.[103]

In the sixteenth century the reified ideology of a universal empire continued to be held. The ideas of equal sovereignty spelled out in the previous centuries could not gain an ideological stronghold as long as the idea of a universal Christian church remained intact. Humanists such as Desiderius Erasmus (1466/69–1536), who were adversaries of Charles V's imperial projects, based the political order in Europe on the concept of a universal Christian community. Erasmus was a subject of Charles V living in the Duchy of Burgundy (the Netherlands). He was appointed councilor to the young Charles and wrote *The Education of a Christian Prince* as a book of counsels for him.[104] In this book he criticized the imperial policies of the Habsburgs, especially their acquisition of countries through marriage and their administration through the regency system. He argued that a good prince should stay in his country and constantly monitor his subjects. Thus, he criticized the imperial peripatetic government of Charles and supported a government within fixed political boundaries. Moreover, he also argued that the emperor should not seek imperial suzerainty over other European states. However, he based these counsels on Christian virtues. The state system was not based on the natural rights of sovereign states, but on the grace of the emperor who should forsake his legal rights derived from *Corpus Iuris Civilis* for the sake of peace.[105] In this way, Erasmian thought reflects the mentality before the great confessional wars in Europe, which would make a durable peace based on a universal Christian community impossible.[106] Thus, Erasmus did not yield a legitimating discourse for the territorial state. His works were very influential among the members of the Imperial Chancery, especially on Chancellor Gattinara, an admirer and friend of Erasmus.[107] Charles's imperial propaganda used the Erasmian call for peace among Christian states in order to substantiate his universal empire.

Legal and political discourse changed drastically towards the end of the sixteenth century. First, the constitutional set-up of the empire was developed by Imperial Diets, especially the Diet of Augsburg (1555), to such an extent that a general knowledge of Roman law and a humanist philosophy were inadequate to analyze imperial affairs. The prevailing opinion – that private law was the true subject matter of law and public law was only a mask for ignorant lawyers – began to change. Public law focused on the question of sovereignty. Some claimed that the empire was a continuation of the Roman Empire and emphasized the 'inalienable rights of the *imperium*,' while others asserted that the empire was a creation of the people and defined sovereignty as 'the right conferred on the prince by the people.'[108]

The end of Charles V's rule also marked the end of the concept of universal monarchy. Moreover, the confessionalization and territorialization of political authority led to the questioning not only of the emperor's universal suzerainty but also his sovereignty within the empire itself. In the late sixteenth century, Bodin formulated a theory of sovereignty (*maiestas*) based on the French model of the territorial state and concluded that the emperor was not a real sovereign, nor the empire a monarchy.[109] Although Bodin's theory questioned the statehood of the empire, its widespread influence urged German political thinkers to address its critique of the imperial constitution and to prove that the empire was indeed a legitimate sovereign state. Thus, the old discussion of whether sovereignty derived from God or from the people was replaced by the discussion of Bodin's theory of sovereignty. The effect of Bodin's theory was an expression of the challenge posed by the emergence of the territorial state to the legitimacy of the empire.

In Germany Bodin's work was received with reservations. Hermann Vuljetus (1555–1634), a Calvinist professor from Marburg, claimed in 1599 that although the emperor was not an absolute ruler (*legibus solutus*), the empire remained a monarchy ruled in an aristocratic manner. He criticized the ahistorical use of concepts from Roman law to understand German feudal imperial institutions. Following Bodin and his follower François Hotman, he argued against the theory of the transfer of rule (*translatio imperii*). Instead, he developed a historical approach, studying the evolution of the empire as a pure monarchy from the time of Charlemagne to its contemporary state. Vuljetus conceptualized the feudal relations between the emperor and the Imperial Estates as a kind of partnership (*consortium*) based on the oath of fealty and the devolution of the usufruct (*dominium utile*) to the vassal.[110] Another Calvinist scholar Johannes Althusius (1557–1638) applied the concept of convenant (*foedus*) from covenantal theology to public law and stipulated a contract between God and the sovereign to lead the chosen people. Contrary to Bodin, Althusius asserted that the empire was a monarchy, in which sovereignty was invested in the person of the emperor but the administration was shared by the emperor and the Imperial Estates. He argued that while *maiestas* could not be divided, administration could be performed by more than one person.[111]

The Peace of Westphalia led to an important debate in German public law between the defenders of the emperor like Dietrich Reinking (1590–1664) who, using Bodin's theory, asserted that the empire was a monarchy, and the enemies of the Habsburgs, such as Hippolithus a Lapide (the pseudonym of Bogislaw Philipp Chemnitz, 1605–1678), who argued that the empire was an aristocracy. The moderates, Veit Ludwig von Seckendorff (1626–1692) and Johannes Limnaeus (1592–1663) asserted that the empire was a mixed form of government, in which the emperor and the Imperial Estates shared sovereignty.[112] Reinking claimed that the sovereign command (*imperium*) originated from God, and the empire was the embodiment of Daniel's fourth monarchy. The emperor was the lord of the whole world and all other kings and princes derived their rights from him. Thus, Reinking repudiated Bodin's conclusion regarding the sovereignty of the empire but accepted his definition of the *maiestas* to assert the sovereignty of the emperor over the empire. According to Reinking, the causes for the empire's decline were papal interventions, the exemptions of the estates (allowing them to sidestep imperial jurisdiction), and internal discord among the estates. Central to Reinking's theory was the argument that the territorial supremacy of the estates was granted to them without diminishing the emperor's *maiestas*. The recipients of these grants owed them to the emperor. Moreover, the parts of *maiestas* that the emperor ceded to a territorial prince became territorial rights which were not supreme and not independent of imperial laws based on the imperial *maiestas*.[113]

Anti-Habsburg sentiment was expressed by a Lapide who argued in his book *On State Reason* (*De Ratione Status*, circa 1640) that the empire was a true aristocracy. The novelty of his approach was his insistence upon basing his discussion on published documents, imperial decrees and other constitutional material rather than on the teachings of Roman law. Based on the study of actual legal documents rather than jurisprudence, he concluded that the empire was a mixed government of three aristocracies: the electors, other princes and free cities. Thus, the main remedy for the collective action failure of the empire was to diminish the powers of the emperor, which had been usurped by the Habsburgs and establish a central government through the Imperial Diet.[114]

However, a Lapide never used historical proof to discredit the argument from Roman law and the four monarchies theory. It was the work of Hermann Conring (1608–1681) which, through the study of history, refuted the late medieval theory that the empire was a continuation of the Roman Empire and the legal system was based on Roman law. Emphasizing the role of university jurists, Conring repudiated the myth that Emperor Lothar III had declared Roman law the official law of the empire in 1135. Conring's historical critique influenced Samuel Pufendorf's analysis of the German Empire.[115]

Samuel von Pufendorf (1632–1694), who, together with Hugo Grotius, is regarded as the founder of natural law and international law, affirms the conceptualization of natural law used in this book. Born in Saxony in 1632, Pufendorf was a first-hand observer of the Thirty Years War and the Peace of Westphalia. Although he is mostly known for his works on natural law, he also produced important works on history and constitutional law. He worked as a professor of law between 1661 and 1670 at the University of Heidelberg and between 1670 and 1677 at the University of Lund. Charles XI of Sweden, who held a seat in the Imperial Diet after Westphalia, appointed him court historian and secretary of state. In 1688 he moved to Berlin as court historian and privy counselor to the Elector of Brandenburg.[116] Thus, Pufendorf's personal career was influenced by the political plight in Germany after the Peace of Westphalia, which revealed two important issues: First, the claim of the universal supremacy of the empire had lost its credibility. Second, with the reinforcement and enhancement of the territorial authorities of the Imperial Estates the question arose whether these rather than the emperor were the carriers of sovereignty.

Pufendorf criticized the theory of the transfer of rule by arguing that the empire created by the pope in 800 was 'a kind of unequal league only entered between *Charles* and the See of *Rome*.'[117] He mocked the proponents of the transfer of rule theory as 'childish' and pointed out that the title of Holy Roman Empire was only honorary and had been the cause of mischief rather than advantage.¹¹⁸ By invoking Hobbes's concept of the 'irregular body,' Pufendorf defined the empire as a 'monstrosity'.¹¹⁹ He asserted that the form of government in the empire fluctuated between a system of states and a limited monarchy. However, after 1648 the maintenance of the empire with divided sovereignty became increasingly impossible.¹²⁰

Pufendorf emphasized that the real weakness of Germany lay not in the imprudent or unchristian policies of the estates or the emperor, but in its constitutional structure, which was leading to collective action failures. Pufendorf's analysis focused on the institutional structure of the empire. His natural law approach revealed the contradiction between the form of the empire and the interests of the Estates. The plight of Germany provided a perfect laboratory for natural law with its basic assumption of the state of nature. In pointing to the institutional structure of the empire as responsible for collective action failures, Pufendorf also justified the self-help behavior of the Imperial Estates.

Thus, natural law provided legitimization for the territorialization of authority within the empire and the rise of absolutist states such as Prussia and Austria. In 1701 the elector of Brandenburg, Friedrich III, declared himself King of Prussia based on Pufendorf's conception of natural right. The Prussian ambassador in Vienna stated that the elector could assume any title for his own duchy since the source of his authority was not the emperor but the will of the people. Faced with the Wars of Spanish Succession, the emperor gave in with the reservation that with its promotion into a kingdom, Prussia would not acquire new rights within the empire.¹²¹

In both Prussia and Austria, absolutist monarchy was legitimized by natural law. Natural law distinguished between private and public spheres, turned the feudal lords into private property owners, and transformed the relationship between the ruler and the subject into an impersonal one between the citizen and the sovereign. It enhanced the law-making capabilities of absolutist monarchies by emphasizing the will of the sovereign as the source of positive law.¹²² It replaced sacral law and custom in legitimizing law-making. Erasmus recommended that the prince maintain the status quo and avoid innovation as much as possible, because novelty in the structure of the state was usually accompanied by upheavals.¹²³ Even if reform improved the status quo, new situations were inherently destabilizing.¹²⁴ In addition, Erasmian political order was based on the Christian conduct of the subjects and the princes. In the age of confessional conflict, however, the very definition of a true Christian was disputed. Natural law based political authority on the consensus of agents defined in minimalist terms, i.e. without cultural or religious identifications.¹²⁵ In this respect, natural law freed generalized power from traditional legitimacy constraints and ascriptive settings. It thereby legitimized reforms in the fields of administration, taxation and foreign policy.

Conclusion

This chapter analyzed how the Holy Roman Empire responded to the survival imperatives of the state system, in which the territorial state became the dominant unit. A neo-realist approach with the emphasis on power shifts cannot explain how the vast empire of Charles V, who was both victorious on the battlefield and rich in material resources, was unable to act as a unitary actor. Charles V could draw on his enormous wealth and victories to the extent that the institutional framework of his empire could translate these into generalized power. Charles lacked institutions that could free resources from ascriptive settings and coordinate and mobilize elites in support of imperial policies. Institutions, such as the Imperial Diet or other parliamentary assemblies in Naples, the Netherlands and Spain, were unwilling to give Charles free resources that could be used against them or simply spent on other parts of the empire. Reforms in the Holy Roman Empire and the attempts of Chancellor Gattinara to establish a centralized administration indicate that the systemic pressures were perceived by Habsburg statesmen. However, imperial reforms creating a collective security system and common jurisdiction, taxation and executive organs only strengthened the Imperial Estates rather than the emperor. In contrast to other European kingdoms, in which survival imperatives led to the concentration and accumulation of political authority in the king's hands to the detriment of the landed nobility, in Germany the same process led to the consolidation of the territorial authority of the Imperial Estates. This phenomenon can be explained by path dependency and institutional layering, which prevented the emergence of a central political authority.

Thus, neo-realist explanations based solely on survival imperatives of the states system cannot explain the foreign policy making of the Holy Roman Empire since it did not constitute an autonomous, unitary actor. The historical sociological focus on state formation illustrates that the empire lacked a centralized administration, a unified political community, a consolidated fiscal system and a coordinated foreign policy. In administration, taxation and foreign policy, several organs and groups were involved in decision making. Under these circumstances, both the empire and the Imperial Estates were far from embodying the autonomy attributed to states by neo-realism. Pufendorf's definition of the empire as a monstrosity expresses this fact lucidly.

Germany's political development in the fifteenth and sixteenth centuries also reveals the shortcomings of constructivism. Indeed, both the Imperial Estates and other European states rejected the idea of a universal empire under the Habsburgs. However, the critique of universal empire did not automatically yield an ideological alternative. The major contribution of this chapter to constructivism is its analysis of the role of the dynamic between legitimating principles and political institutions in determining the compliance pull of ideas. In this respect, the Imperial Diets of the sixteenth and seventeenth centuries (especially Augsburg and Westphalia) contributed greatly to the establishment of emerging doctrines of territorial sovereignty and natural law. These doctrines in turn made it possible for the Imperial Estates to legitimize their political authority and implement absolutist reforms leading to state centralization, fiscal unification and the rationalization of foreign affairs.

Constructivism also fails to explain the failure of imperial reforms. Indeed, one of the main problems for Charles V was the lack of identification of individual countries with the larger imperial project. However, the reason for the lack of a common identity despite a common ruler and imperial ties cannot be understood unless one takes the local political institutions into account. In the sixteenth century, German identity became pervasive in the empire. This, however, did not always guarantee collective action. On the contrary, princes used German identity to strengthen their particular interests and privileges against the central authority of the emperor. The emergence of diverse confessions in the empire exacerbated the problem of coordination. The Peace of Augsburg and Westphalia not only marked the end of the idea of universal empire but also paved the way for a new legitimating discourse: natural law.

Habermas's approach to natural law emphasizes that the most important feature of modern natural law was not its metaphysical content but its method of argumentation based on reason. By emphasizing the need of modern state formation for political legitimacy, the Habermasian approach not only complements the Weberian approach with its narrow focus on the impact of warfare, but also improves the constructivist argument. This approach explains why modern natural law emerged in the seventeenth century and how it was different from preceding intellectual traditions. On the one hand, natural law legitimized the claim of emerging absolutist states, such as Prussia and Austria, to establish a centralized state and control the Territorial Estates. On the other hand, it provided a new organizational principle for the Holy Roman Empire, deriving not from Roman law, ecclesiastical doctrines or Biblical stories, but from the consensus of contracting parties.

The historical sociological approach of this chapter suggests that most of the problems facing the empire cannot be explained simply by changes in material capabilities or ideas. Early modern German political development reveals that neither material capabilities nor identities translate directly into agency in the states system. In order to explain how material and normative sources constitute agency in the states system, a study of institutions is essential.

6
STATE FORMATION IN THE OTTOMAN EMPIRE

As arch-enemies, the Habsburgs and the Ottomans experienced systemic pressures simultaneously. This chapter demonstrates how the Ottomans reacted differently to the survival imperatives of the state system and explains the variation of state formation in both empires in terms of institutional differences. In stark contrast to the Holy Roman Empire, the Ottoman Empire emerged as one of the most centralized states in Europe. So much so that Machiavelli singled out the power of the Ottoman sultan as an example of strong and unified government.[1] In this context, the path dependence argument in the previous chapter seems to pose a problem: if the failure of adaptation of the Holy Roman Empire to the early modern state system and the emergence of Habsburg absolutism can be explained by the low level of central authority, how can one explain the adaptive failure of the Ottoman Empire? Moreover, if the prevailing Weberian argument in historical sociology that wars make states and vice versa is correct, why would a centralized state like the Ottoman Empire in the sixteenth century change into a disintegrating polity with strong centrifugal political forces?

This chapter seeks to answer these questions by studying the challenges of the systemic pressures on the empire in four domains: administration, taxation, foreign policy and legitimation. It argues that the closure of the imperial frontier in the late seventeenth and early eighteenth centuries led to a rationality crisis of the empire which could not be solved within the existing organizational principles. In the seventeenth century while the territorial state was consolidated in Germany after the Thirty Years War, the Ottoman state underwent its own crisis when it had to concede its first main territorial losses in 1699 and 1700 in the Karlowitz and Istanbul Treaties. The treaties marked a break not only with the traditional legitimacy based on Holy War, but also with the institutional design of the empire, which until then was based on the primacy of the military class. For the first time in its history, the scribal class came to dominate the foreign affairs of the empire. While these scribes turned into diplomats they also started to propose domestic political, social and economic reforms. However, reforms to overcome the rationality crisis at the level of the state system could not be formulated as long as the empire failed to change its institutional design and its legitimation discourse. The institutions, which had initially contributed to the success of the Ottoman polity in the fifteenth and sixteenth century, proved inflexible in the seventeenth and eighteenth century.

The Ottoman Empire

In the late thirteenth century, two dominant states in Anatolia were disintegrating. The Seljuk Sultanate, the nominal suzerain of the Ottomans, was challenged by the second wave of Turcoman settlers and Mongol attacks, while the Eastern Roman (Byzantine) Empire was deprived of its capital Constantinople by the Latin invasion between 1204 and 1261. Both states needed the help of Turcoman frontier principalities to secure order in their borderlands. The Ottomans, like the Habsburgs, used this opportunity to establish themselves as a frontier principality in the late thirteenth century. However, unlike the Habsburgs, the Ottomans created the institutional framework of their empire without being constrained by an existing state structure.

Within less than two centuries the Ottomans evolved from a tribal emirate to a highly bureaucratized empire. Their initial success depended on their organization of frontier warriors to wage guerilla warfare and distribute the spoils among their supporters. An inclusionary tribal ideology based on kinship recruited warriors, dervishes and colonizers from Muslim pastoralists as well as Christian settlers. This ideology was expressed in the concept of *gaza* (Holy War) which initially was not equal to *jihad* and did not denote religious fanaticism and orthodoxy. The *gaza* reflected the 'metadox' or 'doxa-naïve' world-view of the frontier society characterized by pragmatic inclusiveness and latitudinarianism without following an orthodox doctrine articulated by religious scholars. The power of the frontier society depended on the enlargement of tribal networks through the mobilization of various religious and ethnic groups for warfare.[2]

As the Ottoman army started to attack cities towards the end of Orhan's rule (*circa* 1324–1362), siege and battlefield warfare necessitated an increase in Ottoman infantry and a reduction of mounted archery.[3] The transition to siege warfare led inevitably to a transformation in the organization of warfare and state formation. The growing Ottoman principality was approached by Muslim scholars and statesmen offering their services. Tribal ideology and structure were incapable of holding together a territory consisting of important cities located along trade routes. Two offices emerging under Murad I (1362–1389) marked the transformation of the Ottoman tribal emirate to a state. First, the office of the military judge (*kazasker*, originally *kadıasker*), a special judge for the military class, reflected a social differentiation between the ruling military class and the taxpaying subjects. Second, the appointment of marcher lords (*uç beğleri*) indicated a differentiation between the political center and the periphery and thereby the degree of Ottoman state centralization.[4]

Early Ottoman state formation laid down the basis for the emergence of a highly centralized world empire. The Ottomans were the founders of the state and, unlike the Habsburgs, were not bound by any pre-existing institutional framework. Thus, in contrast to the Holy Roman Empire, the Ottoman Empire was ruled by a hereditary dynasty with a central bureaucracy and a spatially fixed capital. There were no powerful land-owning nobles or representative institutions such as the Imperial and Territorial Diets. While the offices of the Holy Roman Empire were hereditary entitlements of the electors, the Ottoman sultans increasingly appointed so-called slaves (*kul*), who were recruited through the child levy (*devşirme*) system (also initiated during the reign of Murad I), to their military-administrative positions. The child levy system was based on collecting young Christian boys from villages, converting them to Islam and putting them under state service. The child levy, an overt breach of the protection of non-Muslims granted to them by the *shari'a* under the legal *dhimmi* status, provided the Ottoman sultan with a loyal group of officials, in particular the janissaries and the pages of the court. The system created a cadre of state officials (*ehl-i 'örf*) who owed their social status solely to the sultan; they would never dream of questioning his authority.[5] Although this slave system was never predominant and lasted for only a limited time,[6] its differences from the European feudal system were remarkable. Unlike vassal lords in Europe, upon a slave's death all his property would devolve to the sultan who would keep one tenth of the property for himself and distribute the rest among the inheritors of his slave. Slaves had to accept promotion as well as disgrace and execution without resistance.[7]

Another important characteristic of the early Ottoman emirate was the maintenance of territorial integrity. Had the Ottomans followed Turco-Mongolian inheritance practice they would have partitioned the land among the sons of Osman. Orhan would still have been the commander-in-chief over his brothers but they would have ruled in their own domains. Instead, unigeniture was established very early and was noted by early Ottoman chroniclers as a distinguishing characteristic of the state.[8] The indivisibility of territory was later legalized by the law book of Mehmed II which established sultanic fratricide as a lawful act.[9] The practice of fratricide indicated two principles underlying the succession process: first, Ottoman territory was indivisible and second, none of the sultan's heirs had primacy in succession.[10] Thus, by the time of Mehmed II (1444–1446 and 1451–1481) the Ottoman Empire had become a centralized state which had annexed large territories, made Constantinople its capital and established its central organs and constitutional rules.[11] These rules were outlined in the law book (*kanunname*) of Mehmed II which constitutes the main source for the analysis of Ottoman administration.[12]

Administration

Unlike the Holy Roman Empire, the Ottoman Empire in the sixteenth century relied on a highly centralized bureaucracy that was independent of ascriptive groups. The Ottoman state managed to tie all the military-administrative class, religious establishment, corporate bodies such as guilds and endowments, cities, religious and ethnic groups, and even village communities to the political center. It controlled cities and merchants through price regulations. However, this high level of centralization led to an extreme fragmentation of Ottoman society: individual communities were tied vertically to the state but had no horizontal ties to each other.[13] As such, the Ottoman state ruled over a conglomerate of numerous communities rather than a single political community.[14] This lack of civil society and social institutions of collective action made it harder for the empire to implement reforms in the subsequent centuries as it started to compete with the emerging territorial states of Europe. Unlike the reforms of the territorial states in Germany that relied on the cooperation of corporate bodies (such as Territorial Estates, cities, territorial churches), Ottoman reforms had little social support. Since they destroyed the existing social hierarchy, they destabilized the imperial ruling elite and led to their political fragmentation and ultimately to the failure of collective action.

In its heyday, the Ottoman state was run by the powerful grand vizier (*vezîr-i azam*) who was the head of all viziers and *amīrs* and the absolute deputy of the sultan.[15] The unique feature of the Ottoman grand vizier – compared to the viziers of pre-Ottoman Muslim states – was the concentration in his hands of responsibilities for administration and the conduct of military affairs.[16] The Ottoman grand vizier was the executive of the administration rather than a bureaucrat *ex officio*. This is apparent in the lack of a formal ladder of political advancement (*cursus honorum*) for grand viziers in the law book of Mehmed II.[17] Although, in the fourteenth century, most of the grand viziers came from the ranks of the religious establishment, in the latter half of the fifteenth century Mehmed II started the tradition of appointing the grand viziers from the Christian levies (*devşirme*).[18] The sultan's preference for his slaves over the Muslim scholars, who were usually the offspring of old Turcoman families, represented the increasing autonomy of the ruler from ascriptive groups. Thus, the grand vizier served as the slave of the sultan under pain of death.[19] However, in accordance with his unlimited liability in state affairs, he also enjoyed enormous political power. In the sixteenth century he became the political center of the empire; he convened a state council daily in his own residence and employed an increasingly larger staff of officers and scribes.[20]

The second important official of the empire was the chief treasurer (*başdefterdâr*), who was the deputy of the sultan's property and was responsible for financial affairs.[21] Thus, the fiscal bureaucracy seemed to put a significant limit on the powers of the grand vizier. According to the law book, all income and expenses were to enter or exit the treasury with the orders of the treasurers. Similar to the grand vizier, the chief treasurer was liable only to the sultan.[22] The grand vizier and the chief treasurer constituted an executive dyad sharing the most important secrets of the empire.[23] However, both officers acted in an Imperial Council with other viziers and officials. Although they could balance against the grand vizier,[24] the latter was still responsible not to the Imperial Council, but only to the sultan himself. The only authority to discharge and execute the grand vizier was the sultan, since he was his slave.

The law book regulated the procedure in the Imperial Council; its members were the viziers, the military judges, the treasurers and the affixer of the cipher. The most distinguishing feature of the Ottoman Imperial Council – compared to its pre-Ottoman counterparts – was its degree of centralization.[25] The head of the chancery of the council was the affixer of the cipher who was responsible for the internal state correspondence, the preparation and control of *kanuns* and the drawing of the Sultan's official monogram (*tuğra*).[26] Another important member of the Imperial Council was the military judge as the head of the judiciary. He was the only official besides the grand vizier, the treasurers, and the military judges who could issue orders in the sultan's name.[27] While their pre-Islamic counterparts were responsible only for the judiciary of the military class, Ottoman military judges were at the top of both the military and civilian judiciary.[28] The military judges were also the heads of the religious establishment appointing all judges (*kadı*) and professors (*müderris*) in *madrasas*. They acted as supreme judges in the sessions of the Imperial Council as a high court. The importance of this office in the early Ottoman state is indicated by the fact that the sultans appointed grand viziers from among the military judges until Mehmed II's preference for slaves. The composition of the Imperial Council struck an intricate balance, not only between the military-administrative establishment, the religious establishment and officialdom, but also among the fractions within each establishment. The council institutionalized and regulated competition among the ruling elite, which enabled the sultan to rise above political rivalries. Like the absolutist rulers of the seventeenth century, who controlled the court nobility through the competition for titles, posts and grants, the sultans of the fifteenth and sixteenth centuries controlled the elite through the distribution of fiefs, posts and royal gifts and most importantly through the balance in the council.[29]

Another important administrative organ was the Imperial Court. In the Ottoman Empire, as in Europe, the problem with the separation between court and state administration was that of communication between the bureaucrats and the ruler. A major difference between the court life of the Ottoman Empire and the absolutist courts of Europe was the divide between the inner and outer parts of the Ottoman palace. In Europe the feudal landed nobility was transformed into a submissive court nobility by compulsory attendance at court. The development of the Ottoman state into an empire was accompanied by the sultan's seclusion; he made fewer public appearances and stopped presiding over the Imperial Council.[30] The secluded sultan ruled through the Imperial Council over a vast hierarchy of administrators. Ottoman administrative officials were called the military (*askeri*) class, which reflected the fusion of administration and military. The traditional composition of the Ottoman army was born during the reign of Murad I: a fief-holding cavalry (*sipahi*) in the provinces and the *kapıkulu* (slaves of the Porte) soldiers, including the personal guards of the sultan, the janissaries in the capital. The central army consisted of salaried soldiers stationed in the capital while the cavalry lived on the assigned fief.[31]

Thus, in addition to its role in warfare, the fief-holding cavalry was also responsible for administration and taxation. Provincial administration reflected the organization of the army; the province under a governor-general (*beğlerbeği*) was divided into districts called *sancak* (literally banner) headed by district-governors (*sancak beği*).³² The balance in the Imperial Council was also replicated at the provincial level: the military judge appointed a judge (*kadi*), a member of the religious establishment, to complement and check the authority of the *beğ*, a member of the military-administrative class. While the *beğ* needed the *kadi*'s judicial authority for punishments, the *kadi* needed the *beğ* to execute his decision.³³ Still, governors-general enjoyed enormous powers since they distributed *timars* in the provinces in addition to distributions by the Imperial Council.³⁴ The Ottoman fief (*timar*) was a non-hereditary prebend or fief, which was assigned to a cavalryman called *sipahi* who, in proportion to the size of the fief, had to train a certain number of auxiliary cavalry (*cebelü*).³⁵ Although the legal status of fief-holders never achieved the degree of security acquired by European feudal lords in the late sixteenth century, the council tried to preserve the class of local *timar*-holders against the granting of *timars* by governors-general to their own entourage. However, it could not do this without harming the military power of the *timar*-holders since increased control by the central government led to the distribution of fiefs to officials, protégés of the viziers, pages and ladies of the court to cover the increase in expenses.³⁶ Despite the legal and political control of the central government over the fiefs, the Ottoman cavalry – like the European nobility – served the basic function of tying the peasants to allotted land and extracting taxes.³⁷ The *timar* system not only constituted a pillar of provincial administration but also played a major role in Ottoman state finance.³⁸

In the late sixteenth and seventeenth centuries the Ottomans, like other European states, faced systemic pressures due to the emergence of the territorial state as the dominant unit. The Age of Absolutism was characterized by prolonged technology-intensive warfare and a closely monitored diplomatic system. Both processes favored a state which could free and mobilize more resources and sustain this mobilization over prolonged periods. Although territorial acquisition was still a major goal for states, the centralization of political authority and the enhancement of mobilization capacity became far more important than the size of territory. Changes in European warfare technology and the defeat of the Ottoman army in Europe had important political and social consequences for the Ottoman state. The closure of the imperial frontier and the end of conquest led to a rationality crisis in the Ottoman state, which was soon translated into a legitimation crisis.

In the sixteenth century, the Ottomans managed to build a bureaucratic empire that extended beyond the immediate patrimonial realm of the dynasty.³⁹ However, the central administration of the empire was substantially different from the centralization of the territorial state. It was marked by a fuzzy and ever-expanding imperial frontier, an unequal distribution of political authority of the center in the semi-peripheries and peripheries, a multiplicity of loosely connected ethnic and multi-confessional societies and a pluralistic legal system consisting of Islamic law, sultanic statutory law, local custom and communal privileges. Creating a vast territorial state out of the Ottoman domains would require a unified legal system based solely on the legislation of the state, and the consolidation of fiscal resources, neither of which were possible within the traditional imperial organizational principles.

Systemic pressures, such as changes in warfare technology and diplomacy, challenged the organizational principles of the empire. The need for soldiers with firearms in Central Europe, especially during the long war between 1593 and 1606, caused the Ottomans to make important changes in their military structure leading to important social and political changes. The fief-holding cavalry (*sipahi*) fought with conventional weaponry such as bow and arrow, lance, sword and shield, which were becoming less and less effective against the Austrian musketeers. The Ottomans responded by increasing the number of janissaries from 13,000 in the 1550s to 38,000 in the 1600s. However, when the increase of janissaries did not meet the demands of the military, the Ottomans started to recruit soldiers with firearms from the tax-paying peasantry (*reaya*). These soldiers were called *sekban* and were paid by the government only during wartime. The obliteration of social boundaries between the tax-collecting military class and the tax-paying peasants (*reaya*) antagonized the former who, as the slaves (*kul*) of the sultan, enjoyed a privileged status. Moreover, the long-term mobilization of the *reaya* also led to the emergence of local notables (*ayan*) as important power-holders who helped the government to register *sekbans*.

Thus, while the rapid increase of janissaries led to their domination of the capital between 1617 and 1656, the governors-general found opportunities to use the *sekbans* to increase their power. Unemployed *sekbans* in peacetime either served the governor or wandered through Anatolia extracting money and supplies from the population leading to what is called the *Celali* Rebellions (1596–1607). These rebellions led to the Great Flight (*büyük kaçgun*) of the peasants who were seeking refuge from the tyranny of the *sekbans*. The central government's response, which was to station janissary garrisons in Anatolia, provided an opportunity for the latter to integrate into the provincial urban structure. The emergence of janissaries established in the provinces also led to rivalry between the *kapıkulus* in the capital and those in the provinces, further weakening central authority.[40]

This rivalry led to violent conflicts between the two groups in which the central government and rebellious governors changed sides several times.[41]

In addition to warfare, the increase and intensification of diplomatic activity led to the rise of the scribal class (*kalemiyye*) at the expense of the military-administrative and religious establishments. In the heyday of the empire, the number of Ottoman scribes remained fairly small; they were relatively less institutionalized but their function, the production of documents, was vital for the working of the state.[42] They were recruited mostly from freeborn Muslims in contrast to the prevailing converts selected by the child-levy in the military-administrative class.[43] The most common means of recruitment was called *intisab* or connections either through kinship or household patronage.[44] Despite their intellectual isolation from new ideas and their exclusive focus on document production, the scribes emerged as the vanguards of the reform movement in the eighteenth and nineteenth centuries. Due to their increasing diplomatic contacts with European powers and their rather precarious pre-eminence, they were more interested in the reforms than any other social group. In order to understand the extent of reform, a closer look at changes in the Ottoman state structure is necessary.

One of the most important developments in the seventeenth century was the decline of the Imperial Council. Despite being created by sultanic law, the Imperial Council was a body without legal personality issuing orders in the name of the sultan.[45] For this reason, historian Joseph Matuz asserts that the Imperial Council was only a consultative not a decision making institution.[46] Unlike the Imperial Diet of the Holy Roman Empire, the Imperial Council never became a corporate body consisting of representative colleges. Thus, when the Ottoman imperial frontier closed in the seventeenth century and the capability of the sultan to allocate resources was reduced, the balance between the ruling elites became tenuous and the Imperial Council's meeting became merely symbolic and was unable to provide a formal means of regulating political competition. Increasingly, officials assembled in *ad hoc* consultative councils (*meşveret meclisi*), in which the grand mufti (*şeyhülislam*), who was the head of the religious-scholar establishment (*ilmiyye*) but not a member of the Imperial Council, bestowed legitimacy on decisions.[47]

When the conduct of state affairs was transferred from the sultan's Porte to the grand vizier's Porte in 1656, the chancery of the Imperial Council moved into his house. In 1654 a palace was assigned to the grand vizier as his permanent office and residence.[48] Still, the old office structure of the Imperial Council remained operative while new elements were added to it.[49] Emulating the grand vizier, other viziers and *paşas* also started to maintain offices in their residences. Thus, during the late seventeenth century, *paşa* households became important centers for recruiting the administrative-military and scribal elite of the empire, undermining traditional recruitment through the imperial palace school (*enderun*). Competition among households to expand their patronage networks by getting their protégés appointed to higher posts drastically changed Ottoman officialdom; hence it could no longer be defined merely as an extension of the sultanic household. With the emergence of *paşa* households, the scribes' personal loyalty to their patron became the prevailing ethos.[50]

The rise of the grand vizier's residence and the decline of the Imperial Council were also reflected in the decreased standing of the affixer of the cipher and the military judge in state affairs. The decline of the fief system and the fief-holding cavalry, and the vertical mobility of peasants into the military ranks progressively reduced the significance of military judges who were in charge of sultanic laws regulating fief bestowals and the judiciary military-administrative class. The military judge also lost his prominence among the religious establishment to the grand mufti, a non-member of the council. The affixer of the cipher, though still the titular head of the Ottoman chancery that now worked directly under the grand vizier, only prepared the imperial cipher for documents.[51] Reminiscent of the decline of European chancellors, who became symbolic officers, increasing state correspondence led to the rise of the secretaries and the chief of scribes, nominally an officer under the affixer of the cipher.[52] In this regard, despite different institutional traditions, both the European and Ottoman chanceries seem to respond in the same manner to the increasing burden of correspondence in early modern politics.

The transformation of Ottoman administration reveals the constraints of the ruling elites in adapting the empire to the changing nature of the state system. Although the empire achieved a high level of administrative centralization as early as the fifteenth century, its organizational principles and their embodiments, the political institutions, restrained the reform options of the elites. While reforms changed the social and political structure and made state organs dysfunctional, the existing institutions were not replaced with new formal institutions integrating the new ascending classes, regulating political competition and ensuring collective action. The old formal institutions existed next to emerging mechanisms until the establishment of a cabinet regime in the early nineteenth century, at which time modern ministries evolved from the offices of the chancery of the Imperial Council.[53] For their part, the Habsburgs benefited from the weakening of the constitutional structure of the Holy Roman Empire;

the imperial constitutional structure gave the Habsburgs the legitimacy to construct their territorial state as the princes of their own domains.[54] The co-existence of old dysfunctional institutions with symbolic, legitimating offices and the new informal institutional in charge of the conduct of state affairs led to a gap between political legitimacy and political rationality. Nineteenth-century reformers were aware of this fact. Ahmed Cevdet Paşa, the leading reformer and most prominent figure of the nineteenth century Ottoman codification *Mecelle*, remarked, in his history of the Ottoman state, that '[…] it is more difficult … to change and renovate the laws of a state than to found a state anew.'[55]

Taxation

The same dynamic of reform, coexistence of old and new institutions in the Ottoman Empire, can also be observed in the field of taxation. As with the administrative system, the fiscal system of the empire was also unified in the fifteenth century. The Imperial Council monitored all the revenue sources in the empire through a specialized provincial fiscal bureaucracy with the chief treasurer at its head. Treasurers in the provinces conducted detailed surveys for each newly conquered province and updated them regularly. Since most of the Ottoman land belonged legally to the state, the fiscal system was unified under the sultan's control. Thus, unlike the Habsburgs, the Ottomans could raise vast armies without asking ascriptive groups for contributions or borrowing cash from banking houses. However, this advantage yielded negative feedback in the seventeenth century when the changing nature of warfare and the world economy challenged the fiscal system. As Wallerstein points out, imperial organizational principles were not oriented towards increasing domestic productivity or exploiting other economies through the import of raw materials and the export of manufactured goods.[56] In line with the ideology of universal empire, Ottoman economic policies encouraged the import and discouraged the export of manufactured goods in order to provide Ottoman cities, in particular the capital, with goods in high demand. For these purposes, the Ottomans granted extensive trading and even extraterritorial sovereignty rights to European states.[57] Thus, the control of the state over cities, domestic traders and corporate bodies such as guilds and the lack of civil society at large led to comparative disadvantage in the long run. When systemic pressures increased the need for cash, the Ottoman fiscal system had no financial institutions to pool domestic resources and to provide much needed loans.

The classical Ottoman fiscal system was based on three main pillars: the central treasury (*hazine-i âmire*), the *timars* and the Sultan's treasury (*ceb-i hümâyun*). The Sultan's personal treasury consisted of some revenues directly assigned to this department which the rulers could use as they wished. The central treasury was relatively small and its main sources of revenue were imperial fiefs of the Sultan (*havass-ı hümâyun*). Around 70 percent of the revenues of the central treasury were spent on the Sultan's central army (*kapıkulu*). The revenues from fiefs of several sizes (*has, tımar* or *zeamet*) did not reach the central treasury but were collected by the cavalry or other state officials in return for their services. Given the low level of monetization of the economy, the state could thus save the transaction costs of transferring taxes – mostly in kind – to the center, turn them into cash and send them to its officers and cavalry. This fiscal system was based on two assumptions: that the Ottomans would always win in war and that wars would not be financed by cash. The landed cavalry was not supposed to engage in prolonged warfare since this would curtail the extraction of agricultural surplus. Moreover, the central treasury had a static structure of revenues and was not designed to finance unforeseeable war costs. Warfare for the Ottomans was supposed to be a source of revenue not expenditure. In this regard, the central treasury was susceptible to deficit in the case of prolonged warfare and defeat.[58] The two presumptions of the classical taxation system of the sixteenth century were both challenged in the seventeenth century. Warfare in the seventeenth and eighteenth centuries lasted longer than wars in the sixteenth century.[59] Increasing dependence on infantry with firearms led to an increase in the number of janissary soldiers and the employment of mercenary armies.

In the classical system the fief-holding cavalry, whose expense was met by fief revenues, constituted 30 to 40 percent of the Ottoman army. Increasing dependence on janissaries and mercenaries raised the cash needs of the central treasury. In addition to this, the influx of American silver from Europe and the subsequent price revolution shook the Ottoman economy starting from the 1580s. The devaluation of the Ottoman silver coin, the piastre (*akçe*) led to a decrease in state revenues and in the revenues of fief-holders since these were established as fixed sums. A potential increase in taxes on fief-holders would greatly diminish the livelihood of the *reaya* and favor only the fief-holders and not the central treasury. Starting in the seventeenth century, Ottoman budgets always yielded deficits. Thus, similar to the Habsburgs, instead of changes in the classical *timar* system, the Ottomans resorted to extraordinary taxes collected directly by the treasury and to new tax collection methods.[60]

Between 1687 and 1703 the Ottoman state redistributed its financial resources and discovered new ones.[61] Historian Rhodes Murphey emphasizes the creation of a self-sufficient, regulated economy and a new focus on domestic production as a conscious part of Ottoman reforms.[62] However, legitimation placed limits on new reforms: '[...] the Ottoman sultans could only be as institutionally innovative as their more socially and intellectually conservative subjects would allow.'[63] Thus, the Ottoman bureaucracy tried to solve the fiscal problem within the classical system through transfers from the sultan's treasury, coinage debasements and forced loans (*imdadiye*). It also increased the cash flow to the treasury by applying tax-farming (*iltizam*) more widely. Tax farming emerged parallel to the *timar* system and involved the sale of a tax source by auction for a specific period of time, usually three years, to an individual. Tax farmers (*mültezims*) could divide the revenue unit (*mukataa*) further and sell them to secondary tax farmers. Since the provincial administration was ordered to assist the tax farmers in tax collection, this led to close cooperation between tax farmers and administrators. Tax farmers were usually local notables who thus gained an increasing role in the provincial administration. In 1695 the fiscal bureaucracy came up with a novel solution by selling tax farms to buyers for life. This new system – called the *malikane* (manor) system – combined the fief system and tax farming and was to constitute the fundamental instrument of Ottoman fiscal policy in the eighteenth and nineteenth centuries. Similar to the *timar* system, the new system with lifetime tenure aimed at creating a long term interest for the tax famers, such as increasing efficiency in their tax sources.[64]

In addition to these changes, the Ottoman state introduced new taxes to finance the costs of warfare. The first type of extraordinary tax was called *avarız-ı divaniyye*. This tax was paid by all males – except of course for the military class, the religious establishment and others who enjoyed tax exemptions – entered by the *kadis* in registers (*tawzi defterleri*). During the Habsburg Wars (1593–1606) the *avarız* was turned into a regularly levied tax. An important social consequence of these taxes was the emergence of local notables as the representatives of tax-payers negotiating with the *kadi* or through his mediation with the imperial center. Between 1683 and 1699 and due to the bribes and misappropriations of the kadis, the central government ordered the notables of the province (*ayan-ı vilayet*) to assist the *kadi* not only in levying the *avarız* but also in other tasks. Thus, the *ayan* rose as an indispensible class for the administration of the empire. Because of the enormous burden of these taxes, many of the *reaya* deserted their villages. Similar to the absolutist regimes in Eastern Europe, the government responded by decreeing the return of fugitives.[65]

Another type of tax was the *tekalif-i örfiyye* which, in the seventeenth century, emerged out of the need of Ottoman military commanders (*beğs* and *paşas*) to maintain large retinues of mercenaries. These commanders traveled within the provinces and stayed in villages in order to maintain their soldiers through several exactions from the local population. Some urban centers under the leadership of local notables managed to resist the provincial governors' arbitrary exactions and secure exemption (*muafiyetname*) from the sultan. This also contributed to the rise of local notables as important power-holders which the central government supported as a balance against its governors.[66] In addition to these extra levies, the government also resorted to forced loans called urgent war contributions (*imdad-i seferiyye*) from the wealthy, who then collected levies from the *reaya* as reimbursement. In 1686 after the defeat at the Hungarian border, the government decreed that the local notables in all Ottoman towns, governors, and ladies of the court should contribute to the war effort. The religious establishment (*ulema*) protested fiercely against this and was eventually exempted from the tax. In the provinces, where loans were collected in lump sums, the *kadi* and the notables determined the share for each district. Then, the notables summoned the elderly in the districts to decide how to divide up the responsibility at the district level. Again, the forced loans contributed to the rise of local notables as important agents for provincial administration as well as local representation.[67]

Despite the lack of systematic historical studies of the fiscal distribution of Ottoman warfare, the emergence of local notables and the spread of the *çiftlik* system indicate that the costs and benefits of wars contributed to the rise of new political actors and the demise of the old. A negative effect of prolonged warfare was the neglect of the safety of the roads and the countryside. Since the army was busy at the front, banditry became pervasive. Many office holders depended on the revenues remitted from their subcontracting tax-farmers, who collected the grain, sold it on the market and sent the proceeds to the capital. Due to increasing insecurity in the countryside these subcontractors were unable to send the revenues.[68] This might have led to the formation of a political alliance in the capital among the social groups who benefitted from peace. For instance, the chief of scribes Rami Mehmed Efendi, the Ottoman chief negotiator in Karlowitz, had a lifetime tax-farm.[69] However, more studies are needed to determine what the relationship was between the beneficiaries of the manor system and the supporters of peace and how the benefits of peace weighed against the fixed rewards or the ideological value of war-making.

Ideological legitimation of peace with Christian states was a delicate matter for a universal empire that was established on the idea of the Holy War. In this regard, the Ottoman fiscal system was not entirely oriented towards cost-benefit calculations but burdened by ideological considerations. The fiscal reforms of the seventeenth and eighteenth centuries were implemented without a change in the organizational principles. While the financial bureaucracy experimented with new fiscal instruments, there was no large reform proposal like the Kaunitzian reforms in the Habsburg monarchy. Thus, the Ottoman fiscal system retained its conservative goal of increasing the revenues of the state, disregarding economic productivity and domestic economic actors until the late eighteenth and early nineteenth century, when ideas of economic liberalism began to influence Ottoman economic thinking.

Foreign Policy

The articulation of Ottoman foreign policy was also centralized in the Imperial Council. In the sixteenth century, it reflected the imperial organizational principle that the Ottoman sultan was superior to all other rulers and the leader of the Holy War. Foreign policy was therefore formulated in a manner in which the sultan treated other rulers as his vassals. Since the Ottomans did not regard other states as equals, they did not send permanent ambassadors to them, but allowed some of them to maintain embassies in Istanbul. They also refrained from signing bilateral treaties with other states, especially peace treaties with Christian states. Instead of formal residence diplomacy and official bilateral agreements they used an intricate web of agents and unilaterally granted privileges called capitulations to enter alliances with European states. However, the emergence of the modern state system radically challenged Ottoman foreign policy making. Their defeats by European states led to the haphazard adoption of the emerging rules of international society such as the recognition of mutual sovereignty, the rules of reciprocal diplomacy and the monitoring of the system through diplomatic congresses. Most importantly, adaptation to the modern state system necessitated a reorganization of Ottoman imperial administration and the emergence of a bureaucracy specialized in foreign affairs. However, all these changes led to a legitimation crisis since they contradicted the imperial organizational and legitimating principles. This crisis had increasingly pernicious effects on the adaptation of the Ottoman state to the modern state system.

The Ottoman foreign policy approach of the sixteenth century relied on a synthesis of three traditions of universal sovereignty: the Central-Asian khanate tradition, the Islamic-Iranian sultanic tradition and the Eastern Roman caesarist tradition.[70] Contrary to widespread argument, the Ottoman claim to universal superiority cannot be explained by religion.[71] This belief stems from an uncritical reading of Western and Ottoman sources and taking imperial propaganda for facts. In the sixteenth century, Ottoman sultans claimed to be caliphs, even though they did not rely on the orthodox Sunni doctrine that the caliph be chosen from the Prophet's tribe, the Quraysh. Since the sultans could not claim to be the descendants of this tribe, they based their claim on the reinterpretation of an old Ottoman tribal tradition – the *gaza*. As the Ottoman state became a world empire, the religious establishment reformulated religious doctrine and turned the caliphate into a hereditary title of the Ottoman dynasty.[72] Around the same time, the bilateral diplomacy of the early Ottoman state with Christian states, such the Eastern Roman Empire, Geneva and Venice as well as other Turkish principalities in Anatolia, was changed.[73] As the imperial identity of the state became dominant, bilateral treaties were transformed into unilaterally granted privileges.[74]

The unilateral attitude of the Ottoman Empire was the formal and legal expression of the claim of imperial suzerainty which in fact required the collection and dissemination of information and disinformation, the forging of alliances and the coordination of central imperial decision-making with marcher lords, vassal states and allies. Like most medieval and early modern states, the conduct of foreign policy was diffuse; not only high officials but also local officials, marcher lords, and even members of the religious establishments such as the Greek Orthodox Patriarchate could play a role in the decision making process.[75] Ottoman information-gathering, a crucial element in the planning of military expeditions and the making of alliances, took place on four levels: central intelligence in Istanbul; local intelligence, especially by marcher lords; intelligence from vassal and client states; and espionage and counter-espionage by the Sultan's spies and saboteurs.[76] Unlike the Habsburgs, the Ottomans managed to coordinate all these agents through the central government. Ottoman grand strategy, which emerged during the reign of Süleyman I (1520–1566), involved the formulation of an imperial universalist ideology, the collection of information inside and outside the empire, the formulation of a foreign policy and propaganda, and the mobilization of the empire's resources.[77]

The expansion of the empire depended on its operation in a system of states and thus, on reciprocal relations with other states; in other words, unilateralism did not mean isolationism from European politics.[78] The Ottoman Empire used two major instruments in order to make alliances with Europeans: first, the networks of converts and Christian and Jewish subjects of the sultan, who were used for the gathering of information and diffusion of propaganda without compromising Ottoman imperial pretensions and second, the granting of capitulations to European states. The non-Muslim subjects, slaves recruited through the child levy and other converts gave the empire an important advantage over their European counterparts who did not have any Muslim subjects. Since European diplomats usually lacked knowledge of Turkish and relied mostly on the Greek and Latin subjects of the sultan in the capital for translation, the Ottomans pressed these translators for information. Although no European languages were taught in the Ottoman palace school or in the colleges, known as *madrasas*, the Ottomans employed subjects who were fluent in European languages and who translated official documents.[79] Through their family networks, these functionaries had access to European sources of information and even European courts. They were sent to Europe several times to collect intelligence.[80] Unfortunately, there is still no systematic study of Ottoman diplomats in the period under discussion. But these findings suggest that the Ottoman Empire was far from being isolated from European politics. In addition to their subjects, the Ottomans, in their efforts to gather intelligence, used permanent ambassadors in their capital as well as several functionaries.[81] Their networks helped the Ottomans in the sixteenth century to seek alliances with the enemies of the Habsburgs – France, England and the Protestants in Germany.

The major instrument of Ottoman foreign policy in its reciprocal relations with European states was the granting of privileges. In their relations with Europeans, the Ottomans resorted to the legal fiction that the diplomatic corps were non-Muslim visitors who were granted safe-conduct (*aman*). This provided the Ottomans with a legal basis to establish reciprocal – albeit legally unequal – relations with European states.

> All non-Muslim foreigners (*harbi*) were to be seen as obedient subjects (*dhimmi*) of the *Dar al-islam* on whom the benevolent ruler bestowed various privileges in order to promote the welfare of the Islamic community (*maslaha*). The sultan, acting as head of the people of Islam, would even confirm his policy towards non-Muslims with his promise (*ahd*) to maintain these privileges upon condition of reciprocal loyalty.[82]

These privileges – called capitulations (*ahdname*) – were a continuation of both the Islamic *aman* system and the custom of Byzantine and Mamluk capitulations granted to Europeans.[83] Through capitulations, a foreign enemy (*harbi*) became a foreign resident (*müste'min*), and theoretically, after a certain period of residency, a foreign resident would become a non-Muslim subject of the Sultan (*dhimmi*). According to historian Daniel Goffman, these unilaterally granted capitulations reflected an Islamic world-view, which envisioned the eventual incorporation of all Genoese, Venetian and other merchants into an Islamic society.[84] The final documents expressed the ideological stance of the Ottoman state, which did not distinguish between domestic and international law. As such, the capitulations 'were conceived as instruments of domestic policy in conformity with the law of Islam which in theory cannot recognize the legal existence of statehood outside Dar al-Islam.'[85]

Despite the unilateral formulations, the capitulations still served the function of developing reciprocal relations and providing diplomatic protection that allowed the empire to forge alliances and operate in the state system within the confines of its legitimating principles. The initial drafts of capitulations prepared by Ottoman and Europeans envoys reflected a far more bilateral negotiation process and even the influence of European terminology.[86] Moreover, the capitulations provided more protection to diplomats than they enjoyed in Europe. Basic institutions of residence diplomacy such as consuls, extra-territorial protection, the gathering of intelligence, reciprocity and privileges for the protection of nationals, etc., were developed by Italians in the Ottoman Empire before being transplanted into the Italian peninsula.[87] While European states were unwilling to grant envoys the right to heretical worship, the Ottomans granted all ambassadors jurisdiction over their subjects' affairs and the maintenance of a chapel. In other words, the principle of *cuius regio eius religio* did not apply in the Ottoman Empire.[88] This religious pluralism was an application of the organizational principle of the empire that granted the protection of Islamic law to diverse ethnic and religious communities under its rule.[89] Thus, even the stipulations in the capitulations which contradicted Islamic law were put into effect by the confirmation of the sultan and became part of the already pluralistic Ottoman legal system.[90] In 1651, for instance, the enforcement of the capitulations even led to the dismissal of the mufti at the top of the religious establishment.[91] Thus, unilateralism did not prevent the Ottoman state from fulfilling the stipulations of the capitulations or establishing reciprocal relations with Christian and non-Christian powers.

STATE FORMATION IN THE OTTOMAN EMPIRE 135

By the seventeenth century military defeats and domestic rebellion had destroyed the political consensus on which Ottoman imperial ideology was founded. In the face of increasing interstate competition and changes in warfare technology and statecraft the Ottoman world-view became increasingly incompatible with the characteristic elements of the dominant unit in the state system, the territorial state, whose demarcated political boundaries contradicted the organizational principles of the Ottoman Empire. The changing balance of power turned the traditional Ottoman instruments of foreign policy into instruments of European foreign policy. European states used capitulations to establish their own networks within the empire by granting citizenship to non-Muslim Ottoman subjects and thereby providing them with diplomatic protection. When necessary they also used their extraterritorial rights in the capitulations to evade the sultan's sovereignty and jurisdiction within Ottoman territory when necessary. The resulting rationality crisis of Ottoman foreign policy could have resulted either in the decreasing power of the state or in an immediate legitimation crisis of Ottoman organizational principles. Unable to forge a new consensus, the Ottoman elites opted for reforms within the existing organizational principles which eventually led to the waning of the state and the contraction of the empire. Thus, the legitimation crisis could not be escaped but only delayed.

In the seventeenth century, the Ottomans had to fight the Habsburgs in the West and the Safavids in the East. France, England and the Netherlands, all geographically distant, inimical to Habsburg policies and commercially interested in the Eastern Mediterranean, became important partners for the Ottomans.[92] The Iranian wars (1578–90, 1603–19, 1623–24, 1629–39) and the Habsburg wars (1593–1606) marked the stabilization of the Ottoman borders on the Eastern and Western frontiers. After that, the Ottoman army was unable to acquire any significant territories beyond its frontiers.[93] However, the rise of Russia in the north further complicated the picture. In the early seventeenth century, the Ottomans recognized the equality of the Ottoman sultan with the Habsburg emperor who had been treated as having equal rank with the grand vizier during the reign of Süleyman I. In order to justify this diplomatic defeat the plenipotentiary explained that these titular changes were necessary and permissible in 'this age of dissimulation' (*bu asır mudara asrıdır*).[94] However, the signing of the treaties of Karlowitz (1699) and Istanbul (1700) could not be justified so easily. In July 1697 an imperial rescript announced that the Ottoman state was willing to make peace on the principle of *uti possidetis* (*alahaleh* in Ottoman) that the territory currently held should remain in the possession of the current holder.[95] The signing of a peace treaty with a Christian state and the adoption of an international rule represented a radical break with imperial unilateralism. The ensuing treaties, which were negotiated for the first time by Ottoman diplomats of scribal rather than military origin, set clearly demarcated political boundaries and imposed respect for territorial integrity.[96]

Despite negotiating from weakness and their relative lack of experience, the Ottoman mission made use of precedents and negotiation rules and strategized well, both in proceeding in an inductive fashion and in dealing separately with the allies of the Holy League. The final instruments of peace definitively reflected the end of unilateral diplomacy; they drew clear boundaries between states, created a joint commission for the demarcation of these boundaries and established a timetable for the implementation of the stipulations. In this regard, the acceptance of mutually respected political boundaries and the mutual guarantee of the inviolability of territory created a legitimation crisis for the Ottoman Empire which had based its political legitimacy on the ever-victorious frontier. When finally the treaties were put into effect, the Tatars, who traditionally raided the Polish and Russian territories under the vassalage of the sultan, withdrew their allegiance to the sultan as the titular head of the Abode of Islam.[97] In Istanbul opposition to Sultan Mustafa II led to the rebellion of 1703. The military and religious establishments forged an alliance against the sultan and declared the withdrawal of their allegiance (*hurûc ala s-sultan*). Legal opinions (*fatwas*) were issued to justify the cause of the rebels. The rebels suspended the Friday prayer and the weekly *hutbe* in the capital which represented the allegiance of the population to the ruler. As the rebellion grew, the rebels finally deposed the sultan on the grounds that he had made peace with Christians, ceded Muslim territory to them and made himself subject to Christian law. As a result, Mustafa II, who posed as the last *gazi* by going on campaign in person, was deposed as a traitor.[98]

Ultimately, the treaties of Karlowitz and Istanbul contributed importantly to the bureaucratization and rationalization of the conduct of foreign affairs. During the peak of its imperial power the Ottoman state developed neither a formal institution for diplomatic communication nor a diplomatic corps trained for peace negotiations. Ottoman missions normally consisted of members of the military class. In the course of the 17th century the central bureaucracy – the scribes – took the lead in inter-state negotiations. The chief scribes attended the negotiation of the treaties of Vasvar and Buczacz (1672) with the Habsburgs.[99] Civilian officials represented the empire diplomatically for the first time at Karlowitz. The chief scribe and chief translator were instructed by a rescript from the sultan to negotiate as deputies of the grand vizier and not to act against the honor (*ırz*) and dignity (*namus*) of the sultan. From this date on until the transformation of the chief scribe into the minister of foreign affairs in 1830, the chief scribe always represented the Ottomans in peace negotiations.[100]

The dyad of the Muslim-born chief scribe and the Greek chief translator was to become typical for the conduct of Ottoman foreign affairs in the eighteenth and early nineteenth century. While the former was trained and promoted within the network of *paşa* households, the latter was appointed from the influential Phanariot Greek dynasties.[101] The office of the chief scribe originated from the traditional office in the Imperial Council and became an important bureaucratic post leading possibly to the Grand Vizierate. Despite his ceremonial inferiority the chief scribe was in charge of both the domestic and foreign correspondence of the Imperial Council.[102] In the nineteenth century, the chief scribe evolved from his original role as a secretary for internal, military and foreign affairs to become the minister of foreign affairs.[103]

Thus, Ottoman adaptation to the state system continued despite the ensuing legitimation crisis. The rising scribal class played a major role both in the conduct of foreign affairs and in the introduction of social, political, economic and legal reforms. Mustafa's successor, Ahmed III, sent an ambassador to Vienna to reassure the Habsburgs that the war he was about to wage against the Russians was defensive in nature.[104] The fact that the Ottomans felt the need to give the Habsburgs prior notice and assurances before going to war against Russia reveals that the empire had started using diplomacy as a corollary to warfare in an unprecedented way. The report of the envoy, who was a member of the military class, does not contain any description of Habsburg institutions. This might be due to the fact that the Ottomans, especially the military class, still thought that they had nothing to borrow or copy from the West.[105] In contrast, at the end of the century, Ebu Bekir Ratib Efendi's embassy to Vienna reveals a conscious effort on the part of the Ottomans to learn from Habsburg institutions. In his report to the sultan, the Ottoman diplomat not only described Habsburg military institutions but, more interestingly, their financial institutions. Following the wars with Russia and the Habsburgs (1787–1792) and in order to solve the Ottoman financial crisis, Ebu Bekir Ratib Efendi emphasized the fiscal instruments that enabled the Habsburgs to raise money for warfare. Overall, the report of the envoy reflects the mentality of a reformer, who distinguishes between various adaptable and less adaptable Western institutions.[106]

The Treaty of Küçükkaynarca (1774) with Russia, in which the Ottoman state was forced to cede the Crimea, a Muslim territory, led to an important change in the Ottoman world-view of the eighteenth century. The Austrian proposal to include the Ottoman state in the European society of states was vehemently rejected by Russia, which pretended to be the protector of the Christian subjects of the empire.[107] In addition to Russia's opposition, historian Christoph Neumann points to 'insufficient input of information, ownerless and unorganized decision making, and passivity' as major factors in the exclusion of the Ottoman Empire from the European society of states. Although the consultative councils (*meşveret meclisi*) replaced the Imperial Council as the new assemblies to incorporate new elements in the decision-making process such as the grand mufti, the minutes of the councils reveal a slow and passive decision-making process. Although the inclusion of the religious establishment seemed to secure legitimacy for the conduct of foreign policy, the indecisiveness of these councils suggests that the participants did not feel secure enough to take the initiative.[108] The ineffectiveness of Ottoman foreign policy making in the eighteenth century constitutes a startling contrast to the foreign policy of the centralized institutions of the sixteenth century. Historical evidence suggests that the empire perceived systemic pressures and made changes in the conduct of foreign policy. The stagnation of Ottoman institutions and the crippling of the decision-making process demonstrate that successful adaptation to the modern state system required a larger transformation of imperial organizational principles rather than *ad hoc* small-scale changes.

The eighteenth century scribes, who acted as mediators between Ottoman and Western societies from the late seventeenth century onwards, became major reformers.[109] In the nineteenth century, westernization was formulated and implemented by Ottoman statesmen from diplomatic backgrounds. In this regard, the role of Ottoman diplomats as reformers was analogous to the role of Habsburg diplomats: they realized that the Ottoman state needed large-scale reforms and a break with traditional imperial principles. However, in their reform efforts, Ottoman diplomats were increasingly confronted with a trade-off between the rationality of the international system and the domestic legitimation of the state.

Legitimation

Reforms in the fields of administration, taxation and foreign policy to increase the competitive capability of the Ottoman state were limited by a reified world-view. When faced with the challenge of the European territorial state, the Imperial elites could only devise reforms which remained within the limits of the organizational principles of a world empire based on *gaza*. Although Ottoman elites identified their weaknesses and made efforts to adapt to the new state system in the seventeenth century, they still retained an imperial world-view as the basis of political legitimation. While the German states, after the Reformation and the Thirty Years War, reformulated their political legitimacy in terms of natural law, Ottoman reforms were justified as a return to the Golden Age of Süleyman I. The gap between symbol and reality in the Ottoman Empire restricted the reforms and policy choices of the Ottomans and thus contributed to the waning of the Empire. Constraints on Ottoman institutional learning and the persistence of imperial organizational principles can be explained by using Habermas's approach to the rationalization of world-views.

The idea of a world empire played a crucial role in the reification of the Ottoman world-view. First, a world-view based on a universal empire with an ever-victorious frontier was bound to contradict the institutions and practices of the emerging state system which was based on the balance of power among equally sovereign states. As soon as the Ottoman Empire started to incur losses, the world-view had to be either changed or reified to protect it from criticism. Second, as Joel Mokyr observes, political fragmentation in Europe contributed to the emergence of a market for ideas. Scholars could travel across different countries if faced with persecution.[110] However, in the course of constructing their empire the Ottomans established a hierarchy for the scholarly community with the Sultanic *madrasas* at the top. The Sultanic *kanuns* determined the *cursus honorum*, the salaries of scholars as well as their license to recruit graduates.[111] Since the Ottoman Empire dominated the entire Mediterranean basin, it was very hard for a dissident scholar to find and hold a job and not be persecuted.[112] In contrast, in the Holy Roman Empire, territorialization contributed to the establishment of various universities committed to different confessions and dynasties.

In the sixteenth century, the Ottoman Empire could neither claim descent from the Mongol imperial dynasties as had the Jengizid Özbeks and the Timurid Mughals, nor from the Prophet Muhammed as had the Safavids. Lacking genealogical legitimacy, the Ottomans had to base their legitimacy claims on their military capacity which presumably maintained universal justice consisting of the Islamic *shari'a* and the Sultanic *kanun*.[113] Thus, the Ottoman Empire was marked by the political symbiosis of the military and religious-scholar establishments embodied in the concept of *gaza*. As long as the Ottoman Empire continued to expand, the imperial ideology seemed to be confirmed by daily facts.[114] Problems emerged when facts and validity seemed to drift apart with Ottoman defeats by the Christians. As Habermas would suggest, the cost of maintaining a reified world-view which was protected against the facts, was the limitation of innovation and criticism. The notion of the Golden Age in Ottoman ideology reflects this reified world-view.

Historian Hakan Karateke argues that the Ottomans resorted both to 'normative' and 'factual' legitimacy. The former was couched in the classical Islamic political terminology mainly by a close circle of elites who had a certain level of intellectual background. The latter was based on the fact that the Ottoman dynasty was the ruling dynasty of a state that was expanding through conquest. Conquests were indicators of divine confirmation of Ottoman rule.[115] The Ottomans were aware that they were not ruling the whole world, but their official ideology preached that they were politically superior to others. As the rulers of the old Roman capital, the capital of the caliphs, Baghdad, and the Holy Cities of Mecca, Medina and Jerusalem they had ample support to convince a medieval audience of their claim to universal suzerainty. But even among Muslim states, their imperial claims did not go unchallenged. The Safavid and Mughal Empires raised similar claims to suzerainty.[116] However, such empirical evidence does not falsify an ideology. It is explained away in a reified world-view which leaves no discursive space for the questioning of the ideology. The concept of the ever-victorious frontier was an expression of this gap between fact and validity.[117]

The normative aspect of political authority was expressed in the concept of a world order that had universal validity and was not restricted to a certain era, dynasty or region. Historian Gottfried Hagen points out that the fifteenth-century Ottoman historian Tursun Bey defined social order as a consequence of human sociability. God created humans as social beings who tend to live in societies under conditions of solidarity and mutual aid. Conflicts between societies were caused by natural variations of social differentiation. Since primeval societies were threatened by disruption, a ruler watching over the social divisions was necessary. Thus, the source of royal authority was divine. The same theme was reiterated by İbrahim Müteferrika in the eighteenth century but the main thrust of social cooperation was Islamic law revealed by God to the Prophet.[118] This indicates that the major ideas of natural law, i.e. the sociability of human beings and the necessity of political authority due to anarchy in pre-political society, existed in the writings of Ottoman intellectuals very early on. However, the main difference between Ottoman political thought and European natural law was the way in which these ideas functioned in argumentation which, in the case of the Ottomans, was still based on quotations from authorities rather than procedural rationality.

In Europe, the early modern lawmaking state was predicated on a secular concept of state agency justified by public good and state reason rather than sacral law and custom. In this regard, the extent to which Ottoman political thought attributed agency to the state revealed the ideological limits of Ottoman state formation. Moreover, to what extent divine or human agency was responsible for Ottoman victory also illustrated the legitimation basis of the Empire. This question became crucial in the seventeenth and eighteenth centuries in the investigation of the causes of the Ottoman defeat. Human agency in Ottoman political thought was conceptualized as 'particular will' that is part of 'divine will.' This concept originated from Ibn Sina (Avicenna) and was transmitted to the Ottomans through the work of Celaleddin-i Devvanî (Jalal al-Din al-Dawwanî) and his follower Kınalızade in the sixteenth century. According to Ibn Sina, divine will reached human beings through the mediation of the heavens, which yielded the events witnessed by humans in this world. Thus, human intellect was 'particular will' and stood at the end of a chain originating from divine intellect. The vagueness of the theory regarding the exact limits of human or particular will was also its main strength and popularity in the Ottoman Empire, because it could express several rival explanations.[119]

Celaleddin-i Devvanî's *Ethics* elaborated the theory of four pillars (*erkân-ı erba'a*), according to which the social order rested on four distinct classes reminiscent of Plato's model: men of the pen, men of the sword, men of business and husbandmen. In this regard, social justice depended on the preservation of the hierarchical social order, a view that was also shared by many contemporary European humanists.[120] This hierarchical order was formulated by Devvanî and adopted by Kınalızade as a set of logically following axioms called the 'circle of equity' expressing the harmonious working of different social classes:

> There can be no royal authority without the military. There can be no military without wealth. The subjects produce wealth. Justice preserves the subjects' loyalty to the sovereign. Justice requires harmony in the world. The world is a garden, and its walls are the state. The Holy Law orders the state. There is no support for the Holy Law except through royal authority.[121]

This circular reasoning – starting and ending with royal authority – represents the reified world-view perfectly. Historian Boğaç Ergene emphasizes that, in this scheme, justice was extrinsic to the system of four pillars and not an outcome or an attribute of its ideals. The state was an exogenous agent to the social mechanism and was responsible for its proper working.[122] He argues that official Ottoman ideology combined a pre-Islamic notion of charismatic kingship and the Islamic – quasi-contractual – notion of the caliphate.[123] It was the synthesis of two distinct traditions that gave the critics of the government an opportunity to voice their dissent.[124]

However, this world-view was shaken during the course of the seventeenth century when the imperial frontier slowly closed and new rival groups rose to power. The Karlowitz (1699) and Istanbul (1700) treaties, which mark the first and greatest loss of territory in Ottoman history,[125] were a major blow against imperial Ottoman discourse. The Ottoman polity had already been fragmented during the course of the seventeenth century which witnessed a series of revolts, dethronements of sultans, and increasing lack of discipline in the military-administrative establishment. The military-administrative elite itself was fragmented into numerous groups – *paşa* households – that were competing for political power.[126] In this respect, the 1703 rebellion following the peace with Christian states clearly demonstrates the legitimation crisis of the Ottoman polity that was a result of its changing foreign policy making and the underlying transformation of the social structure.[127]

Ottoman ideology amplified the effects of failure in the state system. As Hakan Karateke asserts,

> [P]recisely because the sultans had exploited the state's military triumphs so heavily, they ran into trouble when the tide of conquest turned. Yet they apparently did not abandon the use of this fundamental support of legitimacy; but as one might suspect, this contradiction eventually reduced its actual value.[128]

For Karateke, it was not coincidental that Ottoman reform began in the military field. Hence the closure of the imperial frontier by the end of the seventeenth century was not merely another military defeat but an official recognition of peace with Christian states. As such, it unleashed a major crisis for the Ottoman imperial world-view.[129] In Karateke's words, military defeats led to an emphasis on 'normative legitimacy.'[130] This is predicted by Habermasian argument presented in chapter three, since the facts of interstate politics did not lead to a questioning of the world-view but rather to its reification.

Thus, seventeenth-century Ottoman political thought reflects the uneasy task of Ottoman intellectuals to explain military defeat and social change. In 1656 Katib Çelebi wrote a defense of the need for rational sciences in his book *The Balance of Truth in Choosing the Most True (Mīzan al-haqq fi'khtiyar al-haqq)*. Here, he not only reiterated the old idea of the natural division of humanity into different societies, but also added that political fragmentation of humankind necessitated peaceful coexistence. 'It must also be known that mankind, ever since the time of Adam, has been divided' said Çelebi,

> Every division has its own tenets and its own mode of behaviour, which seem at variance with those of other divisions. As God Almighty says, 'Every party rejoices in its own' (Kor. 23:55): they all like their own ways and prefer them to others. But after all, some men are intelligent: they ponder and observe the inner purpose of this divergence and find that many advantages underlie it, and they will not interfere with or attack anybody's tenets or code. If these seem wrong in the light of their own religion, they content themselves with disapproving of them silently in their own hearts. Other men are gibbering fools: they do not comprehend the inner purpose of divergence and hold the absurd notion that all mankind ought to share one creed and one code of behaviour. Although unprovoked contention in matters of religion is forbidden, they fall into toils of interference and aggression, and will not leave well alone. It cannot be: they give themselves trouble to no avail.[131]

Çelebi not only demanded peaceful coexistence of different societies, but also urged the empirical study of humankind in its diversity.[132] Notably, Çelebi used traditional Islamic sources. Thus, he provides important evidence for the argument that the reification of the world-view cannot be attributed to inherent qualities of Islam but to the institutional framework. Çelebi's work also presents an important parallel to his European counterparts: the exclusion of religious contention from inter-state politics. In this regard, he offers a foundation for conducting inter-state affairs without religious zeal. Religious differences can be disapproved 'silently' by individual conscience, but should not be made a source of political controversy. Çelebi's writings attest to the potential of Muslim intellectuals for formulating new foundations for political order, in both the domestic and foreign politics of the empire. Çelebi provides an important example for the Ottoman reform movement before the westernization of the nineteenth century.

The attempts of Ottoman intellectuals to justify the reforms contradicting imperial organizational principles intensified in the eighteenth century. Historian Mustafa Naîmâ, who was appointed as the first official palace chronicler immediately after the signing of the 1699 and 1700 treaties, attests to the government's need for legitimacy. In contrast to previous Ottoman intellectuals such as Mustafa Ali in the sixteenth and Koçi Bey in the seventeenth centuries who defended the rights of the declining fief-holding cavalry, Naîmâ became the speaker for the rising civilian scribal class in the eighteenth century.[133] In order to justify peace with Christian states, Naîmâ opened his book with a narrative about the Prophet's Peace of Hudaybiya with the pagan Quraysh tribe in Mecca.[134] He then proceeded with Ibn Khaldun's theory of the decline of empires and tried to justify the Sultan's policy in these terms. The apologetic historiography of Naîmâ was still composed in a traditional genre. However, in the late seventeenth and early eighteenth centuries, a new political writing emerged that abandoned traditional references and moved toward an idea of government based on reason rather than religion.[135] The authors of these writings were members of the scribal class aiming to reform the state. Thus, in the second half of the eighteenth century a growing literature of embassy notes (*sefaretname*) appeared in which the Ottoman envoys dispatched to European capitals narrated their observations on European states and societies. This literature reflected the attempts of the scribal class to draw conclusions from comparisons and formulated preliminary plans for reform. In these efforts, the scribal class faced two gigantic tasks that needed to be dealt with simultaneously: the domestic legitimation crisis and the rationalization of the Ottoman state.

Historian Virginia Aksan observes that Ottoman authors of the late seventeenth and early eighteenth century, who defended the reform movement in the Empire and abandoned the concept of the circle of equity, also supported the idea of peace among equally sovereign states and fixed and defensible boundaries. They introduced the idea of the balance of power and European style discipline and training for the military.[136] In this regard, the work of İbrahim Müteferrika, which inspired successive generations of Ottoman reformers until westernization in the nineteenth century, represented an important milestone in Ottoman political thought. İbrahim, a converted courtier and diplomat, became an influential reformer in the two peaceful decades following the Treaty of Passarowitz in 1718, in which the Ottoman Empire was forced to cede the Banat, including Belgrade and half of Serbia and Wallachia.[137] After the 1730 rebellion, during which the sultan was forced to execute his grand vizier and suspend the reforms, İbrahim wrote a book with the title *The Philosophical Principles of World Order*.[138] In this book, İbrahim explained Ottoman military defeat against the Europeans in terms of obsolete Ottoman military conduct and lack of discipline.[139] He regarded the problem of military discipline and social order as being interconnected. The population had to be divided into four groups so that order could prevail: men of the sword (*ashâb-ı seyf*), men of the pen (*ashâb-ı kalem*), men of cultivation and farming (*ashâb-ı hars-u ziraât*) and men of crafts and trade (*ashâb-ı hırfet-u ticâret*). The dominant social group was the men of the sword, who ruled the people properly in accordance with the opinions of the men of the pen. Thus, for İbrahim order in the military would bring order in society. This reiteration of the circle of equity reflected the dilemma of the reformers; they wanted to implement military reform while retaining the traditional social and political order.

The restructuring of the Ottoman military could be achieved only through a wholesale transformation of Ottoman society, but the state was unable to coordinate the Ottoman elites for large-scale reforms. Thus, İbrahim like many Ottoman writers attributed the failure of the Ottoman state to enforcement, conduct, lack of virtues and knowledge but not to the legitimizing principles and institutions themselves. In order to prove this point, İbrahim asserted that the religion and political order of the enemy were not superior. The enemy did not have divine rules (*ahkâm-ı şeriye*) to solve problems, but had to turn to rules of reason (*ahkâm-ı akliyye*). In contrast, Muslims had divine rules to distinguish rightful (*hak*) from false (*batıl*) claims. The superiority of the Ottoman state was based on Muslim sacral law (*shari'a*) and the inferiority of Europeans was due to the lack of it. Thus, İbrahim Müteferrika retained sacral law as the most important legitimizing discourse of the Ottoman state. Nevertheless, he also articulated some classical statements of modern natural law by arguing that humans were by nature sociable (*tâlib-i ictimâ*) and in need of civilization (*medeniyyet*).[140] When the prophets passed away, peoples of the world came together and appointed rulers in accordance with sacral law (*shari'a*) and reason (*'akl*). In this fashion, İbrahim came very close to the conception of political authority in modern natural law based on social contract. However, natural law according to İbrahim was still a combination of sacral law and reason.

Another novelty of İbrahim's work was the lack of reference to the Golden Age. Ottoman political writing, from the late sixteenth century through the seventeenth century, presumed a Golden Age, usually referring to the reign of Süleyman I which demonstrated the success of sacral law and imperial custom. In order to maintain order and defeat their enemies Ottoman statesmen had to adhere to Muslim principles of moral and political conduct, sacral law and imperial custom. For the Ottoman elites in the late sixteenth and seventeenth centuries the main problem was to explain the failures of the Ottoman state in a manner which would leave the reified world-view unquestioned. The fiction of the Golden Age served as a discursive strategy to attribute the causes of the crisis of the empire to the personal shortcomings of statesmen. Moral decay was the cause of political decay. Thus, reform proposals were limited to restoring the Golden Age. In contrast to earlier authors, İbrahim discussed not only what was wrong with Ottoman institutions but also what made European states victorious, although he still maintained the inherent superiority of sacral Islamic law to secular European law. Only in the nineteenth century would the Ottoman Empire undertake a consciously self-critical reform process which would center on the discussion of which institutions and practices needed to be preserved and which needed to be changed.

The diplomat Ahmed Resmi provides an important example of the changing mentality of the scribal class and anticipates the reformers of the nineteenth century. He was a defender of perpetual peace and solid political boundaries, but he also suggested reforms in the preparation for war.[141] Like Kaunitz, Ahmed Resmi seems to have realized the importance of the territorial state when he argued that imperial overextension – including that of Süleyman I – was against the laws of nature and the results were not worth the effort. The Ottoman state should stay within its borders and thus give no one the pretext to go to war against it.[142] This transition from imperial legitimating principles to the principles of the territorially bounded state was essential for the reforms of the nineteenth century, which transformed the Ottoman Empire into an absolutist monarchy. As Ahmed Resmi's writings reveal, the transition was justified by reference to state interest and strategy rather than to religion. This legitimating discourse was also employed in the making of the The Charter of Alliance of 1808 (*Sened-i İttifak*) – a constitutional contract signed by the sultan, the high officers of the empire and the local notables (*ayans*) assuring loyalty to the state and the sultan and the lives and property of the notables.[143] It was also used as a justification for the promulgation of the Rescript of *Gülhane* (*Gülhane Hatt-ı Hümayunu* also known as the Rescript of *Tanzimat*) (1839) and its reassurance by the Rescript of Reform (*Islahat Fermani*) (1856), which revoked the traditional Islamic division of subjects into Muslims and non-Muslims, established equality of subjects before the law and took the first steps towards the development of a political community of Ottoman citizens.[144] The reforms also established representative assemblies in the provinces and the capital whereby the notables could participate in state affairs.[145] All these new institutions provided the state with organizational principles legitimated by nascent civil society institutions. However, until the emergence of these new organizational and legitimating principles in the nineteenth century, the Ottoman state remained crippled by rationality and legitimacy crises.

Conclusion

This chapter has demonstrated how the Ottoman Empire dealt with the challenges raised by the emergence of the territorial state in the fields of administration, taxation, foreign policy and legitimacy. A neo-realist explanation of Ottoman decline would focus on the changes in material capabilities. However, this institutional analysis reveals that pre-existing Ottoman institutions had difficulties in increasing their resources and capabilities because their organizational principles contradicted the organizational principles of the modern states system. The historical sociology of early modern state formation provides the analytical tools to investigate the restraints on the capability of the elites for reforms. It emphasizes that systemic pressures on the Ottoman state were perceived accurately by Ottoman elites but their social consequences led to a collective action failure. Changes in the organization of warfare and diplomacy led to the rise of new political actors such as mercenaries, local notables and diplomats. They also led to the demise of the fief-holding cavalry and the Imperial Council, while the grand vizier, the grand mufti, the competing *paşa* households, the janissaries, and the governors found new opportunities to increase their political power. These changes made existing Ottoman institutions dysfunctional in ensuring collective action. However, they continued to exist next to new informal mechanisms which, due to their informality, were less predictable, less reliable and of an *ad hoc* nature. The coexistence of old dysfunctional institutions with their symbolic power and the practical informal mechanisms caused what Habermas would call a divergence between validity and facts, or legitimacy and rationality. This divergence explains how a centralized state like the Ottoman Empire was unable to act according to survival imperatives and adapt to the modern state system.

A constructivist approach could explain the persistence of the medieval world-view and Ottoman inertia for large-scale reform, but it must be complemented by an explanation of how new ideas emerged. Most importantly, the constructivist approach would need to explain the timing of ideational change and how certain ideas came to dominate rather than others. In this regard, Habermas's theory of the rationalization of world-views and the institutionalist arguments of path dependence and institutional layering provide insights into the dynamics of ideational change. The analysis of the legitimacy crisis reveals that no large-scale reforms could be formulated until the discourse of the Golden Age was discarded. This chapter traced the changes in political legitimation in the emergence of novel genres such as the political thought of İbrahim Müteferrika and the embassy reports. Both genres exemplify a heightened curiosity about European superiority in warfare, taxation, administration and foreign policy. However, Ottoman intellectuals of the eighteenth century still retained the idea of sacral law as the basis of political legitimacy. This analysis claims that this ideological persistence can be explained by the inflexibility of old imperial institutions that prevented the emergence of the territorial state and by the lack of new formal institutions that would forge a new consensus between the emerging and existing political actors.

7

CONCLUSION

> *We need to be able to generate multiple histories of peace, on the basis of rigorous historical studies of the psychological, social, cultural, moral-legal, economic and political aspects of previous attempts from within international societies to form international political communities.*
>
> Hayward Alker, *Rediscoveries and Reformulations*[1]

This study investigates the adaptation of two dominant states in sixteenth-century Europe, the Holy Roman Empire and the Ottoman Empire, to the early modern state system. Both the Holy Roman and Ottoman Empires were political entities that claimed to represent the universal community of believers: *res publica Christiana* or *dar-al Islam*. The rulers of both empires, Charles V and Süleyman I, commanded resources far beyond the imagination of their predecessors and their contemporaries. Despite these resources, both Habsburg and Ottoman dreams of a universal empire came to an end in the seventeenth century. The survival imperatives of the state system exacerbated the waning of central political authority in the Holy Roman Empire and led to the emergence of various territorial states including the Habsburg absolutist state, which became one of the great powers in the eighteenth and nineteenth centuries. In contrast, the Ottoman Empire was far more centralized than any of the sixteenth-century European states. Facing the challenges of the territorial state as the dominant unit of the state system, the Ottoman Empire failed to reform its political institutions in order to increase its competitiveness. In this regard, this book emphasizes that the survival imperatives of the state system do not produce the same effect in every state. The variance in the outcomes of Habsburg and Ottoman adaptation can be explained by differences in the institutionalization of political power, i.e. the mechanism through which power is legitimately distributed in a society.

Chapters five and six illustrated that systemic pressures challenged the institutions of the Holy Roman and the Ottoman Empires in the fields of administration, taxation, foreign policy conduct and political legitimation. In both empires, the imperial organizational and legitimating principles constituted a barrier to territorial state formation. Thus, the stronger these principles were anchored in political institutions the harder it became for the state to formulate and implement reforms to adapt to survival imperatives. In both empires, the reformers came from the group of officials who were in charge of conducting foreign policy: the diplomats. Prince Kaunitz and Ahmed Resmi Efendi provide two important examples of diplomats as reformers, who finally broke with the traditional legitimating and organizational principles. They realized that the survival of the state depended on implementing reforms that went beyond the immediate changes in military organization and tactics but entailed large-scale social and economic transformations. These diplomats were essential in the emergence of absolutist states. However, the rise of the diplomats also required major changes in the social and political structures that took a different path in the two empires.

In the Holy Roman Empire, the weak central authority of the emperor and the constitutional structure of the corporate state as the legacies of the Middle Ages prevented the emergence of a centralized imperial state but led to the formation of territorial states at the level of the Imperial Estates. In the administrative field the empire had no central executive organs and no standing army at the emperor's disposal. In the fiscal field there was no fiscal unification and no central treasury. The Estates used the administrative and fiscal institutions of the empire that were established in the late fifteenth century, to consolidate their territorial authority. In the conduct of foreign policy the empire could not coordinate the policies of individual Imperial Estates due to the lack of central political institutions. In the field of legitimation the universalist principles based on the idea of the last kingdom of Christians were accompanied by the organizational principles of the corporate state. Both principles, imperial suzerainty and the territorialization of political authority, prevented the transformation of the empire into an absolutist sovereign monarchy. In this context, the Protestant Reformation deepened the crisis of the empire and provided natural law as a legitimating discourse for territorial state formation. After the Peace of Westphalia, the Habsburg dynasty abandoned the pursuit of a universal empire and joined other German princes in building a territorial state in its hereditary domains. The Habsburg monarchy introduced reforms that enabled the state to gain autonomy from ascriptive groups, to establish a centralized administration and achieve fiscal unification. In the conduct of foreign policy these changes enabled a major reorientation of the Habsburg approach to its European alliances, guided by the balance of power rather than by imperial responsibilities. The Habsburgs could act as an autonomous entity according to the survival imperatives of self-help politics only after giving up the pursuit of a universal empire.

In the Ottoman Empire, the Ottoman dynasty managed to achieve a high level of state centralization as early as the fifteenth century; the empire had a relatively centralized administration and fiscal unification monitored by a bureaucracy loyal to the sultan. Compared to the Holy Roman emperor, the Ottoman sultan was far less dependent on ascriptive groups and had far more free resources and generalized power to use for his political goals. Ottoman foreign policy was conducted according to imperial organizational principles through a complex network of converts and non-Muslim subjects. In order to forge alliances with European states, the Ottomans used unilaterally granted capitulations that allowed them to make commitments to non-Muslim states within the confines of Islamic law and imperial organizational principles. In the course of the seventeenth century, the Ottoman Empire was increasingly challenged by the emerging territorial states in Europe. The Treaty of Karlowitz at the end of the century marked not only the ineffectiveness of Ottoman military methods but also revealed the necessity of adapting to the European diplomatic system. However, survival imperatives in the state system were contradictory to the legitimating and organizational principles. Reforms in administration, the conduct of the military and diplomacy entailed significant social transformations. In this regard, the initial imperial institutions made it harder for the Ottomans to change their imperial legitimating discourse. In contrast to natural law which gave considerable power to the Habsburg monarch for implementing reforms, the Ottoman sultan was increasingly bound by imperial custom and sacral law as legitimating discourses. This inability to change the legitimating discourse led to the reification of the Ottoman world-view that restricted institutional learning. Thus, Ottoman institutions remained crippled until the diplomats of the empire gained enough power to initiate a westernization movement in the nineteenth century that changed the entire political structure and legitimating discourse of the empire. The history of the two empires reveals that the adaptation of a state to changing survival imperatives depends on the flexibility of organizational principles embodied in political institutions and legitimating principles expressed in legal and political discourses.

The starting point of this book is the criticism raised against neo-realist systems theory in the 1980s, arguing that the basic unit of the state system — the sovereign independent state — is a historical construct. Critics emphasize that neo-realist neglect of the transition from the feudal to the modern state led to an over-determinant and static concept of the state system unable to explain historical change. In the twenty years since these debates, a few studies, mostly in the constructivist vein, have addressed the question of the historical change of the state system. Since international relations theory has been preoccupied with the ontological debate, these studies have focused on how changes in ideas have led to changes in the identities of states and in international rules. This study argues that a focus on material and ideational resources is inadequate for explaining historical change and emphasizes the institutions that turn these resources into power in the state system.

Undeniably, the availability of material resources explains the level of state power in the state system. However, the effectiveness of a state in using its existing resources depends on the institutions that make them available to policy makers. Thus, this study demonstrates that the rationalization of state apparatus and the construction of institutions enabling collective action and coordination of foreign policy played a crucial role in the rise and demise of great powers. Ideational resources also influence state power since policy makers respond to survival imperatives within the confines of the ideological frameworks available to them. The world-views of policy makers determine the pace and extent of learning and thus the limits of adaptation to new environments. However, the origins and the effects of political ideas are not determined solely by individual genius or intellectual tradition but to a large extent by institutional factors. Political institutions determine why some ideas prevail over others and why some ideas are rejected. Institutional mechanisms that favor certain carriers of ideas over others put limits on discursive reasoning within a given world-view. Thus, as Avner Greif's discussion of institutional change demonstrates, unidirectional causal explanations neglect the long-term and feedback effects of institutional mechanisms. At any given point decision makers can circumvent ideological constraints, but the persistence of a gap between fact and validity will lead to important institutional rigidities and lack of innovation and experimentation. Certain ideas might work at any given point but inhibit adaptation in the long run.

This study uses the historical sociological literature on state formation in order to investigate the changes in state institutions in four domains: administration, taxation, foreign policy and legitimacy. Historical sociology conventionally regards state formation within a narrow definition of rationalization, or merely as bureaucratization. In this context, Jürgen Habermas's theory of communicative action and his critique of Weber's use of rationality to explain early modern state formation provide a fruitful framework to combine the insights of both neo-realism and constructivism. Bureaucratization as a response to intensive modern warfare is only one aspect of rationalization. As the early modern reform projects clearly reveal, the success of reform depends on legitimation. Early modern state formation involved more than just the reorganization of state offices. As a consequence of state formation, the individual was defined by an objective legal order as a legal agent bearing inalienable rights; society was defined as a pre-political field marked by voluntary associations of individuals; the state was defined as a necessity of human sociability and as an autonomous law-maker in accordance with state reason; finally, the state system was defined as a system comprised of equally sovereign states which works according to its own autonomous logic, the balance of power. This study emphasizes two important aspects of state formation which have thus far been neglected by both the state formation literature and international relations theory: the emergence of the legal personality of the state and the emergence of natural law as the basis of political legitimation. While the former provides an organizational tool for the early modern state, the latter justifies the autonomous authority of the ruler. Both aspects are essential for the autonomous modern state that is assumed to be the dominant unit of the modern international system.

In this respect, this book provides a fruitful research agenda for the study of current dynamics of state formation and systemic change in international relations by focusing on institutional change and political legitimation. Under increasing systemic pressure due to a globalizing world economy and state system, states continue to introduce administrative and fiscal reforms, and new institutions for constructing foreign policy. After the end of the Cold War, neo-liberal reforms, including deregulation, the decline of the welfare state, and the liberalization of international markets, indicate that a new wave of state formation is leading to transformations on the levels of the individual, society, the state and the state system. Similar to the Habsburgs and the Ottomans, current policy makers are bound by organizational and legitimating principles that put limits on institutional learning and adaptability. Thus, the theoretical framework developed in this study can be applied to contemporary state formation to help us understand the present evolution of the international system.

In this context, a major question for the discipline of international relations awaits further investigation. This book tackles the question of how pre-modern states differed from modern states and how the transition was harder for some than for others. The question for contemporary international politics is how current states differ from the states of the past and which states can perform better than others. The study of the Habsburg and Ottoman transitions reveal that the imperial organizational principles were unable to produce the necessary reforms to meet the demands of the survival imperative. Thus, medieval empires were unable to compete with the territorial absolutist states emerging in Europe in the sixteenth century. Similar to the empires, today's nation-states are faced with challenges of increasing globalization. As sociologist Manuel Castells points out, the organizational principles of nation-states cannot effectively solve global problems. The nation-state's inability to address current survival imperatives is leading to an efficiency crisis, a crisis of equity, a crisis of identity and a crisis of legitimacy.[2] Thus, like the Habsburgs and the Ottomans, current policy makers face the dilemma between a rationality crisis and a legitimation crisis: global and regional institutions (such as WTO or the EU) created to solve global problems are suffering a democratic deficit and lack of domestic legitimacy while legitimate national institutions (parliaments) are becoming increasingly inefficient and excluded from problem solving. In Habermas's words, the gap between fact and validity is growing as globalization intensifies.

In this respect, the historical account of medieval empires reveals that material and ideational resources cannot always be translated into political power especially during times of major transitions. Both institutions and legitimating discourses influence the organization of the state and its competitiveness in the state system. The life story of the two protagonists cited at the start of the book attests to the limits of imperial power: After abdicating the imperial throne, Charles V isolated himself in the monastery of San Jerómino der Yuste. Although his arch-nemesis Süleyman I continued his military expeditions, after the unsuccessful siege of Vienna there was a change in the tone of his rule. The pomp that earned Süleyman the title Magnificent gave way to a humble and more religious personal life. As an old man who had executed a favorite son and a grandson he wrote:

> Nothing among the people is more esteemed than the state
> Yet there is no state [in this context meaning good fortune] in the world like a breath of health[3]

Students of international relations, as well as the policy makers of today's great powers, have a lot to learn from the disappointments of these two most powerful sixteenth century men.

NOTES

Introduction

1 Ullmann, 1949: 32–33; Stengel, 1939: 2.
2 Kohler, 2001 [1999]: 201–202.
3 Eisenbichler, 1999.
4 Pietschmann, 2002: 340.
5 Pietschmann, 2002: 325–327, 340.
6 O'Gorman, 1965.
7 Rosenthal, 1973.
8 Kütükoğlu, 1998: 73.
9 The Turkish term gaza derives from the Arabic ghazw or ghaziya indicating a military expedition. Although the term dates back to the pre-Islamic Bedouin warfare for camels, it was used for the Prophet's raids against the infidels. Similar religiously sanctioned wars in Transoxania and Khurasan also took the same name. From the ninth century on, the Turkish warriors fighting along the Arab-Byzantine border were called ghazis, participants of gaza. In the fourteenth century, the Turcoman rulers of Anatolia carried the title ghazi as a legitimation of their political and military authority. Mélikoff, 1965; Johnstone, 1965; Kafadar, 1995: xii, 56–57. Cemal Kafadar points out the inaccuracy of equating gaza and jihad by translating them both as holy war. He asserts that both terms were distinguished clearly by popular and canonical works. Jihad is rarely mentioned by early Ottoman chronicles and frontier narratives. While jihad denoted defensive warfare as a religious duty, gaza was an aggressive raid on a voluntary basis. More importantly, non-Muslims (particularly the Christian warriors of the frontier regions) could also join the gaza as ghazis. Kafadar, 1995: 79–80.
10 İnalcık, 1993b; Göçek, 1993; İnalcık, 2009: 110–112; Barkey, 2008: 72–74.
11 Köhbach, 1992; İnalcık, 2002a [1973]: 58.
12 Raby, 2000: 66–72; Necipoğlu, 2000: 22–30.
13 Necipoğlu, 1993: 179.
14 İnalcık, 1993, 59–92; Göçek, 1993: 93–108; Necipoğlu, 1993: 175, 190.

15   Kütükoğlu, 1998: 148.
16   Elias, 2001 [1986].
17   Nexon, 2009: 10–12.
18   Kratochwil, 1986: 28.
19   Naff, 1984.
20   Kennedy, 1989: 11–12.
21   Lenski, 1984 [1966]: 20–21.
22   Issawi, 1993.
23   Contrary to Hendrik Spruyt, who asserts that the 'imperial solution had failed by the early fourteenth century,' the intricate imperial network of the Habsburg dynasty and of the Ottoman Empire both reached their zenith in the states-system of the sixteenth century. Spruyt, 1994: 540.
24   The Holy Roman Empire survived until 1806, when the Habsburg monarchy declared its own empire that lasted until the end of World War I in 1918. Likewise, the Ottoman Empire, torn by the same war, was dissolved by the Turkish Grand National Assembly in 1922. In other words, both empires far outlived the lifetime assigned to them by international relations theorists. For Spruyt's critique with respect to the Holy Roman Empire, see: Teschke, 2003: 37.
25   Braudel, 1992: 9.
26   Wallerstein, 1974: 136.
27   Reston, 2009: 298.
28   Although classical realists are much more versatile in their methodological and ontological orientations, they also approach the history of international relations solely from the perspective of the pursuit of power, disregarding changes in the modalities and definitions of power. Morgenthau, 1962; Wight, 1995.
29   Teschke, 2003: 14–16.
30   Waltz, 2002: 65.
31   Waltz, 2002: 64.
32   Waltz, 1986: 57–58.
33   Schroeder, 1994: 116–129.
34   For the most recent contributions in this vein, see Brooks and Wohlforth, 2008; Schweller, 2006.
35   Tammen et al., 2000; Lemke, 2002.
36   Kennedy, 1989; also see McNeill, 1984:95–98.
37   Ruggie, 1986: 143–145; Hall and Kratochwil, 1993.
38   Fischer, 1992: 443.
39   In sociology this approach is known as decisionism. For a useful review of decisionism and its commonalities with political realism see: Habermas, 2000 [1999]. Carl Schmitt and Niklas Luhmann provide classical versions of the decisionist conception of legitimacy. Schmitt, 1998 [1932]; Luhmann, 1983. Henry Kissinger and Inis Claude provide variations of realist conceptions of legitimacy. Kissinger defines legitimacy as a stable international system, while

for Claude legitimization through the UN means justification of superpowers. Evans and Newnham, 1998: 302; Claude, 1966: 369–370.
40 Buzan and Little, 2000: 41.
41 Hall and Kratochwil, 1993: 487.
42 Giddens, 1987: 13.
43 Barkin and Cronin, 1994; Philpott, 1999.
44 Reus-Smit, 1997: 557.
45 Hall, 1999: 47. Mlada Bukovansky is critical both of Reus-Smit's and Hall's work. She contends that 'neither provides a theoretical purchase on the question of how or why variation came about.' However, her study is not concerned with transformations of organizational principles. Bukovansky, 2002: 41–42.
46 Wendt, 1997: 48.
47 Wendt, 1997: 50–54.
48 Wendt, 2000: 198.
49 Wendt, 2000: 202.
50 Wendt, 2000: 246.
51 Inayatullah and Blaney, 1997: 67; Pasic, 1997: 89. To compensate for his ahistoricism, Wendt suggests that interdependence and transnational convergence of domestic values level off the cultural differences of corporate identities anyway. Wendt, 1997: 55–56.
52 '[…] No nation could come to consciousness as a nation except within an international society.' Mead, 1915: 605.
53 'Nations, like individuals, can become objects to themselves only as they see themselves through the eyes of others. Every appeal to public sentiment is an effort to justify oneself to oneself.' Mead, 1915: 604.
54 Italics in original; Mead, 1915: 607.
55 Jackson, 1993: 27–29.
56 Cooper and Brubaker, 2005.
57 In his discussion of American politics during the First World War, Mead makes clear that American 'fundamental political habits of feeling, thought and action have been such necessary outgrowths of the doctrine that governments must be with the consent of the governed that [Americans] could never associate ourselves with the imperialistic aims which have so largely dominated the alliances and hostilities of European nations.' Mead, 1917.
58 Bloom, 1990: 52.
59 Max Weber's typology of charismatic, traditional and legal-rational legitimacy provides a starting point.
60 Legro, 2005: 11.
61 Legro, 2005.
62 Waltz refers to S.F. Nadels's The Theory of Social Structure. For a brief description of the cultural anthropological and bio-cybernetic conceptions of systems with regard to the theoretical trajectory of Talcott Parsons see: Habermas, 1999b: 338–339.

63 Kratochwil, 1986: 27.
64 Kratochwil, 2000: 96; Albert, 1999; Albert and Brock, 2001.
65 For a critique of Wendt's simplistic duality of materialism and idealism see: Keohane, 2000: 128–129.
66 Habermas, 1973: 11.
67 Ruggie, 1986: 131–157.
68 Habermas, 1973: 13.
69 Greif, 2008: 153–157.
70 Greif, 2008: 156.
71 Marx, 1965 [1848]: 9.
72 Spruyt, 1998.
73 Hobden, 1999: 269.
74 Rosenberg, 1994: 138–139.
75 Teschke, 2003: 265.
76 For Weber, the nuclei of the modern state were developed out of bureaucratic structures of the Middle Ages. See: Weber, 1958b: 210.
77 Spruyt, 1994a; 14, 17; Spruyt, 1994b: 527–557.
78 Spruyt, 1994b: 553; for a recent institutionalist conception of international legitimacy as credibility, see Gelpi, 2003; an earlier account of legitimacy as reputation can be found in Keohane, 1984: 106–107.
79 Spruyt, 1994b: 540.
80 Teschke, 2003: 37. He also fails to incorporate domestic legitimation which leads him to a rather hasty conclusion that French absolutism was a product of the alliance of the Crown and burghers against the nobility and emerged as an exemplar of the modern territorial state. Both of these accounts are highly contestable in historical terms. Perry Anderson argues that absolutism was the most developed form of feudalism. Anderson, 1979 [1974].
81 Nexon, 2009: 1–39.
82 Nexon, 2009: 24–25.
83 Nexon, 2009: 67–98.
84 Nexon, 2009: 99–134.
85 Nexon, 2009: 15.
86 Karen Barkey's recent book applies the same network approach to the study of the Ottoman Empire, see Barkey, 2008.

From Empires to Absolutist States: Political Change in Early Modern Europe

1 Eisenstadt, 1993 [1963]; Kautsky, 1997 [1982]; Doyle, 1986; Esherick, Kayalı and Van Young, 2006; Cooper, 2005a; 2005b and 2005c; Nexon, 2009; Barkey, 2008.
2 Esherick, Kayalı and Van Young, 2006: 5; Also see Nexon, 2009; Barkey, 2008.
3 For the following discussion see Doyle, 1986: 35–47.
4 Doyle describes the imperial government as 'a sovereignty that lacks a community.' Doyle, 1986: 36.

5   Doyle, 1986: 45.
6   Wallerstein, 1974: 15–16.
7   Wallerstein, 1974: 60.
8   Wallerstein, 1974: 33.
9   Wallerstein, 1974: 151.
10 Wallerstein, 1974: 137–138.
11 Eisenstadt, 1993 [1963]: 4.
12 According to these criteria, Eisenstadt distinguishes between patrimonial empires (the Carolingian and the Ahmenid empires), nomad or conquest empires (the Mongolian empires and the Arab emirate under the first caliphs), and centralized historical empires, which include ancient empires as well as absolutist monarchies of early modern Europe. Eisenstadt, 1993 [1963]: 8–11.
13 Eisenstadt, 1968: 43.
14 Eisenstadt, 1962: 280.
15 For definition of free resources: Eisenstadt, 1993 [1963]: xvi.
16 Eisenstadt, 1993 [1963]: xvi-xvii.
17 Eisenstadt, 1993 [1963]: 300–360.
18 Kautsky, 1997 [1982]: 127–131.
19 Kautsky, 1997 [1982]: 3–9.
20 Kautsky, 1997 [1982]: 34–38.
21 Kautsky, 1997 [1982]: 49–75.
22 Kautsky, 1997 [1982]: 118–127.
23 See chapter one for Nexon's work.
24 Barkey, 2008: 9–27; Nexon, 2009.
25 Nexon, 2009: 101.
26 Collins, 1996: 5; Nexon, 2009: 236.
27 Nexon, 2009: 236.
28 Nexon, 2009: 263–264.
29 Barkey, 1997 [1994].
30 Barkey, 1997 [1994]: 2.
31 Barkey, 1997 [1994]: 8–9.
32 See chapter six.
33 Barkey, 1997 [1994]: 24–44.
34 Barkey, 1997 [1994]: 44.
35 Anderson, 1979 [1974]: 15.
36 Anderson, 1979 [1974]: 19–29.
37 Anderson, 1979 [1974]: 31–40.
38 Western absolutism was the reorganization of a feudal class in the face of an urban economy. Absolutism in the West was based on the commutation of dues. In contrast, in the East the typical feudal problem was the existence of few peasants over vast territories. If absolutism was a 'compensation for the disappearance of serfdom' in the West, in the East it was a 'device for the consolidation of serfdom.' Anderson, 1979 [1974]: 195.
39 Giddens, 1987: 148–160.

40 Giddens, 1987: 94.
41 Giddens, 1987: 85.
42 Congresses were international gatherings that settled the relations between states and regulated the distribution of power in the state system with a plethora of treaties. The peace congress of Westphalia was the most famous and largest congress in which this new diplomatic approach was invoked. Giddens, 1987: 85–86.
43 Giddens, 1987: 105–106.
44 Gorski, 2003: 5.
45 Weber, 1958b: 221–224.
46 Parker, 1996: 1–3.
47 McNeill, 1982: 63–116.
48 This argument is best illustrated by the increasing powers of the Imperial Princes of Germany during the conflict between the pope and the emperor. The decline of the authority of the emperor following the Investiture Conflict increased the powers of the Imperial Princes and also gave other European monarchs the justification to refute the universal suzerainty of the empire. It is no coincidence, Hintze claims, that the theorists of corporations were canonists and Romanists, the protagonists of the Investiture Conflict. French absolutism developed during its struggle against the imperial power of the Habsburgs and later became a model for the rest of Europe. Hintze, 1962a [1902]: 39–49. For the Investiture Conflict see chapter four.
49 Tilly, 1998: 4. In a circular fashion, Tilly argues that states make war and wars make states.
50 Capital includes tangible mobile sources and enforceable claims on such resources. Coercion involves all concerted application of action that usually causes loss or damage to the persons or groups who are aware of both the action and the potential damage. Tilly, 1998: 17–20.
51 Tilly, 1998: 21–31.
52 Mann, 1997 [1986]: 482–483.
53 Mann, 1997 [1986]: 453–458.
54 Mann, 1997 [1986]: 478–481.
55 Elias, 2001 [1969]: 202–203. In France the transformation of feudal society into court society took place during the reign of Francis I (1515–1547). Elias, 2001 [1969]: 272–273.
56 Rosenthal, 1998: 68–85.
57 Rosenthal, 1998: 95–97.
58 Gorski, 2003: 37.
59 Gorski, 2003: 36.
60 Nexon, 2009: 282–286.
61 Nexon, 2009: 287.
62 Nexon, 2009: 64–65.
63 Nexon, 2009: 85.
64 Nexon, 2009: 73.

65   Collins, 1996: 1.
66   Collins, 1996: 2.
67   Blanning, 2008: 206.
68   By unified parliament Anderson does not refer to the later distinction between the House of Lords and House of Commons, which he regards as an intra-class differentiation. Unified parliament simply indicates the representation of the knights and towns alongside the barons and bishops. Anderson, 1979 [1974]: 115.
69   Anderson, 1979 [1974]: 127.
70   Brewer, 1990: 4.
71   Brewer, 1990: 3–24.
72   Blanning, 2008: 217.
73   Blackbourn and Eley, 2003 [1984]: 10–12.
74   Blackbourn and Eley, 2003 [1984]: 33.

Institutions and World-Views

1   Greif, 2008 [2006]: 3–27.
2   Greif, 2008 [2006]: 29.
3   Greif, 2008 [2006]: 30.
4   Greif, 2008 [2006]: 36–39.
5   Greif, 2008 [2006]: 40–45.
6   Greif, 2008 [2006]: 46.
7   Greif, 2008 [2006]: 46–52.
8   Greif, 2008 [2006]: 124–152.
9   Greif, 2008 [2006]: 158–170.
10   Greif, 2008 [2006]: 187–209.
11   Thelen, 2003.
12   Kuran, 1997a [1995]: 105–117.
13   Habermas, 1973: 12.
14   Habermas, 1973: 13.
15   Habermas, 1973: 18.
16   For Habermas's critique of Weber, see Habermas, 1999a [1981]: 278, 331, 344–346, Habermas gives three examples from Weber's work which attest to this tendency: the interpretation of natural law, his equation of legitimacy with legality and his concern about endangerment of the formal qualities of law through material rationalization; 355–356. Also see: Habermas, 1998d [1986]: 580.
17   Habermas, 1973: 68–70.
18   The more these values can be manipulated by the state, the less legitimating power they have. As Taiwo points out, 'the basis for the obligation to obey the law must be extralegal.' Taiwo, 1996: 98.
19   Humphreys, 1985: 256.
20   Eder, 1976, 158–159.

21 Raeff, 1983; Strakosch, 1967.
22 Habermas, 1999a [1981]: 94.
23 Habermas, 1999a [1981]: 104.
24 Habermas, 1999a [1981]: 106–108.
25 Habermas, 1999a [1981]: 97.
26 Habermas, 1999a [1981]: 73–75.
27 Habermas, 1999a [1981]: 250–251.
28 Habermas, 1999a [1981]: 107.
29 Habermas, 1999a [1981]: 73–75.
30 Habermas, 1999b [1981]: 166.
31 Habermas, 1999b [1981]: 220.
32 Habermas, 1999a [1981]: 339, 405–406.
33 Thus, Habermas builds on both Weber and Durkheim, who conceptualized legal evolution as a process of disenchantment. Habermas, 1999a [1981]: 350; for his rendering of Durkheim, Habermas, 1999b [1981]: 119.
34 Habermas, 1999a [1981]: 350 and for the table see: 1999b [1981]: 260.
35 Habermas, 1999b [1981]: 261.
36 Olufemi Taiwo stresses, 'what law is is a different question from how it is enforced.' He continues: 'Sanction theories of law tend to ignore the fact that what is essential to law is that it prescribes behavior and provides consequences to follow when its presciptions are infringed.' Taiwo, 1996: 63.
37 Habermas, 1999b [1981]: 261; Eder, 1976: 32–33.
38 Habermas, 1999b [1981]: 264; Eder, 1976: 35–36.
39 This symbiosis of morality, political power and institutional structure cannot be analyzed properly by the positivistic conception of law. Habermas, 1998d [1986]: 585–587.
40 Habermas, 1999a [1981]: 351.
41 Habermas, 1998b: 124.
42 Habermas, 1999a [1981]: 351–354.
43 Reynolds, 1997: 36–37.
44 Benhabib, 1995.
45 Toulmin, 1971: 54.
46 Toulmin, 1971: 33–35.
47 Toulmin, 1971: 55–56.

Legal Evolution and State Formation: A Comparison of Roman Law and Islamic Law

1 Duff, 1938: 1–2.
2 Runciman states that 'the state is … an association that cannot be identified with its members, its constitution, its powers, or its purposes. In law, such associations are known as fictions. But states, surely, are real.' Runciman, 2003: 29; Gierke also insists that legal personality is real: Gierke, 1990 [1868].
3 Tierney,1982:19.

4   Kuran, 2005: 787.
5   As Weber illustrates, both private and public organizations share administrative technologies. However, Weber distinguishes between three forms of organization: an endowment (*Stiftung*) with fixed membership which is not associationally organized; a corporation (*Korporation*) with fixed membership which can be altered; and an institution (also translated as compulsory association, *Anstalt* as opposed to a voluntary association *Verein*) with no organized body of members but having organs representing the members. Members of the institution have no influence on management. Weber 2002 [1921]: 425; Weber, 1978b [1921]: 707–708. Weber defined the modern state as a compulsory political organization with continuous operations (*politischer Anstaltsbetrieb*), Weber 2002 [1921]: 29; Weber, 1978a [1921]: 54. However he also emphasized that the boundaries between the three organizational forms are blurred.
6   Kuran, 2005.
7   Hendrik Spruyt suggests that the ability to make credible commitments helped sovereign states displace other forms of state, such as the city-state and the empire. Spruyt, 1994: 28.
8   'The state is not itself a collectivity, because … no collection of individuals can be liable for the action of the state, no matter how those liabilities are distributed. Rather, the state is the institution to which we ascribe liability…' Runciman, 2003: 34; See also Weber 2002 [1921]: 424; Weber, 1978b [1921]: 707; Burch, 1998: 118.
9   Legal historian Otto von Gierke discusses the role of corporations in generating meaningful identities for their members. Gierke, 1990 [1868]: 4.
10 Maitland, 2003: 66.
11 Historians like Gierke distinguish between the abstract Roman concept of corporation and the organic Germanic concept of fellowship, arguing that the latter has a stronger power of communal identification. Gierke 1990 [1868].
12 Ullmann, 1975: 36–38.
13 Digest 3.4.1.2 cited by Tierney, 1982: 23. Weber argues that the origins of the corporation lie in Roman municipal law (*Gemeinderecht*). After the Latin War, sovereign city states acquiring Roman citizenship retained their municipal autonomy. Weber, 2002 [1921]: 430; Weber, 1978b [1921]: 715.
14 Hintze, 1962a [1902].
15 Gierke, 2005 [1913]: 1.
16 Ullmann, 1966: 7–13.
17 Reynolds, 1997 [1984]: 10, Tierney, 1982: 20–21; Berman, 1995 [1983]: 215–221; Ullmann, 1966.
18 Reynolds, 1997 [1984]: 34–35.
19 Berman, 1995 [1983]: 88–94.
20 Prior to the Protestant Reformation, the church owned one fourth to one third of the land in most of Western Europe. Berman, 2006 [2003]: 167. The incorporation of the church also led to a reaction on the part of secular rulers

who used incorporation against the passage of land into the church's hands. Reynolds, 1997 [1984]: 59–64.
21 Gierke 2005 [1913]: 1, 25
22 Gierke 2005 [1913]: 46, 276.
23 Nov. 9, pref.; 24 pref.; 47 c.1; etc. Ullmann, 1975: 70.
24 Experts on the Byzantine Empire point out that the dominance of the ruler over the church should not be exaggarated. Papadakis and Kazhdan, 1991.
25 Berman, 1995 [1983]: 88–92, 94.
26 In Hintze's view, the Carolingian state could no longer sustain caesaropapism. Hintze, 1962 [1902]: 41–42. Berman, however, provides historical evidence that even the Carolingians upheld a caesaropapist ideology. Berman, 1995 [1983]: 63.
27 The crusades in 1096, 1147 and 1189 and the colonization of northern and eastern Europe in the late eleventh and twelfth centuries were important enterprises of the new papacy. Berman, 1995 [1983]: 95–103. The papacy was also the first institution to invoke the notion of power not bound by law (*potestas legibus soluta*) for its claims to world dominion. Ullmann, 1975: 56–59; d'Entrèves, 1957: 66–67.
28 Berman, 1995 [1983]: 107–119.
29 Lewis, 1994: 3–4.
30 Lewis argues, 'the notion that religion and political authority, church and state, are different and that they can or should be separated is, in a profound sense, Christian.' Lewis, 1994: 179.
31 Crone, 2004: 13–16.
32 Dreyfus and Rabinow, 1983: 202.
33 Crone, 2004: 268.
34 Crone, 2004: 15.
35 Hodgson, 1977a: 13–17.
36 Weiss, 2006: 114–115.
37 Hodgson, 1977a: 53–54.
38 Hodgson, 1977a: 30.
39 For this discussion see Hodgson, 1977a: 335–362.
40 Crone, 2004: 4.
41 A similar stasis occurred in Europe after the barbarian invasions.
42 Sourdel, 1975; For Islamic theories of the universal empire with an emphasis on the Ottomans see Köprülü, 2002 [1931]: 113–119.
43 Barkey, 2008: 69.
44 Other schools could still be applied in courts if litigants did not observe the Hanefi school.
45 For the institution of the religious and scholarly hierarchy in the Ottoman Empire see Repp, 1986.
46 Barkey, 2008: 102.
47 Weber 2002 [1921]:462–467; Weber, 1978b [1921]: 792–802.
48 Weber 2002 [1921]: 395–396.

49 Weber 2002 [1921]: 398.
50 In his critique of Weber, Habermas claims that the form of abstract and general laws can be justified as reasonable only with reference to moral principles. Weber neglects the compliance pull of certain values that inform and guide individual preferences. Moral obligation means that some values obligate everyone equally. Thus, Weber does not differentiate value judgments (*Wertschätzungen*) from the formal aspects of the binding force of norms. The validation of norms does not vary with the substantive content of the values. Habermas, 1998d [1986]: 548–549.
51 Habermas, 1999a [1981]: 362–363. Weber describes the rationality of modern law merely in terms of purposive-rational instrumentality rather than in terms of the value-rational economic and administrative action. For Habermas's critique of Weber see 1999a [1981]: 278, 331, 344–346, Habermas gives three examples from Weber's work which attest to this tendency: the interpretation of natural law, his equation of legitimacy with legality and his concern about endangering the formal qualities of law through material rationalization; 355–356.
52 Habermas, 1999a [1981]: 354–355.
53 Turner, 1974.
54 Jonsen and Toulmin, 1989 [1988]: 106.
55 Jonsen and Toulmin, 1989 [1988]: 231–249.
56 For the rise of Cartesian and Newtonian theories in response to the wars of religion, see Toulmin, 1992 [1990].
57 Ullmann, 1975: 55.
58 Ullmann, 1975: 67.
59 Radding and Ciaralli, 2007: 36. While the Visigothic Code (*Leges Visigothorum*) of King Euric (466–485) was heavily influenced by Roman law, the Lombard law-book (*Leges Langobardorum*) was overwhelmingly Germanic in substance and structure. It was applied and taught at Pavia at least down until the eleventh century. Ullmann, 1975: 195–197. Although in a letter of 603 Gregory the Great had cited passages from the Novels, the Code and the Digest, the papacy under Gregory's successors in the seventh and eighth centuries did not refer to them at all. Occasional references reappear in the ninth century. All this suggests that the texts of Justinian's law were available but of little or no use. Radding and Ciaralli, 2007: 40–47; Ullmann calls the period between the sixth and the late eighth centuries a gestation period, Ullmann: 1975: 71.
60 It is hardly surprising that the Lombards had no use for Roman law. Although over generations people might have used Roman legal practices, the social and political context of the Lombards was substantially different from Roman antiquity. Radding and Ciaralli point out that even after the Germanic conquests Romanized populations continued using documents to validate legal transactions and follow Roman rules. They might also have transmitted Roman legal language from generation to generation simply by copying documents from older transactions and using them as templates. 2007: 39–40.

61 The Vulgate functioned as the transmitter of Roman law and prepared the ground for the reception from the eleventh century onwards. Ullmann, 1975: 42–44.
62 Ullmann, 1975: 78–79.
63 Evans, 1996: 67–71; Maas, 1992: 100–101.
64 Ullmann, 1975: 55, 99; Habermas, 1990: 58.
65 Ullmann, 1975: 86.
66 Ullmann, 1975: 104.
67 Strauss, 1986: 66.
68 The Great Schism also facilitated the breakdown of a universal papal authority and the emergence of independent and sovereign kingdoms. Tierney, 1982: 2–3.
69 Ullmann, 1975: 106–111.
70 Ullmann, 1975: 54. Both the Latin term canon and the Arabic term *kanun* derive from the Greek kanon (κανών), which originally meant 'any straight rod' and then came to denote 'a measure of rule.' In the third and fourth centuries, local Christian synods (ecclesiastical councils) in North Africa and in Arles issued kanons as did the first ecumenical synod at Nicaea in 325. In the papyri of the fourth and fifth centuries the term kanon was finally used for 'assessment for taxation,' 'imperial taxes,' and 'tariff.' After the Muslim conquest of Egypt and Syria the term was adopted by Islamic fiscal terminology. De Bellefonds, 1975; Berman, 1995 [1983]: 199.
71 Gratian's dialectical method was a special application of the deductive method, aiming at the elimination of contradictions. The dialectical method assumed that the human mind was a divine gift not capable of contradicting itself. Since the same was valid for laws as products of the human mind, it was the task of the interpreter to solve seeming contradictions. By distinguishing changeable laws from immutable laws, the method attempted to achieve uniformity. As we shall see later, the basic assumptions of this scholastic method were very similar to the assumptions of the Muslim jurists. Ullmann, 1975: 163–165.
72 Berman, 2006 [2003]: 102–108.
73 Weiss, 2006: 172.
74 Khadduri, 1955: 27–28. Majid Khadduri and Wael Hallaq suggest that the Prophet's Sunna, one of the sources of Islamic law, basically originated from Arabian customary law. Khadduri, 1955: 29; Hallaq 1997: 10–11.
75 Weiss, 2006: 2–3. Bernard Weiss claims that 'the Umayyad Caliphate (661–750) and the Abbasid Caliphate (750–950) did for Islam what the Davidic kingdom had done for the religion of Israel, i.e. provide the political context necessary for the development of genuine law.' Weiss, 2006: 4.
76 Khadduri, 1955: 29.
77 Hallaq, 1997: 15.
78 Khadduri, 1955: 29–30. Hallaq argues that in fact the term *ra'y* had a double meaning by the middle of the second century of Islam: it meant both free reasoning based on practical considerations and free reasoning based on an

authoritative text and motivated by practical concerns. Only in later centuries did the second type of reasoning prevail over the first and the term *ra'y* was abandoned. Hallaq, 1997: 19.
79 Khadduri, 1955: 30–31.
80 Hallaq, 1997: 34.
81 Hallaq, 1997: 101.
82 Weiss, 2006: 31.
83 Weiss, 2006: 114–115.
84 Weiss defines textualism as 'the approach to the formulation of law that seeks to ground all law in a closed canon of foundational texts and refuses to accord validity to law that is formulated independently of these texts.' Weiss, 2006: 38.
85 Weiss, 2006: 68–70.
86 Khadduri, 1955: 36.
87 Hallaq, 1995: 33–34.
88 Khadduri, 1955: 35.
89 Weiss, 2006: 124.
90 Weiss, 2006: 113.
91 Weiss, 2006: 114.
92 Weiss, 2006: 4–5.
93 Marxist and Weberian studies of the state ignore the fact that law has a dual function for the state. First, it is an organizational tool. Raeff, 1983. Second, law embodies values which evade political authority. These values, which cannot be controlled by the state, procure legitimacy. Habermas, 1998b: 178; Taiwo, 1996: 98.
94 For the following discussion see Habermas, 1998c [1986]: 581–585; Unger, 1976: 49–52, 58–63; Eder, 1976: 159–160.
95 Accordingly, regulatory law is expected to emerge first and foremost in areas of inter-communal relations and only later and less completely inside communities. This was indeed the case with the Ottoman and Holy Roman Empires. The regulatory laws in the empires did regulate the external relations of communities, such as guilds, estates, cities and village communities in terms of taxation, privileges and representation. However, the state did not regulate their internal affairs. Thus, the members of those communities remained first and foremost members of their particular legal community and only secondarily, members of a common imperial legal community.
96 Such a division between state and society is rare in pre-modern societies, since the pure instrumentality of regulatory law cannot procure legitimacy by itself and requires legitimation by custom and sacral law. China provides an exception in this respect since sacral rules never became independent of government. Unger, 1976: 52. However, in China the belief in the divine nature of the emperor might have made the ruler's law sacred by definition.
97 Eder, 1976: 165.
98 Taiwo, 1996: 1; 37–38; Pakaluk, 2002:131.

NOTES

99 d'Entrèves, 1957: 9–11.
100 Eder, 1976: 160–166; Unger, 1976: 52–85.
101 In Habermas's words, the rationality of modern natural law becomes practical rationality, which is the rationality of an autonomous morality. Habermas, 1998c [1986]: 588–590.
102 Although natural law theories of the seventeenth and eighteenth centuries have metaphysical connotations, their model of contracting parties leads to a procedural justification of law, which means the justification by reference to principles, the validity of which is subject to criticism. Habermas, 1999a [1981]: 357–358. This aspect of early modern natural law becomes apparent only if one takes account of the procedural rationality rather than the content of natural law. In this context, Habermas criticizes Weber for not distinguishing sufficiently between the particular value contents (*Wertinhalten*) of cultural transmissions and the universal standards of value (*Wertmaßstäben*). The pluralism of the value contents (*Wertmaterien*) has nothing to do with the difference of aspects of validity (*Geltungsaspekten*). Habermas, 1999a [1981]: 340.
103 Since 1489, the Estates were arranged into three curia (colleges): the Electors, the Imperial Princes and the Cities. Unlike in France and England, where the feudal state (*Lehenstaat*) was transformed into a monarchical territorial state in the fifteenth century, the empire turned into a corporate state (*Ständestaat*), in which the imperial princes came to be regarded as the trustees of separate territories rather than as vassals of the emperor, Duchhardt, 1991: 13–16. For the emergence of the corporate state in Germany see two outstanding studies. Spangenberg, 1964 [1912] is more specific, Du Boulay, 1983 provides a general history of medieval Germany.
104 Strauss, 1986: 100; Ullmann, 1975: 62–63, 193; Berman, 1995 [1983]: 145.
105 Gierke, 2005 [1913]: 204–209.
106 Gierke, 2005 [1913]: 223–233.
107 Berman, 2006 [2003]: 31.
108 The prince of Lower Saxony protected Luther against the emperor and the pope, despite remaining a Catholic. Berman, 2006 [2003]: 49.
109 Berman, 2006 [2003]: 6.
110 Berman, 2006 [2003]: 109–110.
111 Berman, 2006 [2003]: 97, 128.
112 Brackets are mine. Berman, 2006 [2003]: 26.
113 Berman, 2006 [2003]: 79–82. Melanchton's approach to natural law, grounded in the Bible, was also adopted by another influential legal theorist, Johann Oldendorp, Berman, 2006 [2003]: 89.
114 For a helpful study of the impact of natural law on Prussian state formation see Hellmuth, 1985 and on Austrian state formation see Strakosch, 1967.
115 For insightful studies of the notion of *gaza* see Linder, 1983; Kafadar, 1996.
116 Eighteenth-century Orientalists mistakenly regarded fiqh as the sole legal system in the empire. Timur, 2000: 74–77; see also Barkan, 1943: XVII

(Footnote). Ironically, contemporary Islamist arguments still uphold the Orientalist claims: Akgündüz, 1990: IX-X; Karaman, 1974: 160.

117 Secularist historians assert that the pinnacle of Ottoman expansion can be attributed to the secular political orientation of the empire, while the decline after the sixteenth century was marked by the rise of Islamic religious law in opposition to secular law. İnalcık, 2000a [1958]: 319; İnalcık, 2000b [1958]: 27; Barkan, 1943.

118 The first argument takes this point to be indicative that every sultanic decree was in fact in harmony with Islamic law. The second argument, on the other hand, rightly points to the political authority of the ruler as the source of public law, but exaggerates the secular character of the Ottoman legal system. Barkan, 1943: XIII; Akgündüz, 1990: 78.

119 Akgündüz, 1990: 66–67.

120 Akgündüz, 1990: 47–49.

121 The sultanic kanuns determined the *cursus honorum*, the salaries of the scholars as well as their license to recruit graduates. Articles 25 and 28 of the law book of Mehmed II regulate the scholarly hierarchy, Akgündüz, 1990: 317–343; also see Repp, 1986.

122 Joel Mokyr observes that political fragmentation in Europe contributed to the emergence of a market for ideas. Scholars could travel to different countries if faced with prosecution. Mokyr, 2006.

123 The development of the tradition of kanun started as early as the Umayyid period, becoming a theoretical subject in al-Mawardi's work. These kanuns dealt specifically with issues regarding land taxes and registration and were heavily influnced by Sasanid practices. These laws were justified by the concept of maslahat, i.e. public good. Except for a Khariji minority, most of the mainstream Sunni scholarship maintained the idea that Muslims were obliged to submit to the Imam's authority. İnalcık, 2000a [1958]: 321. Khadduri, 1955: 152–155; Hassan, 2001: 178–179; Timur, 2000: 74. In the Ottoman Empire, Turkish customs as well as the customs of conquered lands made the greatest impact on imperial administration. Barkan, 1943: XVI.

124 Barkan, 1943: XXXVII.

125 Repp, 1986: 131–133; Barkan, 1943: XIX.

126 Repp, 1986: 131; Barkan, 1943: XIX; Akgündüz, 1990: for the full text of the decree: 65–66.

127 Gerber, 1994: 16.

State Formation in the Holy Roman Empire

1 Du Boulay, 1983: 20.

2 The name of the dynasty derives from a fortress - the Habichtsburg (castle of goshawk) – that they built between Zürich and Basel in 1020. Bérenger, 1994: 11; Du Boulay, 1983: 32.

3 Bérenger, 1994: 34–36; Du Boulay, 1983: 32.

4   Bérenger, 1994: 58–61; Du Boulay, 1983: 33.
5   When the Luxemburg male line became extinct, the dynasty's domains were acquired by the Habsburgs, who were connected to the Luxemburgs through marriage. Thus, after Frederick III (1440–1493), the Holy Roman emperors were chosen from among the Habsburgs until the end of the empire in 1806 - with the notable exception of Charles VII from the Wittelbach dynasty, who ruled briefly between 1742–1745.
6   Accordingly, the elections would take place in Frankfurt, the coronation in Aachen, the first imperial summit (*Reichsversammlung*) in Nürnberg. Thus, the elected German king or the king of Rome (*römischer König*) would travel to Rome in order to be crowned by the pope as the emperor (*Kaiser*). The electoral princes (*Kurfürsten*) consisted of the king of Bohemia, the count of Palatine (*Pfalzgraf*), the duke of Saxony, the margrave (*Markgraf*) of Brandenburg and the archbishops of Mainz, Trier and Cologne. Schmidt, 1999: 14; Wilson, 1999: 18–19; Du Boulay, 1983: 40.
7   Bérenger, 1994: 4, 58, 60–61; Barraclough, 1984: 358. In comparison, the Ottoman dynasty progressively discontinued the practice of using dynasty members as administrators and achieved a far more centralized administration.
8   Prior to the formal organization of the Imperial Diet, the emperor had negotiated with individual princes and cities rather than with collective groups of power holders. Duchhardt, 1991: 30–31. Modern scholarship refutes previous attempts to define the diet as a forerunner of a modern parliament. It was an assembly of privileged princes and later counts, prelates and cities. But it had no connection to the Territorial Diets (*Landtag*), which included the estates within a certain territory under a prince. Wilson, 1999: 40.
9   The spiritual princes, the archbishops of Mainz, Cologne and Trier were simultaneously the arch-chancellors of Germany, Italy and Burgundy. The elector of Mainz was also the imperial arch-chancellor (*Reichserzkanzler*), who was the head of the imperial administration and responsible for the internal as well as the external correspondence of the emperor. The four secular princes were the king of Bohemia, the count of Palatine, the duke of Saxony and the margrave of Brandenburg. The Electors of Palatine and Saxony were simultaneously imperial vicars (*Reichsvikare*), who took over the imperial authority during an interregnum or in the absence or inability of the king. The elector of Palatine also had the authority to preside over the court trying the emperor. Duchhardt, 1991: 32. Over the years, several changes were made in the composition of the Electoral College. In 1648 the prince of Bavaria, in 1692 the prince of Hanover and in 1803 the princes of Salzburg, Württemberg, Hessen-Kassel and Baden acquired voting rights. The Bohemian voting right was suspended from 1648 to 1708. Wilson, 1999: 41, Duchhardt, 1991: 34–36.
10 While princes had full individual votes (*Virilstimmen*), counts and prelates had collective votes (*Kurialstimmen*). The voting rights in the curia also reflected the territorialization of political power with the right of representation

being assigned to a certain territory. Thus, votes would be transferred with inheritance and sale of territories. This is how some dynasties, especially the electoral princes, accrued several votes in the curia. The curia of imperial princes changed enormously in terms of numbers, while the curia of electors stayed stable through the early modern era. Wilson, 1999: 41; Duchhardt, 1991: 36–38.

11 Duchhardt, 1991: 38–39.
12 Wilson, 1999: 22.
13 Duchhardt, 1991: 26–27.
14 The Imperial Chancery reflected the patchwork of Charles's realms: its first division used Latin and German and was assigned to deal with the business of the state (*negocia status*); the second used German and dealt with the Holy Roman Empire; the third used Latin and specialized in the affairs of the Italian domains; the fourth focused on Austrian matters; the fifth processed petitions. The Imperial Chancery was dominated by Spaniards. For over two years, the German divisions lacked a head. Instead, a Castilian secretary Alfonso de Valdés, who could not read German, was appointed the controller-general and registrar. A German scribe assisted him. Headley, 1983: 32–33; 59–85.
15 Kohler, 2001 [1999]: 129–134; Headley, 1983: 30–32.
16 Kohler, 2001 [1999]: 121.
17 The peripatetic government of Charles V tended towards a cabinet regime in which the ruler worked with a close circle of a few trusted servants. Thus, the emperor followed the general European trend of working with a close circle of secretaries who facilitated the increasing state correspondence with other states, rather than reviving the medieval office of the chancellor. For similar trends all over Europe see Headley, 1983: 15–19.
18 Walter, 1958: 9–14. Historian Heinz Duchhardt argues that the decades between 1525 and 1555 can be described as the process of rationalization and bureaucratization of German territories. He emphasizes three aspects of this process: territorial church organization; territorial legal unification; and finally, the emergence of the financial state (Finanzstaat). Duchhardt, 1990: 121–132.
19 Schmidt, 1999: 72–74; Berman, 2006 [2003]: 39–70. Also see chapter four.
20 Berman, 2006 [2003]: 79–82.
21 Duchhardt, 1990: 109, 114.
22 Charles's proposal to integrate the German, Austrian, and Italian domains with the Netherlands in an Imperial Federation (*Reichsbund*) was rejected outright by the estates. Kohler, 2001 [1999]: 319–323.
23 Schmidt, 1999: 89.
24 Bérenger, 1994: 151.
25 His brother Ferdinand, as the elected king of the Romans (the title of the prospective emperor) and Charles's successor, decided to close the session without the announcement. Charles's abdication would be put into effect the next year. Kohler, 2001 [1999]: 350–351; Bérenger, 1994: 152–153.

26 According to Charles's plans his son Philipp II would succeed his brother Ferdinand on the imperial throne. Ferdinand's son Maximilian would follow Phillip and Phillip's son Phillip III would become emperor after Maximilian. However, neither the Austrian branch nor the Imperial Estates supported the plan. Kohler, 2001 [1999]: 327–33; Bérenger, 1994: 221–224.

27 Bérenger, 1994: 153.

28 Ferdinand II's Edict of Restitution in 1629 excluded Calvinists from the peace settlement. This decision alienated not only the two Calvinist electors of Saxony and Brandenburg but also the Catholic estates. Schmidt, 1999: 162.

29 Robertson, 1998: 33.

30 In this regard, the Counter-Reformation, which stimulated conflict in the empire, served as a tool for the constitution of the Habsburg Danubian monarchy. Ingrao, 2000: 49; Wilson, 1999: 24, 27.

31 The electoral authority of Palatine and Upper Palatine was transferred to the Wittelbach family while the original Palatine family received another electoral right for the Rheinish Palatine (*Rheinpfalz*). The peace also recognized the independence of Basel and the Swiss confederation (*Eidgenossenschaft*) from the empire as well as the sovereignty of the Republic of the Netherlands. Alsace-Lorraine was left to France and thus excluded from the imperial system. Sweden received important territories in the empire (Odermündung, Vorpommern, Wismar, Bremen and Verden) and thereby got a seat and vote in the Imperial Diet. Schmidt, 1999: 180.

32 Schmidt, 1999: 182.

33 Schmidt, 1999: 185–186.

34 Ferdinand ruled as the archduke of Austria (1521–1564), as the king of Bohemia, Hungary and Croatia (1526–1564) and as the emperor (1556–1564). Bérenger, 1994: 155–166. For Ferdinand's biography see Kohler, 2003.

35 The Privy Council consisted of the aulic dignitaries, chiefs of the ministerial departments, the high steward of the court (*Obersthofmeister*), the grand marshal of the court, the vice chancellor of the empire representing the imperial arch-chancellor, i.e. the archbishop of Mainz, the court chancellor and an aulic councilor.

36 Szabo, 1994: 73.

37 Szabo, 1994: 4.

38 Szabo, 1994: 75–83.

39 Szabo, 1994: 78. Separation of administrative and judicial powers allowed the central government to curtail the power of the estates by creating a new type of government which could not be exercised by the estates. Up to this point matters of administration, which were usually provincial issues, were dealt with both by the central authority at the court and by the two chancelleries, the Bohemian and the Austrian Aulic Chancelleries (*Böhmische and Österreichische Hofkanzlei*) representing the respective autonomous administration of the estates. Strakosch, 1967: 29–30.

40 Strakosch, 1967: 30–31.

41 Kaunitz was a fervent supporter of neo-Stoicism with a strong disdain for confessional intolerance, a connoisseur of arts, a devotee of the Catholic Enlightenment, who called himself a *philosophe*. Szabo, 1994: 22–35.
42 Szabo, 1994: 90.
43 The chamberlain of Emperor Sigismund had to spend 5,000 florins a day on the court's food during the stay in Constance in 1417, which once included numerous imperial districts where the court would have been staying for free. If Sigismund's complaints are true, he was only receiving 13,000 florins per annum from the empire. Du Boulay, 1983: 25–26.
44 Du Boulay, 1983: 27–28.
45 Wilson, 1999: 49–51.
46 Tracy, 2002: 53–54.
47 Tracy, 2002: 54–63.
48 Kohler, 2001 [1999]: 139–140; For the budget projection of 1534 see Tracy, 2002: 18–19.
49 Tracy, 2002: 19.
50 Bérenger, 1994: 127.
51 Only the Bank of Barcelona could secure long-term consolidated credit in the context of the kingdom of Aragon. In Castile and the Netherlands public credit was available in the form of the sale of rents (*Rentenverkauf*). However, credit was very important for financing Habsburg projects. 850,000 gulden were raised in a short time for the election of Charles V as the Holy Roman emperor. Kohler, 2001 [1999]: 141–143.
52 Kohler, 2001 [1999]: 144–145.
53 For example, the Welsers ruled Venezuela for twenty years until 1556. Tarver and Frederick, 2006: 27.
54 Kohler, 2001 [1999]: 143–144.
55 Tracy, 2002: 17–18.
56 Kohler, 2003: 177–184.
57 Even the travels of the Habsburgs - a necessity of peripatetic government – required significant financing. When Charles V planned a trip to Germany to attend the Imperial Diet in Speyer in 1531, he had to wait for money in order to pay his cavalry companies (*compagnies d'ordonnance*) from the Netherlands, who refused to accompany him until they were paid some of what they were previously owed. Tracy, 2002: 51.
58 However, even the most powerful territorial princes still regarded the imperial framework as the modus operandi of their territorial state formation. Hence, they could not ignore the complaints of the Territorial Estates at the imperial high courts. Schmidt, 1999: 207.
59 Hochedlinger, 2003: 31.
60 Hochedlinger, 2003: 33–34.
61 Hochedlinger, 2003: 34.
62 Hochedlinger, 2003: 36–39.
63 Rosenthal, 1998.

64	Szabo, 1994: 114.
65	Szabo, 1994: 116–118.
66	Szabo, 1994: 118–136.
67	Szabo, 1994: 141.
68	Strakosch, 1967: 8–9.
69	Charles V's base in Spain was regarded as an important tool of his monarchical aims against the Imperial Estates. Kohler, 1990: 62.
70	Kohler, 1990: 66.
71	Kohler, 1990: 1–2.
72	Kohler, 1990: 9.
73	Kohler, 2001 [1999]: 180–200.
74	Several fliers addressed to farmers, artisans and soldiers charged Charles with attempting to impose an Austrian monarchy over Germany and curtail the rights of the Imperial Estates. Schmidt, 1999: 94–96.
75	Schmidt, 1999: 66.
76	Kohler, 1990: 16.
77	Kohler, 1990: 11–15.
78	For financing the defense, Ferdinand had to visit Vienna, Linz, Innsbruck, Graz, Prague, Brünn, Breslau, Bautzen, Lübben, Laibach and Cilli, Pressburg, Agram and Stuttgart. Turetschek, 1986: 19–40.
79	Turetschek, 1986: 41–65.
80	Schmidt, 1999: 119.
81	Kohler, 1990: 33–47.
82	The estates after Westphalia were still far from the concept of sovereignty that Jean Bodin wrote about in the second half of the sixteenth century. Schmidt, 1999: 102–104.
83	Müller, 1976: 13–21; Duchhardt, 1990: 18–19.
84	Müller, 1976: 22–23.
85	Later, when more Habsburg-friendly imperial chancellors took office, the Imperial Chancery was able to regain some of its influence in foreign policy. Müller, 1976: 24–27.
86	Schmidt, 1999: 199–200.
87	Müller, 1976: 28–31.
88	Müller, 1976: 35, 43, 57.
89	Schmidt, 1999: 232.
90	Duchhardt, 1990: 20–21.
91	Duchhardt, 1990: 23, 26–27.
92	Finally, upon Charles's death, the imperial crown was returned to the Habsburgs. Maria Theresa's husband Francis Stephan of Lorraine was elected emperor in 1745 and the Habsburg-Lorraine dynasty held the imperial title until the dissolution of the Empire. Schmidt, 1999: 266–269.
93	Schmidt, 1999: 271.
94	McGill, 1971.
95	*Translatio imperii* was an invention of Innocent III, which presumed that the

church transferred the empire from the Greeks to the Germans. Ullmann, 1949: 32–33.
96 Stengel, 1939: 2.
97 Yates, 1975: 2. The Empire was not called the Roman Empire until 1034, and the Holy Roman Empire until 1254. Berman, 1995 [1983]: 89. Finally, at the end of the fifteenth century, it came to be associated with a certain people and called the Holy Roman Empire of the German Nation (*Heiliges Römisches Reich deutscher Nation*). Schmidt, 1999: 10; Heinz Duchhardt points out that the term first appeared in an imperial law in 1486, Duchhardt, 1991: 16.
98 In practice, the supremacy of the emperor had five important legal consequences: first, *crimen laesae maiestatis* (crime against the sovereign) could only be committed against the emperor; second, the authority to promulgate universal legal rules belonged only to the emperor; third, the creation of public notaries was the exclusive prerogative of the emperor; fourth, the legitimation of an illegitimate child was also an exclusive privilege of the emperor; fifth, an appeal could be made to the emperor against the sentence of a king. Prior to the conflict between Robert and Henry, French, Spanish, Danish and English writers had been defending the kings' rights against the Staufen emperors. Previously Popes Innocent III and his successor Boniface VIII had recognized that the French king was de facto independent, but de jure dependent on the empire. Clement V, for the first time formulated a general rule of the equality of kings with the emperor. Opposition to universal empire in the thirteenth century was expressed in the statement that the king 'does not recognize a superior in temporal matters' (*superiorem in temporalibus non recognoscere*). This did not question the ultimate superiority of the emperor. However, the real blow to the emperor came in the fourteenth century when kings assumed the right to be emperors in their own domains (*rex imperator in regno suo*). Ullmann, 1949; Stengel, 1939.
99 Bosbach, 1986: 38–42.
100 The motto on a coin minted in 1548 attests to the ambition of Charles V: like the sun in the skies, there is [one] Caesar on earth (*quod in celis sol hoc in terra Caesar est*). Schmidt, 1999: 94.
101 In the same vein as medieval Ghibellinism, Charles's imperial chancellor Gattinara invoked the idea of a jurist-emperor along similar lines as Dante. Thus, the recovery of Roman law envisioned buttressing the jurisdiction of the emperor against the pope. Charles, with his huge power, appeared to be a better candidate for such an emperor than any of his medieval predecessors. Robertson, 1998; Headley, 1998; Bosbach, 1998; Yates, 1975.
102 Competing with the French king for office, Habsburg propaganda made use of anti-Latin feeling by referring to German identity. Schmidt, 1999: 49, 53. For Charles's universalist claims see Bosbach, 1986: 35–63.
103 Bosbach, 1986: 63.
104 For the context of Erasmus's book see Erasmus, 2006 (1997): vi–xxiv.
105 Erasmus states that 'the emperor would prefer to give up rather than pursue

the rights to the ancient monarchy, which jurists have conferred on him in their writings.' Erasmus, 2006 (1997): 106, see pages 102–110 on the subject.
106 Sloane, 1991; Toulmin, 1992 [1990].
107 Headley, 1983: 2–3.
108 Gross, 1975 [1973]: xx-xxii.
109 Gross, 1975 [1973]: 1–7, 135.
110 Schmidt, 1999: 186–191, Gross, 1975 [1973]: 135–139.
111 Gross, 1975 [1973]: 103–119.
112 Schröder, 1999: 962–963.
113 Gross, 1975 [1973]: 195–204.
114 Gross, 1975 [1973]: 235–254.
115 Gross, 1975 [1973]: 255–292; Hochstrasser, 2000: 47–60.
116 Krieger, 1960: 201–202.
117 Pufendorf, 2007 [1696]: 41–42.
118 Pufendorf, 2007 [1696]: 45–47.
119 Pufendorf, 2007 [1696]: 159–178.
120 Hochstrasser, 2000: 46.
121 Schmidt, 1999: 209.
122 Hellmuth, 1985; Strakosch, 1967.
123 Erasmus, 2006 (1997): 65–73.
124 Erasmus, 2006 (1997): 79–91.
125 Tuck, 2001: 6.

State Formation in the Ottoman Empire

1 'Anyone who attacks the Turks must, …, expect to find them entirely united, and would do well to rely entirely upon his own forces rather than upon the disorder of the enemy.' Machiavelli, 1981 [1513]: 22.
2 For different views on the concept of gaza see Lindner, 1983: 1–50; Kafadar, 1996; see also chapter one.
3 Imber, 2002: 252–257.
4 Kafadar, 1996.: 142–143.
5 Vryonis, 1956; Wittek, 1955; Ménage, 1965; İnalcık, 1965a; Imber, 2002: 128–142.
6 Darling, 1996: 46.
7 Lybyers, 1978 [1913]: 55–56. The slave system, as the specific characteristic of the Ottoman state, was morally and politically abhorrent to the European aristocracy with its own rights, honors and privileges. The Venetian ambassadors, who were part of the patrician class, in their Relazioni to the Senate expressed their awe at the complete surrender of Ottoman viziers to the death penalty given by the Sultan. Valensi,1994 [1987].
8 Kafadar, 1996: 136–137.
9 Despite its overt breach of the *shari'a*, the law book justified this rule on the basis of the consensus of the scholars. The clause reads as follows: 'For the

welfare of the state, the one of my sons to whom God grants the sultanate may lawfully put his brothers to death. A majority of the ulema consider this permissible.' İnalcık, 2002a [1973]: 59. In the late sixteenth century the Ottomans suspended the tradition of sending princes to the provinces and held them in the palace quarters called the cage (*kafes*). In the second half of the seventeenth century, the principle of seniority became the rule of succession.

10   İnalcık, 2002 [1973]: 60–61; Imber, 2002: 96–115.
11   İnalcık, 2000f [1959]: 31.
12   İnalcık, 1978a: 564–565; the following analysis relies on two printed versions of the text: a detailed one published with a facsimile by Akgündüz, 1990: 317–343 and a summarized version by Hammer, 1977 [1815]: 87–101. For convenience I will use the enumeration of the articles by Akgündüz.
13   Barkey, 1997 [1994]: 24–44.
14   Kautsky, 1997 [1982]: 118–120.
15   He held the exalted seal (*mühr-i şerif*) and his orders should be treated as the sultan's orders. Mumcu, 1976: 42–44. The term vizier derives from the Arabic *wazīr* or helper. Zaman, 2002: 185–188.
16   Kunt, 1983: 5. The Grand Vizierate had been an administrative and not military office in pre-Ottoman Muslim states. In the Seljukid, Mamluk and Ilkhanid states viziers were exclusively in charge of fiscal and administrative matters, while military affairs were under the control of the governor-general (*beğlerbeği*). Köprülü, 2002 [1931]: 35–40. This had been also the case in the Ottoman emirate until Murad I appointed a religious scholar, Çandarlı Kara Halil Hayreddin who combined both religious and military charismatic characteristics. Uzunçarşılı, 1974: 11–12; In the Ottoman Empire the vizierate seems to have emerged in the reign of Orhan (1326–1360). However, it became institutionalized during the time of his successor Murad I (1360–1389), when Çandarlı Kara Halil Hayreddin Paşa was appointed grand vizier. Mumcu, 1976: 22–23.
17   The grand vizier as the absolute representative carries the final political responsibility. Thus, the sultan himself becomes infallible and free of responsibility. Hassan, 2001: 207–208.
18   Between 1385 and 1453 the Çandarlı family provided the viziers and the grand viziers, all of whom had served as judges (*kadıs*) in their early careers. Özdemir, 2001: 52–53. This change corresponds to the pattern of replacement of the men of the pen (*arbab al-kalam*) by the men of the sword (*arbab al-sayf*) in the Mamluk sultanate of Egypt which was noted by Ibn Khaldun. İnalcık, 2002b; for a detailed history of the Çandarlı family see: Uzunçarşılı, 1974. The same pattern can be observed in medieval European chanceries where the chancellor was simultaneously a spiritual office holder. In England the office of Lord Chancellor was taken from the religious establishment during the reign of Henry VIII; Hintze, 1908 [1962]: 283.
19   Out of approximately two hundred grand viziers about twenty were executed when they were discharged. Lybyer, 1978 [1912]: 167.

20 This trend reached its climax in 1654 when the grand vizier Derviş Mehmed Paşa founded his own chancery. Matuz, 1974: 21. For the power of the grand vizier see: Lybyer, 1978 [1912]: 164–165; Hammer, 1977 [1815]: 62.

21 '*Cümle malımın nâzırı olub, umûr-ı âlem ana müfevvazdır.*' The term *daftar* derives from the Greek διφθέρα (*diphthera*) 'to hide.' The word was already used in ancient Greece to refer to parchment and writing materials. Lewis, 1965a: 77–81. Fuat Köprülü argues that the office of the treasurer was adopted from Seljukid and Ilkhanid state practice. Köprülü, 2002 [1931]: 54–58; Hassan, 2001: 210–211. The treasurer presided over a hierarchy of provincial and central finance officers. Lewis, 1965b; İnalcık, 1965b.

22 In the late sixteenth century when the Sultan's treasury had become in practice the state treasury, a treasurer accused of corruption was not tried by the Imperial Council on the grounds that he was directly responsible to the Sultan. Kunt, 1995: 752.

23 'And in all affairs of government, let my grand vizier consult with my other viziers and with my Treasurer. Let no one except them be knowledgeable about these affairs.' (*Ve cümle umûr-ı saltanatı vezîr-i a'zâm, sâir vüzerâ ile ve defterdârım ile müşâvere edeler. Anlardan başka kimesne vâkıf olmaya*). The last sentence of Article 20 states that 'And let my Chief Treasurer consult his affairs with the grand vizier. Not even the second vizier should hear about the secret affairs.' (*Ve başdefterdârım dahi umûrunu vezîr-i a'zâm ile müşâvere edeler. Umûr-ı mahfıyyeyi vezîr-i sânî dahi duymaya*).

24 Mumcu, 1976: 44–47.

25 As opposed to the multiplicity of councils in the Seljukid state, the Ottomans combined multiple functions in their Imperial Council. Mumcu, 1976: 11–20.

26 Köprülü, 2002 [1931]: 50–54; Mumcu, 1976: 47–49; Babinger, 1993.

27 Military judges existed both in the Mamluk state and the Seljukid emirate of Anatolia. The Ottoman state had two military judges for Rumelia and Anatolia. The former had precedence over the latter. Köprülü, 2002 [1931]: 46–49.

28 In pre-Ottoman Islamic states, military judges were responsible for the military judiciary, while the civilian judiciary was headed by a chief judge (*qadi al-qudat*). The military class consisted of people who held a fief from the sultan; Şentop, 2005: 10.

29 Elias, 2001 [1969].

30 Necipoğlu, 1991: 3–30, 90–110; Hassan, 2001: 232.

31 See kapıkulus in Bayerle, 1997: 94. In addition to these two major forces, the Ottomans also levied soldiers from the towns called *azabs* and organized the early lightly armed cavalry as raiders (*akıncıs*). Imber, 2002: 252–286.

32 Each district in turn was divided into subdivisions of the provincial army. İnalcık, 2000j: 502; Imber, 2002: 180–184.

33 İnalcık, 2002a [1973]: 104; Imber, 2002: 190–191; Kunt, 1983: 9.

34 Röhrborn, 1973: 39–40.

35 The Ottomans seem to have adopted Byzantine feudal terminology, which suggests that the Byzantine feudal system provided a model for the Ottomans.

The Ottoman *timar* is the Persian synonym for the Byzantine *pronoia*, meaning 'care' or 'horse-grooming'. The Turkish word was *dirlik*, meaning 'livelihood'. The Greek word for peasant-holding on a fief was *zeugarion*, meaning 'yoke' or 'pair of oxen' which was translated into Turkish as *çift* or *boyunduruk*. The Byzantine unit of land measurement was *stremma*, the 'twisting' referring to the measuring rope. The Ottoman unit of measurement was called a *dönüm*, meaning 'turning.' Incidental taxes were called *bad-i hava* or 'wind or air' in Ottoman terminology. The Byzantine counterpart of these taxes was called *aër* or *aërikon*. Imber, 2002: 195; For an argument against the Byzantine origins see: Köprülü, 2002 [1931]: 76–102; also see Kunt, 1983: 9, 12–13.

36 This was a major point of Ottoman reformers in the seventeenth century. In his reform proposal, Koçi Bey argued that bestowals should not be made in the court but in the provinces where they are known to the locals. Röhrborn, 1973: 49–52.

37 In Perry Anderson's view, the Ottoman *timar* was not a genuine fief, because the *sipahi* had no seigneurial jurisdiction over the peasants and played no role in the agrarian economy. Moreover, while the peasants had hereditary security of tenure over the land they worked on, the *sipahis* did not. Anderson, 1979 [1974]: 368–369. However, there is ample evidence that the state was trying to protect the rights of the existing *timar*-holders against newcomers. Moreover, the *timar*-holder was called the lord of the land (*sahib-i arz*) and lord of the peasants (*sahib-i rai'yyet*). He had exclusive jurisdiction over the land and peasants in order to implement the regulations of the *kanuns*. He could bring a fugitive peasant back to the *timar* within ten and later fifteen years. The peasants were called independent (*hür*) in the sense that the *timar*-holder could not impose more obligations than stipulated by the *kanun*. In organizing their productive activities peasants were free. İnalcık, 2000j: 503–505.

38 A decree in 1586 ordered that *timars* over 20 000 *akçe* could only be bestowed by the court. Moreover, the grand viziers and the commanders could bestow vacant *timars*, which were registered in the vacancy registers (*mahlûl defteri*). Röhrborn, 1973: 55–64. In addition to governors-general, the viziers started to bestow *timars* to their entourage. For new forms of *timar* bestowals see: Röhrborn, 1973: 64–84.

39 Barkey, 1997 [1994]: 25.
40 İnalcık, 1978b: 288–291.
41 For the transformation of the Ottoman army and administration see İnalcık, 1978b: 288–311.
42 Findley, 1980: 87.
43 Findley, 1980: 53.
44 Aksan, 1995: 3; Findley, 1980: 94.
45 İnalcık, 1993a: 13.
46 Matuz, 1974: 12.
47 Şentop, 2005: 4–6.
48 Although the building was changed several times due to changes in the office holders, fires and rebellions, the grand viziers continued to retain a large

household with offices for the bureaucracy and archives. Uzunçarşılı, 1988 [1945]: 249–254.
49 Findley, 1970: 339.
50 Findley, 1980: 35–37, 79. Although the recruitment of the officials took over the master-apprentice patterns of the guild tradition, it failed to produce an autonomous body of professionals with their own collective identity. Findley, 1980: 100.
51 Until around 1592 the affixer of the cipher was in full charge of state affairs and constituted a higher promotion for the chief of scribes. In the seventeenth century while the chief of scribes became the practical head of bureaucracy, the affixer of the cipher became a titular and ceremonial post. In the nineteenth century scribes of secondary rank started to be promoted to the post until its abolishment in 1836. Abou-El-Haj, 1963: 31–36.
52 Headley, 1983: 15–19 and see chapter five on Gattinara's failure to reform the Imperial Chancery.
53 In the nineteenth century modern state ministries would grow out of three officers in the grand vizier's offices: *kahya bey* (minister of the interior), *çavuş başı* (minister of justice) and *reisülküttab* (minister of the exterior). Findley, 1970: 336.
54 Thus, Max Kortepeter points out that in Hungary the Ottomans failed to confront the centralization of the Habsburg domains. Kortepeter, 1985.
55 Cited in Findley, 1980: vii.
56 See chapter two.
57 Genç, 2002: 43–67.
58 Cezar, 1986: 28–30.
59 In the seventeenth century the siege of Crete (1645–1669) lasted almost 24 years. The wars with the Habsburgs started in 1663, lasted until 1699, and involved Poland, Russia and Venice against the Ottomans.
60 İnalcık, 1978b: 311–313.
61 Murphey argues that Ottoman institutions took lessons from the defeat of 1683 in Vienna. Rather than labeling these responses as decline or stagnation Murphey regards the process as a transformation of the Ottoman bureaucracy. Especially during the authoritarian rule of the Köprülü family as grand viziers in the second half of the seventeenth century important changes were made in the state structure. Murphey, 1993: 427.
62 Murphey, 1993: 435.
63 Murphey, 1993: 438.
64 In the records, tax farming can be traced back to the fifteenth century. Over the two centuries until the seventeenth century its use increased steadily. Darling, 1996: 122; İnalcık, 1978b: 327–328; Cezar, 1986: 29–34; Genç, 2002: 104–117.
65 This finding provides important evidence against Perry Anderson's understanding of the Ottoman polity. Anderson claims that the *çiftlik* system never turned into feudalism because it was never systematically legalized

and the peasants were not legally bound to the soil. Anderson, 1979 [1974]: 365–387. The evidence put forward in this chapter suggests that the *çiftlik* system had in practice the same consequence for peasant mobility as Eastern absolutism in general. The peasants were in practice if not legally enserfed. Faroqhi, 2007: 63; İnalcık, 1978b: 313–317.

66   İnalcık, 1978b: 317–322.
67   İnalcık, 1978b: 322–327.
68   Faroqhi, 2007: 59.
69   Abou-El-Haj, 1963: 29–30.
70   İnalcık, 1993b; Göçek, 1993; Necipoğlu, 1993: 175, 190.
71   For the attribution of Ottoman imperial claims to Islam see Hurewitz, 1961; Naff, 1984. In this vein, the historian Bernard Lewis argues that Arabs and Turks appreciated ancient Greek and Byzantine civilizations, but had no interest in Central and Western Europe. There was no attempt to learn non-Islamic languages. The statesmen often relied on their non-Muslim subjects or refugees in their service. Lewis, 1994: 14–15. According to Lewis, in the early stages of Ottoman advancement in Europe there were no treaties and very little negotiation. The state of permanent war between Islam and the infidels was occasionally interrupted by truces dictated by Istanbul to its defeated enemies. Lewis, 1994: 19.
72   Gerber, 1994: 89–90; Imber, 2002: 125–127; İnalcık, 2002a [1973]: 55–58; Findley, 1980: 8.
73   Ottoman sultans occupying the Eastern Roman throne regarded themselves as true heirs to the Roman imperial tradition. Whereas Charles V was acknowledged simply as the king of Spain, his successor Ferdinand was referred to as the king of Austria (Nemçe kralı). The Ottoman sultans refused to address the Holy Roman emperors as Caesars, on the grounds that there could be only one Caesar on earth. Köhbach, 1992; İnalcık, 2002a [1973]: 58.
74   Kołodziejczyk, 2000: 3–7.
75   Sebastian, 1994: 333–335; Faroqhi, 2007: 6–8.
76   Ágoston, 2007: 82.
77   Ágoston, 2007: 77.
78   Between 1384 and 1600 the Ottoman sultan sent 145 temporary envoys to Venice alone. Yurdusev, 2004: 27.
79   Yunus Bey and İbrahim Ağa of Greek origin, whose family lived under a Venetian colony; İbrahim Bey, a Polish renegade; the translator Mahmud, son of a Jewish merchant from Vienna, the translator Murad from Hungary. Ágoston, 2007: 85–86.
80   Yunus Bey went to Venice at least six times, as well as to Vienna and Hungary. İbrahim Bey visited Venice, his homeland Poland, Vienna and France. The Viennese-born Mahmud was sent to Vienna, where he also visited his family. He made official business trips to Transylvania, Poland, Italy, France and Prague, where he died in 1575. The Hungarian Murad and another Hungarian Ferhad were also sent to Hungary. Ágoston, 2007: 90.

NOTES

81 In 1569, news of the fire in the Venetian arsenal reached the capital through Joseph Nassí, a member of the Jewish Mendes family with a vast commercial network in Europe. This information was crucial in the Ottoman decision to launch an attack on Venice. Similarly in 1588, when the English ambassador broke the news of the defeat of the Spanish armada to the grand vizier, he discovered surprisingly that the Ottoman government had already received the news from Don Alvaro Mendes (alias Solomon Abenaes), who was the brother-in-law of Queen Elizabeth's physician. Ágoston, 2007: 83.

82 De Groot, 2003: 576.

83 Yurdusev, 2004: 17.

84 Goffman, 2007: 65–66; However, as the capitulation of the Adriatic city of Ragusa demonstrates, it was possible to avoid absorption into the Islamic state despite acquiring vassal status. No Ottoman judge (*kadi*) ever took office in Ragusa, which indicates that the city was not considered as part of the *Dar al-islam*. Moreover, the city also retained its minting rights and was allowed to keep consuls abroad. Italians emulated Ragusan capitulations to reside in the Ottoman state indefinitely without losing their nationality. De Groot, 2003: 580–582.

85 De Groot, 2003: 603.

86 Kołodziejczyk, 2000: 55.

87 Goffman, 2007: 62, 70–71; Goffman, 2002: 186; Yurdusev also builds on Goffman Yurdusev, 2004: 25.

88 Goffman, 2007: 72; Yurdusev, 2004: 30.

89 The historian Bernard Lewis emphasizes that the Ottoman capital in the seventeenth century was probably the only city in Europe where Christians of all confessions could live and worship in security. Lewis, 1994: 81.

90 Timur Kuran's studies reveal how European rules of business became part of Ottoman economic practice via capitulations. Many cases from the Ottoman court registers reveal that the terms of the capitulations were indeed implemented by a kadi in the Islamic court system. Kuran, 2008.

91 The grand mufti Baha'i Mehmed Efendi placed the British ambassador in Istanbul under house arrest due to a jurisdictional dispute between the British consul and the kadi of İzmir. For this breach of diplomatic custom, the grand mufti was discharged and sent to exile in the Aegean island of Lesbos, only to be reinstated two years later. Lewis, 1960: 915.

92 Hurewitz, 1961: 146.

93 Faroqhi, 2007: 52.

94 In 1649, during the negotiation for the prolongation of peace for 22 years, the Ottoman plenipotentiary vizier Hasan Paşa reported to the grand vizier about the special concession to the Habsburgs: from then on the Habsburg emperor would be addressed in the Turkish formal second person pronoun *siz* (equivalent of the French *vous*) instead of the informal pronoun *sen* (French *tu*). The Ottoman sultan would use the singular first person pronoun *ben* instead of *biz* (the royal we). Moreover, the Habsburg ruler would be called 'emperor' instead of 'king of Hungary.' De Groot, 2003: 579–580.

95 For the definition of uti possidetis see Abou-El-Haj, 1963.
96 Abou-El-Haj, 1963; Abou-El-Haj, 1969: 467–475; Abou-El-Haj, 1974b: 131–137.
97 Abou-El-Haj, 1969: 467–469, 474.
98 Abou-El-Haj, 1984.
99 Abou-El-Haj, 1963: viii-ix, 20.
100 The rescript designated the grand vizier with full authority to negotiate on behalf of the sultan. The grand vizier, in turn, appointed the chief of scribes Rami Mehmed Efendi as the head negotiator and the chief translator (*dragoman*) Iskerletzade Alexander as a member of the Ottoman peace delegation. Abou-El-Haj, 1963: 20–21; Findley, 1970: 336. The chief translator was born of a Greek father and an Italian mother, had studied first in the Patriarchate School and later, in the Greek College in Rome and the Universities of Padua and Bologna. He held a degree in medicine and was proficient in all major European languages (Latin, Italian, French, Spanish, German) as well as Oriental languages (Greek, Turkish, Arabic and Persian). Abou-El-Haj, 1963: 23–31. The chief of scribes Rami Mehmed was a Muslim trained in Ottoman bureaucracy. He first joined the chancery of the Imperial Council as an apprentice. Through his connection to the famous poet Nabi Efendi, who was in the service of Musahib Mustafa Paşa, the brother-in-law of the sultan, he entered the paşa's household (*kapı*, literally port). Although the paşa was soon discredited at the court and sent to a mission outside the capital, Rami Mehmed followed him and gained experience acting as the chief scribe of the paşa's household. In 1690 he was promoted to the Imperial Chancery as *beylikçi*, the executive assistant to the chief of scribes. Finally, in 1694 he was appointed as the chief of scribes by the grand vizier Ali Paşa. Abou-El-Haj, 1963: 25–28.
101 The chief translators, however, were not part of the larger bureaucratic scheme. They differed not only in their ethnic and religious background, their education and recruitment, but also in their *cursus honorum*. As the second most important post following the chief of scribes, the office of the chief translator did not lead to a higher office in the capital. Former translators were usually appointed as deputies (*voyvoda*) to rule Moldavia or Wallachia. Findley, 1970: 338, especially f.n. 1.
102 The chief of scribes was not a member of the Imperial Council but merely one of its servants. They were not the executive power-holders of the state (*erkan-ı devlet*) but high-level officers of the state (*rical-i devlet*). As such, he had no right to speak in the Imperial Council; in the grand vizier's council he would sit on the carpet next to the grand vizier instead of on the cedar couch (*sedir*) until the nineteenth century. Uzunçarşılı, 1988 [1948]: 247.
103 Abou-El-Haj, 1963: 36–53; the chief of scribes was the head of the Office of the Imperial Council, which consisted of three sections. Next to the Office of the Imperial Council, the chief of scribes also headed the office of all the incoming and outgoing correspondence of the grand vizier (*Mektub-i Sadr-i*

Ali) and the office of the personal secretary of the grand vizier (*Âmedi*). For detailed schemes of these offices see: Bayerle, 1997: 21, 129, 144; Findley, 1970: 335–338.

104　During the visit the Ottoman envoy Seyfulah Ağa assured the Habsburg authorities that Poland would not be invaded under any circumstances. Although the Habsburg's mediation was rejected, the Ottoman envoy received a warm welcome in Vienna. Seyfullah Ağa noted 'in all we had pleasant exchanges. Although they are the enemies of Religion and we know what goes on in their souls, they outwardly showed the greatest respect and friendship. And we did all in our power to reciprocate.' Erünsal, 2000: 23.

105　This is indeed İsmail Erünsal's conclusion after analyzing the text in detail. Erünsal, 2000.

106　Stein, 1985.

107　The inclusion of the empire in the European balance would implicate compensation for the gains and losses of the empire in war. However, Russia treated the empire as an illegitimate state in order to advance its expansion politics in the Balkans. Faroqhi, 2007: 68–69.

108　Neumann, 1993.

109　Aksan, 1995: xii; xviii.

110　Mokyr, 2006.

111　Articles 25 and 28 of the law book of Mehmed II regulate the scholarly hierarchy, Akgündüz, 1990: 317–343; also see Repp, 1986.

112　Neighboring Iran, ruled by the Shiite Safavid dynasty, would not provide a possible job market. Mughal India was geographically too far away at least for most scholars. Francis Robinson emphasizes that the emergence of the Safavid state cut off the interaction of Ottoman scholars with learning centers in Iran, Khorasan, Transoxiana and India. Robinson, 1997: 156.

113　Fleischer, 1984: 57–58.

114　As the historian Hakan Karateke points out, 'when a pre-modern empire is steadily engaged in warfare, the political authority must constantly justify or support its rule by visible successes.' Karateke, 2005a: 17.

115　Karateke, 2005a.

116　Ziegler, 2004: 338; Fleischer, 1984.

117　'Imperial systems are not territorially demarcated because they claim to rule the whole world, in other words, for them the whole Earth potentially constitutes their territory. If some parts of the world are not under their rule and do not offer allegiance, it is a temporary situation. One day or another, they are bound to fall under their imperial domain. There was then no need for territorial demarcation or boundary delimitation.' Yurdusev, 2004: 18.

118　Hagen, 2005: 61.

119　Mardin, 1969: 28–29.

120　Mardin, 1969: 30–32; This model can also be found in the pre-Islamic Indo-Persian political traditions. With the increasing popularity of Plato and Aristotle the model was used by al-Farabi (d.950), al-Miskawayh (d.1030), Ibn Sina (d.1037) and Ibn Rushd (d.1198). Ergene, 2001: 55–56.

121 Fleischer, 1986: 262.
122 Ergene, 2001: 57.
123 Ergene, 2001: 63.
124 In this context, Ergene emphasizes that Mustafa Ali could base his criticism on the notion that the sultan and his subjects have mutual rights and obligations and that the former is responsible for maintaining the just social division. Ergene, 2001: 75.
125 Lewis, 1994: 19–20.
126 Abou-El-Haj, 1974a: 438–447.
127 Abou-El-Haj, 1984.
128 Karateke, 2005a: 43.
129 Abou-El-Haj, 1969.
130 Karateke, 2005a: 36.
131 Katib Chelebi, 1957 [1656]: 29.
132 Katib Chelebi, 1957 [1656]: 29–30.
133 Abou-El-Haj, 1991: 37–40.
134 Naîmâ Mustafa Efendi, 1967: 39.
135 Aksan, 1993, 53–69.
136 Aksan, 1993: 64.
137 Quartet, 2005 [2000]: 40–41.
138 Erginbaş, 2005: 43–44; Şen, 1995: 72–73.
139 Şen, 1995: 140–144.
140 Erginbaş, 2005: 46–49.
141 Aksan, 1995: 169.
142 Aksan, 1995: 197–198.
143 Akyıldız, 2004: 83–102.
144 Veldet, 1999: 159, 166.
145 Akyıldız, 2004: 45–81.

Conclusion

1 Alker, 1996: 387.
2 Castells, 2005.
3 '*Halk içinde mu'teber bir nesne yok devlet gibi; Olmaya devlet cihanda bir nefes sıhhat gibi.*' Brackets are mine. Cited and translated by Gökyay, 1993: 382.

BIBLIOGRAPHY

Abou-El-Haj, R. 1963. *The Reisülküttab and Ottoman Diplomacy at Karlowitz*. Unpublished PhD Dissertation: Princeton University.Abou-El-Haj, R. 1969. 'The Formal Closure of the Ottoman Frontier in Europe: 1699–1703,' *Journal of the American Oriental Society* 89(3): 467–475.

Abou-El-Haj, R. 1974a. 'The Ottoman Vezir and Paşa households 1683–1703: A Preliminary Report,' *Journal of the American Oriental Society* 94(4): 438–447.

Abou-El-Haj, R. 1974b. 'Ottoman Attitudes Toward Peace Making: The Karlowitz Case,' *Der Islam* 51: 131–137.

Abou-El-Haj, R. 1984. *The 1703 Rebellion and the Structure of Ottoman Politics*. Leiden: Nederlands Historisch-Archaeologisch Instituut te İstanbul.

Abou-El-Haj, R.1991. *Formation of the Modern State: The Ottoman Empire Sixteenth to Eighteenth Centuries*. New York: SUNY Press.

Ágoston, G. 2007. 'Information, Ideology, and Limits of Imperial Policy: Ottoman Grand Strategy in the Context of Ottoman-Habsburg Rivalry,' in *The Early Modern Ottomans: Remapping the Empire*. Edited by Virginia H. Aksan and Daniel Goffman. 75–103. Cambridge: Cambridge University Press.

Akgündüz, A. 1990. *Osmanlı Kanunnâmeleri ve Hukukî Tahlilleri, I. Kitap: Osmanlı Hukukuna Giriş ve Fâtih Devri Kanunnâmeleri*. İstanbul: FEY Vakfı Yayınları.

Aksan, V.H. 1993. 'Ottoman Political Writing, 1768–1808', *International Journal of Middle East Studies* 25(1): 53–69.

Aksan, V.H. 1995. *An Ottoman Statesman in War and Peace: Ahmed Resmi Efendi 1700–1783*. Leiden: E.J. Brill.

Akyıldız, A. 2004. *Osmanlı Bürokrasisi ve Modernleşme*. İstanbul: İletişim Yayınları.

Albert, M. 1999. 'Observing World Politics: Luhmann's Systems Theory of Society and International Relations,' *Millennium* 28(2): 239–265.

Albert, M. and Brock, L. 2001. 'What Keeps Westphalia Together? Normative Differentiation in the Modern System of States,' in *Identities, Borders, Orders: Rethinking International Relations Theory*. Edited by Mathias Albert, David Jacobson and Yosef Lapid. 29–49. Minneapolis and London: University of Minnesota Press.

Alker, H. 1996. 'The Presumption of Anarchy in World Politics: On Recovering the Historicity of World Society,' in *Rediscoveries and Reformulations: Humanistic Methodologies for International Studies*. 355–393. Cambridge: Cambridge University Press.

Anderson, P. 1979 [1974]. *Lineages of the Absolutist State*. London and New York: Verso.

Babinger, F. 1993. 'Nishandji,' in *The Encyclopedia of Islam Vol. VIII*. Edited by E. Bosworth, E. van Donzel, W.P. Heinrichs and G. Lecomte. 62. Leiden: E.J. Brill.

Barkan, Ö.L. 1943. *XV ve XVI ıncı Asırlarda Osmanlı İmparatorluğunda Ziraî Ekonominin Hukukî ve Malî Esasları, I. Cilt: Kanunlar*. İstanbul: Burhaneddin Matbaası.

Barkey, K. 1997 [1994]. *Bandits and Bureaucrats: The Ottoman Route to State Centralization*. Ithaca and London: Cornell University Press.

Barkey, K. 2008. *Empire of Difference: The Ottomans in Comparative Perspective*. Cambridge: Cambridge University Press.

Barkin, S.J. and Cronin, B. 1994. 'The State and the Nation: Changing Norms and the Rules of Sovereignty in International Relations,' *International Organization* 48(1): 107–130.

Barraclough, G. 1984. *The Origins of Modern Germany*. New York and London: W.W. Norton & Company.

Bayerle, G. 1997. *Pashas, Begs and Effendis: A Historical Dictionary of Titles and Terms in the Ottoman Empire*. İstanbul: The ISIS Press.

Benhabib, S. 1995. 'The Debate over Women and Moral Theory Revisited,' in *Feminists Read Habermas: Gendering the Subject of Discourse*. Edited by Johanna Meehan. 181–203. New York and London: Routledge.

Bérenger, J. 1994. *A History of the Habsburg Empire 1273–1700*. Translated by C.A. Simpson. London and New York: Longman.

Berman, H.J. 1995 [1983]. *Law and Revolution: The Formation of the Western Legal Tradition*. Eighth Printing. Cambridge, Massachusetts and London, England: Harvard University Press.

Berman, H.J. 2006 [2003]. *Law and Revolution II: The Impact of the Protestant Reformations on the Western Legal Tradition*. Cambridge, Massachusetts and London, England: The Belknap Press of Harvard University Press.

Blackbourn, D. And Eley, G. 2003 [1984]. 'Introduction,' *The Peculiarities of German History: Bourgeois Society and Politics in the Nineteenth-Century Politics*. 1–35. Oxford and New York: Oxford University Press.
Bloom, W. 1990. *Personal Identity, National Identity and International Relations*. Cambridge: Cambridge University Press.
Bosbach, F. 1988. *Monarchia Universalis: Ein Politischer Leitbegriff der Frühen Neuzeit*. Göttingen: Vandenhoeck & Ruprecht.
Bosbach, F. 1998. 'The European Debate on Universal Monarchy,' in *Theories of Empire, 1450–1800*. Edited by David Armitage. 81–98. Aldershot: Ashgate Variorum.
Braudel, F. 1992. *Karl V.: Die Notwendigkeit des Zufalls*. Frankfurt am Main and Leipzig: Insel Verlag.
Brewer, J. 1990. *The Sinews of Power: War, Money and the English State, 1688–1783*. Cambridge, Massachusetts: Harvard University Press.
Brooks, S.G. and Wohlforth, W.C. 2008. *World Out of Balance: International Relations and the Challenge of American Primacy*. Princeton and Oxford: Princeton University Press.
Bukovansky, M. 2002. *Legitimacy and Power Politics: The American and French Revolutions in International Political Culture*. Princeton: Princeton University Press.
Burch, K. 1998. *'Property' and the Making of the International System*. Boulder and London: Lynne Rienner Publishers.
Buzan, B. and Little, R. 2000. *International Systems in World History: Remaking the Study of International Relations*. New York: Oxford University Press.
Castells, M. 2005. 'Global Governance and Global Politics,' *Political Science and Politics* 38(1): 9–16.
Cezar, Y. 1986. *Osmanlı Maliyesinde Bunalım ve Değişim Dönemi: XVIII.yy dan Tanzimat'a Mali Tarih*. İstanbul: Alan Yayıncılık.
Claude, I.L. 1966. 'Collective Legitimization as a Political Function of the United Nations,' *International Organization* 20(3): 367–379.
Collins, J.B. 1996. *The State in Early Modern France*. Cambridge: Cambridge University Press.
Crone, P. 2004. *God's Rule: Government and Islam*. New York: Columbia University Press.
Cooper, F. 2005a. 'Introduction,' in *Colonialism in Question: Theory, Knowledge, History*. 3–32. Berkeley, Los Angeles and London: University of California Press.
Cooper, F. 2005b. 'The Rise, Fall, and Rise of Colonial Studies,' in *Colonialism in Question: Theory, Knowledge, History*. 33–55. Berkeley, Los Angeles and London: University of California Press.

Cooper, F. 2005c. 'States, Empires, and Political Imagination,' in *Colonialism in Question: Theory, Knowledge, History.* 153–203. Berkeley, Los Angeles and London: University of California Press.

Cooper, F. and Brubaker, R. 2005. 'Identity,' in *Colonialism in Question: Theory, Knowledge, History.* 59–90. Berkeley and Los Angeles: University of California Press.

Darling, L. 1996. *Revenue-Raising and Legitimacy: Tax Collection and Finance Administration in the Ottoman Empire 1560–1660.* Leiden, New York and Köln: E.J. Brill.

De Bellefonds, Y.L. 1975. 'Kanūn,' in *The Encyclopedia of Islam Vol. IV.* Edited by C.E. Bosworth, E. van Donzel, B. Lewis and Ch. Pellat. 556–557. Leiden: E.J. Brill.

De Groot, A.H. 2003. 'The Historical Development of the Capitulatory Regime in the Ottoman Middle East from the Fifteenth to the Nineteenth Centuries,' *Oriento Moderno* 22 (3): 575–604.

Doyle, M.W. 1986. *Empires.* Ithaca and London: Cornell University Press.

Dreyfus, H.L. and Rabinow, P. 1983. *Michel Foucault: Beyond Structuralism and Hermeneutics.* Chicago: The University of Chicago Press.

Du Boulay, F.R. 1983. *Germany in the Later Middle Ages.* New York: St. Martin's Press.

Duchhardt, H. 1990. *Altes Reich und Europäische Staatenwelt 1648–1806.* München: R.Oldenbourg Verlag.

Duchhardt, H. 1991. *Deutsche Verfassungsgeschichte 1495–1806.* Stuttgart, Berlin and Köln: Verlag W. Kohlhammer.

Duff, P.W. 1938. *Personality in Roman Private Law.* London: Cambridge University Press.

Eder, K. 1976. *Die Entstehung staatlich organisierter Gesellschaften: Ein Beitrag zu einer Theorie sozialer Evolution.* Frankfurt am Main: Suhrkamp.

Eisenbichler, K. 1999. 'Charles V in Bologna: The Self-Fashioning of a Man and a City,' *Renaissance Studies* 13(4): 430–439.

Eisenstadt, S.N. 1962. 'Religious Organizations and Political Process in Centralized Empires,' *The Journal of Asian Studies* 21(3): 271–294.

Eisenstadt, S.N. 1968. 'Empires,' in *International Encyclopedia of the Social Sciences, Vol. 5.* Edited by David L.Sills. 41–49. New York: The MacMillan Company and The Free Press.

Eisenstadt, S.N. 1993 [1963]. *The Political Systems of Empires.* New Brunswick and London: Transaction Publishers.

Elias, 2001 [1969]. *Die Höfische Gesellschaft: Untersuchungen zur Soziologie des Königtums und der höfischen Aristokratie.* Frankfurt am Main: Suhrkamp.

d'Entrèves, A.P. 1957. *Natural Law: An Introduction to Legal Philosophy*. 4th imp. London: Hutchinson University Library.
Erasmus, D. 2006 [1997]. *The Education of a Christian Prince with the Panegyric for Archduke Philip of Austria*. Cambridge: Cambridge University Press.
Ergene, B. 2001. 'On Ottoman Justice: Interpretations in Conflict (1600–1800),' *Islamic Law and Society* 8(1): 52–87.
Erginbaş, V. 2005. *Forerunner and the Ottoman Enlightenment: İbrahim Müteferrika and His Intellectual Legacy*. Unpublished MA Thesis. İstanbul: Sabancı University.
Erünsal, İ.E. 2000. 'Seyfullah Agha's Embassy to Vienna in 1711: The Ottoman Version,' *Wiener Zeitschrift für die Kunde des Morgenlandes* 90: 7–28.
Esherick, Kayalı and Van Young, 2006. 'Introduction,' in *Empire to Nation: Historical Perspectives on the Making of the Modern World*. Edited by Joseph W. Esherick, Hasan Kayalı, and Eric Van Young. 1–31. Lanham: Rowman and Littlefield Publishers.
Evans G. and Newnham, J. 1998. *The Penguin Dictionary of International Relations*. London: Penguin.
Evans, J.A.S. 1996. *The Age of Justinian: The Circumstances of Imperial Power*. London and New York: Routledge.
Faroqhi, S. 2007. *The Ottoman Empire and the World Around It*. London and New York: I.B.Tauris.
Findley, C.V. 1970. The Legacy of Tradition to Reform: Origins of the Ottoman Foreign Ministry,' *International Journal of Middle East Studies* 1(4): 334–357.
Findley, C.V. 1980. *Bureaucratic Reform in the Ottoman Empire: The Sublime Porte, 1789–1922*. Princeton: Princeton University Press.
Fischer, M. 1992. '800–1300: Communal Discourse and Conflictual Practices,' *International Organization* 46(2): 427–466.
Fleischer, C. 1984. 'Royal Authority, Dynastic Cyclism, and 'Ibn Khaldûnism' in Sixteenth-Century Ottoman Letters,' in *Ibn Khaldun and Islamic Ideology*. Edited by Bruce B. Lawrence. 46–68. Leiden: E.J. Brill.
Fleischer, C. 1986. *Bureaucrat and Intellectual in the Ottoman Empire: The Historian Mustafa Âli (1541–1600)*. Princeton, NJ: Princeton University Press.
Fodor, P. 1986. 'State and Society, Crisis and Reform, in 15th–17th Century Ottoman Mirror for Princes,' *Acta Orientalia Academiae Scientiarum Hungaricae*, 60 (2–3): 217–240.
Gelpi, C. 2003. *The Power of Legitimacy: Assessing the Role of Norms in Crisis Bargaining*. Princeton, NJ: Princeton University Press.
Genç, M. 2002. *Osmanlı İmparatorluğu'nda Devlet ve Ekonomi*. İstanbul: Ötüken Neşriyat.

Gerber, H. 1994. *State, Society and Law in Islam: Ottoman Law in Comparative Perspective*. Albany: SUNY Press.

Giddens, A. 1987. *The Nation-State and Violence*: Volume Two of A Contemporary Critique of Historical Materialism. Berkeley and Los Angeles: University of California Press.

Gierke, O. 1990 [1868]. *Community in Historical Perspective: A translation of selections from Das Deutsche Genossenschaftsrecht*. Translated by M. Fischer. Selected and Edited by Antony Black. Cambridge: Cambridge University Press.

Gierke, Otto Friedrich v. 2005 [1913]. *Das Deutsche Genossenschaftsrecht, Vol. 4*. Berlin: Weidmann (Elibron Replica Edition).

Goffman, D. 2002. *The Ottoman Empire and Early Modern Europe*. Cambridge: Cambridge University Press.

Goffman, D. 2007. 'Negotiating with the Renaissance State: the Ottoman Empire and the New Diplomacy,' in *The Early Modern Ottomans: Remapping the Empire*. Edited by Virginia H. Aksan and Daniel Goffman. 61–74. Cambridge: Cambridge University Press.

Gorski, P. 2003. *The Disciplinary Revolution: Calvinism and the Rise of the State in Early Modern Europe*. Chicago: The University of Chicago Press.

Göçek, F.M. 1993. 'The Social Construction of an Empire: Ottoman State Under Süleyman the Magnificent,' in *Süleymân the Second and His Time*. Edited by Halil İnalcık and Cemal Kafadar. 93–108. İstanbul: Isis Press.

Gökyay, 1993. 'Ideology and Literature During the Expansion of the Ottoman Empire,' in *Süleymân the Second and His Time*. Edited by Halil İnalcık and Cemal Kafadar. 381–394.. İstanbul: Isis Press.

Greif, A. 2008. *Institutions and the Path to the Modern Economy: Lessons from Medieval Trade*. Cambridge: Cambridge University Press.

Gross, H. 1975 [1973]. *Empire and Sovereignty: A History of the Public Law Literature in the Holy Roman Empire, 1599–1804*. Chicago and London: The University of Chicago Press.

Habermas, J. 1973. *Legitimationsprobleme im Spätkapitalismus*. Frankfurt: Suhrkamp.

Habermas, J. 1979. 'History and Evolution,' *Telos* 39: 5–44.

Habermas, J. 1990. *Strukturwandel der Öffentlichkeit: Untersuchungen zu einer Kategorie der bürgerlichen Gesellschaft*. New Edition. Frankfurt: Suhrkamp.

Habermas, J. 1998a. [1986]. 'Recht als Kategorie der gesellschaftlichen Vermittlung zwischen Faktizität und Geltung,' in *Faktizität und Geltung: Beiträge zur Diskurstheorie des Rechts und des demokratischen Rechtsstaats*. 15–60. Frankfurt: Suhrkamp Verlag.

Habermas, J. 1998b. 'Zur Rekonstruktion des Rechts (I): Das System der Rechte' in *Faktizität und Geltung: Beiträge zur Diskurstheorie des Rechts und des demokratischen Rechtsstaats.* 109–165. Frankfurt am Main: Suhrkamp Verlag.

Habermas, J. 1998c. 'Zur Rekonstruktion des Rechts (2): Die Prinzipien des Rechtsstaates' in *Faktizität und Geltung: Beiträge zur Diskurstheorie des Rechts und des demokratischen Rechtsstaats.* 166–237. Frankfurt am Main: Suhrkamp Verlag.

Habermas, J. 1998d [1986]. 'Recht und Moral (Tanner Lectures 1986)' in *Faktizität und Geltung: Beiträge zur Diskurstheorie des Rechts und des demokratischen Rechtsstaats.* 541–599. Frankfurt am Main: Suhrkamp Verlag.

Habermas, J. 1998e [1990]. 'Staatsbürgerschaft und nationale Identität' in *Faktizität und Geltung: Beiträge zur Diskurstheorie des Rechts und des demokratischen Rechtsstaats.* 632–660. Frankfurt am Main: Suhrkamp Verlag.

Habermas, J. 1999a [1981]. *Theorie des Kommunikativen Handelns: Band I, Handlungsrationalität und gesellschaftliche Rationalisierung.* Frankfurt a.M.: Suhrkamp Verlag.

Habermas, J. 1999b [1981]. *Theorie des kommunikativen Handelns, Band II: Zur Kritik der funktionalistischen Vernunft.* Frankfurt: Suhrkamp.

Habermas, J. 2000 [1999]. 'Bestiality and Humanity: A War on the Border between Law and Morality,' in *Kosovo: Contending Voices on Balkan Interventions.* Translated by John Torpey. Edited by William Joseph Buckley. 306–316. Michigan: Eerdmans Publishing.

Hagen, G. 2005. 'Legitimacy and World Order,' in *Legitimizing the Order: The Ottoman Rhetoric of State Power.* Edited by Hakan T. Karateke and Maurus Reinkowski. 55–83. Leiden and Boston: E.J. Brill.

Hall R.B. and Kratochwil, F.V. 1993. 'Medieval Tales: Neo-realist 'Science' and the Abuse of History,' *International Organization* 47(3): 479–491.

Hall, R.B. 1999. *National Collective Identity: Social Constructs and International System.* New York: Columbia University Press.

Hallaq, W.B. 1997. *A History of Islamic Legal Theories: An Introduction to Sunnī Usūl Al-Fiqh.* Cambridge: Cambridge University Press.

Hallaq, W.B. 1995. 'Was the gate of ijtihad closed?', *Law and Legal Theory in Classical and Medieval Islam*, Brookfield, Vermont, Variorum, Chapter V, 33–34.

Hammer, J. 1977 [1815]. *Des Osmanischen Reichs Staatsverfassung und Staatsverwaltung, vorgestellt aus den Quellen seiner Grundgesetze. Erstel Theil: Die Staatsverfassung.* Hildesheim: Georg Olms Verlagsbuchhandlung.

Hassan, Ü. 2001. *Osmanlı: Örgüt – İnanç – Davranış'tan Hukuk – İdeolojiye.* Second Print. İstanbul: İletişim Yayınları.

Headley, J.M. 1983. *The Emperor and His Chancellor: A Study of the Imperial Chancery under Gattinara.* Cambridge: Cambridge University Press.

Headley, J.M. 1998. 'The Habsburg World Empire and the Revival of Ghibellinism,' in *Theories of Empire, 1450–1800.* Edited by David Armitage. 45–79. Aldershot: Ashgate Variorum.

Hellmuth, E. 1985. *Naturrechtsphilosophie und Bürokratischer Werthorizont: Studien zur preußischen Geistes- und Sozialgeschichte des 18. Jahrhunderts.* Göttingen: Vandenhoeck: Ruprecht.

Hintze, O. 1962a [1902]. 'Staatenbildung und Verfassungsentwicklung: Eine historisch-politische Studie,' in *Staat und Verfassung: Gesammelte Abhandlungen zur Allgemeinen Verfassungsgeschichte.* Edited by G. Oestreich. 34–51. Göttingen: Vandenhoeck & Ruprecht.

Hintze, O. 1962b [1908]. 'Die Entstehung der modernen Staatsministerien: Eine vergleichende Studie,' *Staat und Verfassung: Gesammelte Abhandlungen zur Allgemeinen Verfassungsgeschichte,* edited by Gerhard Oestreich, 275–320. Göttingen: Vandenhoeck & Ruprecht.

Hobden, S. 1999. 'Theorising the international system: perspectives from Historical Sociology,' *Review of International Studies* 25: 257–271.

Hochedlinger, M. 2003. *Austria's Wars of Emergence: War, State and Society in the Habsburg Monarchy 1683–1797.* London: Longman.

Hochstrasser, T.J. 2000. *Natural Law Theories in the Early Enlightenment.* Cambridge: Cambridge University Press.

Hodgson, M.G.S. 1977a. *The Venture of Islam: Conscience and History in a World Civilization II: The Expansion of Islam in the Middle Periods.* Chicago and London: The University of Chicago Press.

Hodgson, M.G.S. 1977b. *The Venture of Islam: Conscience and History in a World Civilization III: The Gunpowder Empires and Modern Times.* Chicago and London: The University of Chicago Press.

Hook, J. 1972. 'Clement VII, the Colonna, and Charles V: A Study of the Political Instability of Italy in the Second and Third Decades of the Sixteenth Century,' *European History Quarterly* 2(4): 281–299.

Humphreys, S. 1985. 'Law as Discourse,' *History and Anthropology* 1: 241–264.

Hurewitz, J.C. 1961. 'Ottoman Diplomacy and the European States System,' *The Middle East Journal* 15(2): 141–152.

Imber, C. 2002. *The Ottoman Empire, 1300–1650: The Structure of Power.* Houndmills and New York: Palgrave Macmillan.

Inayatullah, N. and Blaney, D.L. 1997. 'Knowing Encounters: Beyond Parochialism in International Relations Theory,' in *The Return of Culture and Identity in IR Theory.* Edited by Y. Lapid and F. Kratochwill. 65–84. Boulder: Lynne Rienner Publishers.

İnalcık, H. 1965a. 'Ghulam (The Ottoman Empire),' in *The Encyclopedia of Islam Vol. II.* Edited by B. Lewis, Ch. Pellat and J. Schacht. 1085–1091. Leiden and London: E.J. Brill and Luzac & Co.

İnalcık, H. 1965b. 'Daftardar,' in *The Encyclopedia of Islam Vol. II.* Edited by B. Lewis, Ch. Pellat and J. Schacht. 83. Leiden and London: E.J. Brill and Luzac & Co.

İnalcık, H. 1978a. 'Kanūnname,' in *The Encyclopedia of Islam Vol. IV.* Edited by C.E. Bosworth, E. van Donzel, B. Lewis and Ch. Pellat. 562–566. Leiden: E.J. Brill.

İnalcık, H. 1978b. 'Military and Fiscal Transformation in the Ottoman Empire, 1600–1700,' in *The Ottoman Empire: Conquest, Organization and Economy: Collected Studies.* 283–337. London: Variorum Reprints.

İnalcık, H. 1993a. 'Decision Making in the Ottoman State,' in, *Decision Making and Change in the Ottoman Empire* edited by Caesar E. Farah, 9–18. Kirksville, Missouri: The Thomas Jefferson University Press.

İnalcık, H. 1993b. 'State, Sovereignty and Law during the Reign of Süleymân,' in *Süleymân the Second and His Time.* Edited by Halil İnalcık and Cemal Kafadar. 59–92. İstanbul: Isis Press.

İnalcık, H. 2000a [1950]. 'İslâm Arazi ve Vergi Sisteminin Teşekkülü ve Osmanlı Devrindeki Şekillerle Mukayesesi,' *Osmanlı İmparatorluğu: Toplum ve Ekonomi,* 15–30. İstanbul: Eren Yayıncılık.

İnalcık, H. 2000b [1952]. '1431 Tarihli Timar Defterine Göre Fatih Devirnden Önceki Timar Sistemi,' in *Osmanlı İmparatorluğu: Toplum ve Ekonomi,* 109–114. İstanbul: Eren Yayıncılık.

İnalcık, H. 2000c [1953]. 'Stefan Duşan'dan Osmanlı İmparatorluğuna: XV. Asırda Rumeli'de Hıristiyan Sipahiler ve Menşeleri,' in *Osmanlı İmparatorluğu: Toplum ve Ekonomi.* 67–108. İstanbul: Eren Yayıncılık.

İnalcık, H. 2000d [1958]. 'Osmanlı Hukukuna Giriş; Örfi-Sultanî Hukuk ve Fâtih'in Kanûnları,' in *Osmanlı İmparatorluğu: Toplum ve Ekonomi,* 319–341. İstanbul: Eren Yayıncılık.

İnalcık, H. 2000e [1958]. 'Türk – İslâm Devletlerinde Devlet Kanunu Geleneği', *Osmanlı'da Devlet, Hukuk, Adâlet.* 27–36. İstanbul: Eren Yayıncılık, .

İnalcık, H. 2000f [1959]. Osmanlılar'da Raiyyet Rüsûmu,' in *Osmanlı İmparatorluğu: Toplum ve Ekonomi.* 31–65. İstanbul: Eren Yayıncılık.

İnalcık, H. 2000g [1965]. 'Adâletnâmeler,' in *Osmanlı'da Devlet, Hukuk, Adâlet.* 75–190. İstanbul: Eren Yayıncılık.

İnalcık, H. 2000h [1989]. 'Köy, Köylü ve İmparatorluk,' *Osmanlı İmparatorluğu: Toplum ve Ekonomi,* 1–14. İstanbul: Eren Yayıncılık.

İnalcık, H. 2000i [1998]. Şerî'at ve Kanun, Din ve Devlet', *Osmanlı'da Devlet, Hukuk, Adâlet.* 39–46. İstanbul: Eren Yayıncılık.
İnalcık, H. 2000j. 'Tīmar,' in *The Encyclopedia of Islam Vol. X.* Edited by P.J. Bearman, Th. Bianquis, C.E. Bosworth, E. van Donzel and W.P. Heinrichs. 502–507. Leiden : E.J. Brill.
İnalcık, H. 2002a [1973]. *The Ottoman Empire: The Classsical Age 1300–1600.* Second Impression. London: Phoenix Press.
İnalcık, H. 2002b. 'Wazīr – In the Ottoman Empire,' in *The Encyclopedia of Islam Vol. XI.* Edited by P.J. Bearman, Th. Bianquis, C.E. Bosworth, E. van Donzel and W.P. Heinrichs.194–197. Leiden : E.J. Brill.
İnalcık, H. 2004 [1979]. 'A Case Study in Renaissance Diplomacy: The Agreement between Innocent VIII and Bayezid II on Djem Sultan,' in *Ottoman Diplomacy: Conventional or Unconventional?* Edited by A.N. Yurdusev. 66–88. London: Palgrave Macmillan.
İnalcık, H. 2009. *Devlet-i Aliyye: Osmanlı İmparatorluğu Üzerine Araştırmalar – I.* İstanbul: Türkiye İş Bankası Kültür Yayınları.
Ingrao, C.W. 2000. *The Habsburg Monarchy, 1648–1815.* Cambridge: Cambridge University Press.
Issawi, C. 1993. 'The Ottoman-Habsburg Balance of Forces,' in *Süleymân the Second and His Time.* Edited by Halil İnalcık and Cemal Kafadar. 145–151. İstanbul: Isis Press.
Jackson, R.H. 1993. *Quasi-states: Sovereignty, International Relations and the Third World.* Cambridge: Cambridge University Press.
Johnstone, T.M. 1965. 'Ghazw,' in *The Encyclopedia of Islam Vol. II.* Edited by B. Lewis, Ch. Pellat and J. Schacht.1055–1056. Leiden and London: E.J. Brill and Luzac & Co.
Jonsen A.R. and Toulmin, S. 1989 [1988]. *The Abuse of Casuistry: A History of Moral Reasoning.* Berkeley, Los Angeles and London: University of California Press.
Kafadar, C. 1996. *Between Two Worlds: The Construction of the Ottoman State.* Berkeley, Los Angeles, London: University of California Press.
Karaman, H. 1974. *Mukayeseli İslâm Hukuku,* İstanbul, İrfan Yayınevi.
Karateke, H.T. 2005a. 'Legitimizing the Ottoman Sultanate: A Framework for Historical Analysis,' in *Legitimizing the Order: The Ottoman Rhetoric of State Power.* Edited by Hakan T. Karateke and Maurus Reinkowski. 13–52. Leiden and Boston: E.J. Brill.
Karateke, H.T. 2005b. 'Opium for the Subjects? Religiosity as a Legitimizing Factor for the Ottoman Sultan,' in *Legitimizing the Order: The Ottoman Rhetoric of State Power.* Edited by Hakan T. Karateke and Maurus Reinkowski. 13–52. Leiden and Boston: E.J. Brill.

Katib Chelebi 1957 [1656]. *The Balance of Truth*. Translated by G.L. Lewis. London: George Allen and Unwin Ltd.
Kautsky, J.H. 1997 [1982]. *The Politics of Aristocratic Empires*. New Brunswick and London: Transaction Publishers.
Khadduri, M. 1955. *War and Peace in the Law of Islam*. Baltimore: Johns Hopkins Press.
Kennedy, P. 1989. *The Rise and Fall of Great Powers: Economic Change and Military Conflict from 1500 to 2000*. New York: Vintage Books.
Keohane, R. 1984. *After Hegemony: Cooperation and Discord in the World Political Economy*. Princeton, NJ: Princeton University Press.
Keohane, R. 2000. 'Ideas part-way down,' *Review of International Studies* 26: 125–130.
Köhbach, M. 1992. '*Çasar* oder *imperator*? – Zur Titulatur der römischen Kaiser durch die Osmanen nach dem Vertrag von Zsitvatorok (1606),' *Wiener Zeitschrift für die Kunde des Morgenlandes* 82: 223–234.
Kohler, A. 1990. *Das Reich im Kampf um die Hegemonie in Europa 1521–1648*. München: R. Oldenburg Verlag.
Kohler, A. 2001 [1999]. *Karl V. 1500–1558: Eine Biographie*. Third Edition. München: Verlag C.H. Beck.
Kohler, A. 2003. *Ferdinand I. 1503–1564: Fürst, König, Kaiser*. München: Verlag C.H. Beck.
Kołodziejczyk, D. 2000. *Ottoman-Polish Diplomatic Relations (15th-18th Century)*. Leiden, Boston, Köln: Brill.
Köprülü, F. 2002 [1931]. *Bizans Müesseselerinin Osmanlı Müesseselerine Tesiri*. Third Print. İstanbul: Kaynak Yayınları.
Kortepeter, M.C. 1985. 'Habsburg and Ottoman in Hungary in the 16th and 17th Centuries,' *Beihefte zur Wiener Zeitschrift für die Kunde des Morgenlandes* 13: 55–66.
Kratochwil, F. 1986. 'Of Systems, Boundaries and Territoriality: An Inquiry Into the Formation of the States System,' *World Politics* 39(1): 27–52.
Kratochwil, F. 2000. 'Constructing a New Orthodoxy? Wendt's 'Social Theory of International Politics' and the Constructivist Challenge,' *Millennium* 29(1): 73–101.
Krieger, L. 1960. 'History and Law in the Seventeenth Century: Pufendorf,' *Journal of the History of Ideas* 21(2): 198–210.
Kunt, M.I. 1983. *The Sultan's Servants: The Transformation of Ottoman Provincial Government 1550–1650*. New York: Cambridge University Press.
Kunt, M.I. 1995. 'Sadr-ı A'zam,' in *The Encyclopedia of Islam Vol. VIII*. Edited by E. Bosworth, E. van Donzel, W.P. Heinrichs and G. Lecomte. 62. Leiden: E.J. Brill.

Kuran, T. 1997a [1995]. *Private Truths, Public Lies: The Social Consequences of Preference Falsification*. Cambridge, MA and London, England: Harvard University Press.

Kuran, T. 1997b. 'Islam and Underdevelopment: An Old Puzzle Revisited,' *Journal of Institutional and Theoretical Economics* 153(1): 41–71.

Kuran, T. 2004a. 'Islamic statecraft and the Middle East's delayed modernization,' in *Political Competition, Innovation and Growth in the History of Asian Civilizations*, edited by P. Bernholz and R. Vaubel, 150–183. Cheltenham and Northampton: Edward Elgar.

Kuran, T. 2004b. 'The Economic Ascent of the Middle East's Religious Minorities: the Role of Islamic Legal Pluralism.' *The Journal of Legal Studies* 33(2): 475–515.

Kuran, T. 2005. 'The Absence of the Corporation in Islamic Law: Origins and Persistence.' *The American Journal of Comparative Law* 53(4): 785–834.

Kuran, T. 2008. Islam and Economic Underdevelopment: Legal Roots of Organizational Stagnation in the Middle East. Unpublished Manuscript.

Kütükoğlu, M. 1998. *Osmanlı Belgelerinin Dili*. İstanbul: Kubbealtı Akademisi Kültür ve Sanat Vakfı.

Lambton, A.K.S. 1975. 'Khalīfa,' in *The Encyclopedia of Islam Vol. IV*. Edited by C.E. Bosworth, E. van Donzel, B. Lewis and Ch. Pellat. 947–950. Leiden: E.J. Brill.

Legro, J.W. 2005. *Rethinking the World: Great Power Strategies and International Order*. Ithaca and London: Cornell University Press.

Lemke, D. 2002. *Regions of War and Peace*. Cambridge: Cambridge University Press.

Lenski, G.E. 1984 [1966]. *Power and Privilege: A Theory of Social Stratification*. Chapel Hill and London: The University of North Carolina Press.

Lewis, B. 1960. 'Baha'ī Mehmed Efendi,' in *The Encyclopedia of Islam Vol. I*. Edited by H.A.R. Gibb, J.H. Kramers, E. Lévi-Provençal, J. Schacht. 915. Leiden and London: E.J. Brill and Luzac & Co.

Lewis, B. 1965a. 'Daftar,' in *The Encyclopedia of Islam Vol. II*. Edited by B. Lewis, Ch. Pellat and J. Schacht. 77–81. Leiden and London: E.J. Brill and Luzac & Co.

Lewis, B. 1965b. 'Daftardar,' in *The Encyclopedia of Islam Vol. II*. Edited by B. Lewis, Ch. Pellat and J. Schacht. 83. Leiden and London: E.J. Brill and Luzac & Co.

Lewis, B. 1994. *Islam and the West*. New Oxford and New York: Oxford University Press.

Lindner, R. 1983. *Nomads and Ottomans in Medieval Anatolia*. Bloomington, Indiana: Research Institute for Inner Asian Studies, Indiana University.

Luhmann, N. 1983. *Legitimation Durch Verfahren*. Frankfurt: Suhrkamp Verlag.

Lybyer, A.H. 1978 [1913]. *The Government of the Ottoman Empire in the Time of Suleiman the Magnificent*. New York: AMS Press.

Maas, M. 1992. *John Lydus and the Roman Past: Antiquarianism and Politics in the Age of Justinian*. London and New York: Routledge.

Machiavelli, N. 1981 [1513]. *The Prince*. Translated and edited by Daniel Donno. New York: Bantam Books.

Maitland, F.W. 2003. *State, Trust and Corporation*. Edited by D. Runciman and M. Ryan, Cambridge: Cambridge University Press.

Mann, M. 1997 [1986]. *The Sources of Social Power Volume I: A History of Power from the Beginning to A.D. 1760*. Cambridge: Cambridge University Press.

Mardin, S. 1969. 'The Mind of the Turkish Reformer 1700–1900,' in *Arab Socialism: A Documentary Survey*. Edited by Sami A. Hanna and George H. Gardner. Leiden: E.J. Brill.

Marx, K. 1965 [1852]. *Der 18. Brumaire des Louis Bonaparte*. Allgäu: Insel Verlag.

Matuz, J. 1974. *Das Kanzleiwesen Sultan Süleymans des Prächtigen*. Wiesbaden: Franz Steiner Verlag.

McGill, W.J. 1971. 'The Roots of Policy: Kaunitz in Vienna and Versailles, 1749–1753,' *Journal of Modern History* 43(2): 228–244.

McNeill, W.H. 1982. *The Pursuit of Power: Technology, Armed Force, and Society since A.D. 1000*. Chicago: The University of Chicago Press.

Mead, G.H. 1915. 'The Psychological Basis for Internationalism,' *Survey* 33: 604–607.

Mead, G.H. 1917. 'America's Ideals and the War,' *Chicago Herald* August 2, 1917.

Mélikoff, I. 1965. 'Ghazī,' in *The Encyclopedia of Islam Vol. II*. Edited by B. Lewis, Ch. Pellat and J. Schacht.1043–1045. Leiden and London: E.J. Brill and Luzac & Co.

Ménage, V.L. 1965. 'Devshirme,' in *The Encyclopedia of Islam Vol. II*. Edited by B. Lewis, Ch. Pellat and J. Schacht. 210–213. Leiden and London: E.J. Brill and Luzac & Co.

Mokyr, J. 2006. 'Tolerance and Mobility: Origins of the European Economic Enlightenment, 1450–1750,' *Paper Presented at the Institute for Economic Research on Civilizations (IERC) at the University of Southern California* on 03-08–2006.

Moraw, P. 1989. 'Cities and Citizenry as Factors of State Formation in the Roman-German Empire of the Late Middle Ages,' *Theory and Society* 18(5): 631–662.

Morgenthau, H.J. 1962. *Politics Among Nations: The Struggle for Power and Peace.* New York: Alfred A. Knopf.
Moss, A. 1998. 'The Politica if Justus Lipsius and the Commonplace-Book,' *Journal of the History of Ideas* 59(3): 421–436.
Mumcu, A.1976. *Hukuksal ve Siyasal Karar Organı Olarak Divân-ı Hümayun.* Ankara: Ankara Üniversitesi Hukuk Fakültesi Yayınları.
Müller, K. 1976. *Das Kaiserliche Gesandtschaftswesen im Jahrhundert nach dem Westfälischen Frieden (1648–1740).* Bonn: Ludwig Röhrscheid Verlag.
Murphey, R. 1993. 'Continuity and Discontinuity in Ottoman Administrative Theory and Practice during the Late Seventeenth Century,' *Poetics Today* 14(2): 419–443.
Naff, T. 1984. 'The Ottoman Empire', in *The Expansion of International Society.* Edited by Hedley Bull and Adam Watson 143–170. Oxford: Clarendon Press.
Naîmâ Mustafa Efendi 1967. *Naîmâ Tarihi, I.* Translated by Zuhurî Danışman. İstanbul: Zuhurî Danışman Yayınevi.
Necipoğlu, G. 1991. *Architechture, Ceremonial, and Power: The Topkapı Palace in the Fifteenth and Sixteenth Centuries.* Cambridge: The MIT Press.
Necipoğlu, G. 1993. 'Süleymân the Magnificent and the Representation of Power in the Context of Ottoman-Hapsburg-Papal Rivalry,' in *Süleymân the Second and His Time.* Edited by Halil İnalcık and Cemal Kafadar. 163–194. İstanbul: Isis Press.
Necipoğlu, G. 2000. 'Osmanlı Sultanlarının Portre Dizilerine Karşılaştırmalı Bir Bakış,' in *Padişahın Portresi: Tesavir-i Âl-i Osman.* 22–61. İstanbul: Türkiye İş Bankası Kültür Yayınları.
Neumann, C. 1993 'Decision Making without Decision Makers: Ottoman Foreign Policy circa 1780,' in, *Decision Making and Change in the Ottoman Empire* edited by Caesar E. Farah, 9–18. Kirksville, Missouri: The Thomas Jefferson University Press.
Nexon, D.H. 2009. *The Struggle for Power in Early Modern Europe: Religious Conflict, Dynastic Empires and International Change.* Princeton: Princeton University Press.
O'Gorman, J.F. 1965. 'An Interpretation of Andrea del Sarto's Bogherini Holy Family,' *The Art Bulletin* 47(4): 502–504.
Özdemir, H. 2001. *Osmanlı Devletinde Bürokrasi.* İstanbul: Okumuş Adam Yayıncılık.
Pakaluk, M. 2002. 'Natural Law and Civil Society,' in *Alternative Conceptions of Civil Society.* Edited by Simone Chambers and Will Kymlicka. 131–148. Princeton and Oxford: Princeton University Press.

Papadakis, A. and Kazhdan, A. 1991. 'Caesaropapism,' in *The Oxford Dictionary of Byzantium V.1*. Edited by A.P. Kazhdan, A.M. Talbot, A. Cutler, T.E. Gregory, N.P. Ševčenko. 364–365. New York and Oxford: Oxford University Press.

Parker, G. 1996. *The Military Revolution: Military Innovation and the Rise of the West, 1500–1800*. Cambridge: Cambridge University Press.

Pasic, S.C. 1997. 'Culturing International Relations Theory: A Call for Extension,' in *The Return of Culture and Identity in IR Theory*. Edited by Y. Lapid and F. Kratochwill. 85–104. Boulder: Lynne Rienner Publishers.

Philpott, D. 1999. 'Westphalia, Authority, and International Society,' *Political Studies* 47: 566–589.

Poggi, G. 1978. *The Development of the Modern State: A Sociological Introduction*. Stanford: Stanford University Press.

Pufendorf, S. 2007 [1696]. *The Present State of Germany*. Translated by Edmund Bohun, Edited and with an Introduction by Michael Seidler. Indianapolis: Liberty Fund.

Quataert, D. 2005. *The Ottoman Empire*. Second Edition. Cambridge: Cambridge University Press.

Raby, J. 2000. 'Oyun Başlıyor,' in *Padişahın Portresi: Tesavir-i Âl-i Osman*. 64–95. İstanbul: Türkiye İş Bankası Kültür Yayınları.

Radding, C.M. and A. Ciaralli. 2007. *The Corpus Iuris Civilis in the Middle Ages: Manuscripts and Transmissions from the Sixth Century to the Juristic Revival*. Leiden and Boston: Brill.

Raeff, M. 1983. *The Well-Ordered Police State: Social and Institutional Change through Law in the Germanies and Russia, 1600–1800*. New Haven and London: Yale University Press.

Repp, R. 1988. 'Qanūn and Sharī'a in the Ottoman Context', *Islamic Law: Social and Historical Contexts*. Edited by Aziz Al-Azmeh. 124–145. London and New York: Routledge.

Repp, R. 1986. *The Müfti of Istanbul: A Study in the Development of the Ottoman Learned Hierarchy*. London: Ithaca Press.

Reston, J. Jr. 2009. *Defenders of the Faith: Charles V, Suleyman the Magnificient, and the Battle for Europe, 1520–1536*. New York: The Penguin Press.

Reus-Smit, C. 1997. 'The Constitutional Structure of International Society and the Nature of Fundamental Institutions,' *International Organization* 51(4): 555–589.

Reynolds, S. 1997 [1984]. *Kingdoms and Communities in Western Europe, 900–1300*. Second Edition. Oxford: Clarendon Press.

Robertson, J. 1998. 'Empire and Union: Two Concepts of the Early Modern European Political Order,' in *Theories of Empire, 1450–1800*. Edited by David Armitage. 11–44. Aldershot: Ashgate Variorum.

Rosenberg, J. 1994. *The Empire of Civil Society: A Critique of Realist Theory of International Relations*. London: Verso.

Rosenthal, E.E. 1973. 'The Invention of the Columnar Device of Emperor Charles V at the Court of Burgundy in Flanders in 1516,' *Journal of the Warburg and Courtauld Institutes* 36: 198–230.

Rosenthal, J.L. 1998. 'The Political Economy of Absolutism Reconsidered,' in *Analytical Narratives*. Edited by Robert Bates, Avner Greif, Margaret Levi, Jean-Laurent Rosenthal and Barry R. Weingast. 64–108. Princeton, NJ: Princeton University Press.

Röhrborn, K. 1973. *Untersuchungen zur Osmanischen Verwaltungsgeschichte*. Berlin and New York: Walter de Gruyter.

Ruggie, J.G. 1986. 'Continuity and Transformation in the World Polity: Toward a Neo-realist Synthesis' in *Neorealism and Its Critics*. Edited by Robert Keohane. 131–157. New York: Columbia University Press.

Runciman, D. 2003. 'The concept of the state: the sovereignty of a fiction,' in *States and Citizens: History, Theory and Prospects*. Edited by Quentin Skinner and Bo Stråth. 28–38. Cambridge: Cambridge University Press.

Schmidt, G. 1999. *Geschichte des Alten Reiches: Staat und Nation in der Frühen Neuzeit 1495–1806*. München: Verlag C.H. Beck.

Schmitt, C. 1998 [1932]. *Legalität und Legitimität*. Berlin: Duncker & Humblot.

Schröder, P. 1999. 'The Constitution of the Holy Roman Empire After 1648: Samuel Pufendorf's Assessment in his *Monzambano*,' *The Historical Journal* 42(4): 961–983.

Schroeder, P. 1994. 'Historical Reality vs. Neo-Realist Theory,' *International Security* 19(1): 108–148.

Schweller, R.L. 2006. *Unanswered Threats: Political Constraints on the Balance of Power*. Princeton: Princeton University Press.

Sebastian, P. 1994. 'Ottoman Government Officials and their Relations with the Republic of Venice in the Early Sixteenth Century,' in *Studies in Ottoman History in Honour of Professor V.L. Ménage*. Edited by Colin Heywood and Colin Imber. 319- 337. İstanbul: The Isis Press.

Şen, A. 1995. *İbrahim Müteferrika ve Usûlü'l-Hikem fî Nizâmi'l-Ümem*. Ankara: Türkiye Diyanet Vakfı Yayınları.

Şentop, M. 2005. *Osmanlı Yargı Sistemi ve Kazaskerlik*. İstanbul: Klasik Yayınları.

Skocpol, T. 1977. 'Wallerstein's World Capitalist System: A Theoretical and Historical Critique,' *American Journal of Sociology* 82(5): 1075–1090.

Skocpol, T. 1984. 'Emerging Agendas and Recurrent Strategies in Historical Sociology,' in *Vision and Method in Historical Sociology*. Edited by Theda Skocpol. 356–391. Cambridge: Cambridge University Press.

Sloane, T.O. 1991. 'Schoolbooks and Rhetoric: Erasmus's Copia,' *Rhetorica* 9(2): 113–129.
Sourdel, D. 1978. 'Khalīfa,' in *The Encyclopedia of Islam Vol. IV*. Edited by C.E. Bosworth, E. van Donzel, B. Lewis and Ch. Pellat. 937–947. Leiden: E.J. Brill.
Spangenberg, H. 1964 [1912]. *Vom Lehnstaat zum Ständestaat: Ein Beitrag zur Entstehung der landständischen Verfassung*. Aalen: Scientia Verlag.
Spruyt, H. 1994a. *The Sovereign State and Its Competitors: An Analysis of Systems Change*. Princeton: Princeton University Press.
Spruyt, H. 1994b. 'Institutional Selection in International Relations: State Anarchy as Order,' *International Organization* 48(4): 527–557.
Spruyt, H. 1998. 'Historical Sociology and Systems Theory in International Relations,' *Review of International Studies* 5(2): 340–353.
Stein, J.M. 1985. 'Habsburg Financial Institutions Presented as a Model for the Ottoman Empire in the Sefaretname of Ebu Bekir Ratib Efendi,' *Beihefte zur Wiener Zeitschrift für die Kunde des Morgenlandes* 13: 233–241.
Stengel, E.E. 1939. 'Kaisertitel und Suveränitätsidee: Studien zur Vorgeschichte des modernen Staatsbegriffs,' *Deutsches Archiv für Erforschung des Mittelalters* 3: 1–49.
Strakosch, H.E. 1967. *State Absolutism and the Rule of Law: The Struggle for the Codification of Civil Law in Austria 1753–1811*. Sydney: Sydney University Press.
Strauss, G. 1986. *Law, Resistance, and the State: The Opposition to Roman Law in Reformation Germany*. Princeton: Princeton University Press.
Szabo, F.A.J.1994. *Kaunitz and Enlightened Absolutism 1753–1780*. Cambridge: Cambridge University Press.
Taiwo, O. 1996. *Legal Naturalism: A Marxist Theory of Law*, Ithaca and London, Cornell University Press.
Tammen, R.L., Kugler, J., Lemke, D, Alsharabati, C., Efird, B. and Organski, A.F.K., 2000. *Power Transitions: Strategies for the 21st Century*. New York: Chatham House Publishers.
Tarver, H.M. and Frederick, J. 2006. *The History of Venezuela*. New York: Palgrave Macmillan.
Teschke, B. 2003. *The Myth of 1648: Class, Geopolitics, and the Making of Modern International Relations*. London: Verso.
Thelen, K. 2003. 'How Institutions Evolve: Insights from Comparative Historical Analysis,' in *Comparative Historical Analysis in the Social Sciences*. Edited by James Mahoney and Dietrich Rueschemeyer. 208–240. Cambridge: Cambridge University Press.
Tierney, B. 1982. *Religion, Law and the Growth of Constitutional Thought, 1150– 1650*. Cambridge: Cambridge University Press.

Tilly, C. 1998. *Coercion, Capital, and European States, AD 990–1992*. Cambridge, MA and Oxford, UK: Blackwell.
Timur, T. 2000. *Osmanlı Kimliği*. Fourth Print. Ankara: İmge Kitabevi.
Toulmin, S. 1971. 'The Concept of 'Stages' in Psychological Development,' in *Cognitive Development and Epistemology*. Edited by Theodore Mischel. 25–60. New York and London: Academic Press.
Toulmin, S.E. 1992 [1990]. *Cosmopolis: The Hidden Agenda of Modernity*. Chicago: The University of Chicago Press.
Tracy, J. 1978. *The Politics of Erasmus: A Pacifist Intellectual and His Political Milieu*. Toronto, Buffalo and London: University of Toronto Press.
Tracy, J. 2002. *Emperor Charles V, Impresario of War: Campaign Strategy, International Finance, and Domestic Politics*. Cambridge: Cambridge University Press.
Truschek, C. 1986. *Die Türkenpolitik Ferdinands I. von 1529 bis 1532*. Vienna: Verlag Notring.
Tuck, R. 1993. *Philosophy and Government 1572–1651*. Cambridge: Cambridge University Press.
Turner, B.S. 1974. 'Islam, capitalism and the Weber theses,' *The British Journal of Sociology* 25(2): 230–243.
Ullmann, W. 1949. 'The Development of the Medieval Idea of Sovereignty,' *The English Historical Review* 64 (250): 1–33.
Ullmann, W. 1966. *The Individual and Society in the Middle Ages*. Baltimore, Maryland: The Johns Hopkins Press.
Ullmann, W. 1975. *Law and Politics in the Middle Ages: An Introduction to the Sources of Medieval Political Ideas*. Ithaca: Cornell University Press.
Unat, F.R. 1992. *Osmanlı Sefirleri ve Sefaretnameleri*. Edited by Bekir Sıtkı Baykal. 3rd Edition. Ankara: Türk Tarih Kurumu Basımevi.
Unger, R.M. 1976. *Law in Modern Society: Toward a Criticism of Social Theory*. New York: The Free Press.
Uzunçarşılı, İ.H. 1974. *Çandarlı Vezir Ailesi*. Ankara: Türk Tarih Kurumu.
Uzunçarşılı, İ.H. 1988 [1945]. *Osmanlı Devleti'nin Saray Teşkilâtı*. Third Print. Ankara: Türk Tarih Kurumu.
Valensi, L. 1994 [1987]. *Venedik ve Bâb-ı Âli: Despotun Doğuşu*. Translated by A.Turgut Arnas. İstanbul: Bağlam Yayınları.
Veldet, Hıfzı 1999. 'Kanunlaştırma Hareketleri ve Tanzimat,' in *Tanzimat I*, 139–209. İstanbul: Milli Eğitim Bakanlığı.
Vryonis, S. 1956. 'Isidore Glabas and the Turkish *Devshirme*,' *Speculum* 31(3): 433–443.
Wallerstein, I. 1974. *The Modern World-System I: Capitalist Agriculture and the Origins of the European World-Economy in the Sixteenth Century*. San Diego: Academic Press.

Walter, F. 1958. *Die Theresianische Staatsreform von 1749*. Vienna: Verlag für Geschichte und Politik.

Waltz, K.N. 1986. 'Reductionist and Systemic Theories,' in *Neorealism and Its Critics*. Edited by Robert Keohane. 47–69. New York: Columbia University Press.

Waltz, K.N. 2002. 'Structural Realism After the Cold War,' in *America Unrivaled: The Future of the Balance of Power*. Edited by G. John Ikenberry. 29–67. Ithaca and London: Cornell University Press.

Weber, C. 1998. 'Reading Martin Wight's 'Why Is There No International Theory?' as History,' *Alternatives* 23(4): 451–469.

Weber, M. 1958a. 'Science as a Vocation,' in *From Max Weber: Essays in Sociology*. Translated and edited by H.H. Gerth and C. Wright Mills. 129–156. New York: Oxford University Press.

Weber, M. 1958b. 'Bureaucracy,' in *From Max Weber: Essays in Sociology*. Translated and edited by H.H. Gerth and C. Wright Mills. 196–244. New York: Oxford University Press.

Weber, M. 1978a [1921] *Economy and Society: An Outline of Interpretive Sociology: Volume I*. Edited by Guenther Roth and Claus Wittich. Berkeley: University of California Press.

Weber, M. 1978b [1921] *Economy and Society: An Outline of Interpretive Sociology: Volume II*. Edited by Guenther Roth and Claus Wittich. Berkeley: University of California Press.

Weber, M. 2002 [1921] *Wirtschaft und Gesellschaft: Grundriss der Verstehenden Soziologie*. 5th Edition. Mohr Siebeck.

Weiss, B.G. 2006. *The Spirit of Islamic Law*. Athens, Georgia: The University of Georgia Press.

Wendt, A. 1997. 'Identity and Structural Change in International Politics,' in *The Return of Culture and Identity in IR Theory*. Edited by Y. Lapid and F. Kratochwill. 47–64. Boulder: Lynne Rienner Publishers.

Wendt, A. 2000. *Social Theory of International Politics*. Cambridge: Cambridge University Press.

Wight, M. 1995. 'Why is There No International Theory?,' in *International Theory: Critical Investigations*. Edited by James Der Derian. 15–35. New York: New York University Press.

Wilson, P.H. 1999. *The Holy Roman Empire 1495–1806*. New York: MacMillan Press.

Wilson, P.H. 2000. *Absolutism in Central Europe*. London and New York: Routledge.

Wittek, P. 1955. 'Devshirme and Shari'a,' *Bulletin of the School of Oriental and African Studies, University of London* 17(2): 271–278.

Yates, F.A. 1975. *Astraea: The Imperial Theme in the Sixteenth Century*. London: Routledge and Kegan Paul.

Yurdusev, A.N. 2004. 'The Ottoman Attitude Toward Diplomacy,' in *Ottoman Diplomacy: Conventional or Unconventional?* Edited by A.N. Yurdusev. 5–35. London: Palgrave Macmillan.

Zaman, M.Q. 2002. 'Wazīr,' in *The Encyclopedia of Islam Vol. XI*. Edited by P.J. Bearman, Th. Bianquis, C.E. Bosworth, E. van Donzel and W.P. Heinrichs.185–188. Leiden : E.J. Brill.

Ziegler, K-H. 2004. 'The Peace Treaties of the Ottoman Empire with European Christian Powers,' in *Peace Treaties and International Law in European History: From the Late Middle Ages to World War One*. Edited by Randall Lesaffer. 338–364. Cambridge: Cambridge University Press.

INDEX

Abbasids 67, 69, 167
absolutism 5, 6, 7, 9, 10, 14, 15, 17, 20, 23-44, 48, 50, 51, 57, 63, 74, 81, 86, 90-93, 97-101, 107, 108, 113, 115, 117, 122, 129, 146, 149, 150, 154, 159, 160, 161, 182
Abu Hanifa 76
Ahmed III 137
Aksan, Virginia 144, 180, 185, 186
A Lapide, Hippolithus 111
al-Mansur 67, 77
al-Shafi'i 76
Althusius, Johannes 111
Anderson, Perry 31, 32, 41, 159, 160, 162, 180, 181, 182
Augsburg 21
Austria 1, 3, 87, 91, 92, 96, 98, 105, 106, 107, 108, 109, 113, 115, 173, 182

Baghdad 4, 67, 140
Barkey, Karen 27, 28, 156, 159, 160, 165, 178, 180
Battle of Mühlberg 90
Battle of Pavia 101, 166
Belgrade 4, 102, 144
Benhabib, Seyla 56, 163

Berman, Harold 63, 82, 164, 165, 167, 169, 172, 176
Blanning, Tim 40, 42, 162
Bloom, William 12, 158
Bodin, Jean 63, 107, 110, 111, 175
Bohemia 92, 97, 98, 105, 171, 173
Braudel, Fernand 6, 157
Brewer, John 41, 162
Burgundy 2, 109, 171

Celali Rebellions 124
Charlemagne 6, 65, 108, 111
Charles IV 88
Charles V 1, 2, 3, 6, 16, 34, 40, 89, 90, 91, 94, 95, 96, 97, 100, 101, 102, 103, 106, 109, 110, 112, 114, 115, 149, 154, 171-182
Charles VI 105
Chemnitz, Bogislaw Philipp 111
Clement V 108, 176
Clement VII 1
Collins, James 40, 160, 162
Conring, Hermann 112
Constantine 62
Constantinople 3, 65, 73, 118, 120
constructivism 7, 10, 11, 12, 15, 18, 30, 59, 86, 115, 147, 148, 152, 153

corporation 61, 62, 63, 64, 67, 75, 164
Corpus Iuris Civilis 62, 63, 72, 73, 78, 108, 109
Counter-Reformation 6, 91, 93, 173
Crone, Patricia 66, 165

Dante 2, 176
Devvanî 141
Doyle, Michael 24, 159, 160

Ebu Bekir Ratib Efendi 137
Eder, Klaus 54, 162, 163, 168, 169
Eisenstadt, Shmuel 25, 26, 159, 160
Elias, Norbert 35, 157, 161, 179
England 6, 19, 30, 31, 37, 41, 42, 86, 87, 88, 91, 98, 106, 107, 133, 135, 169, 178
Erasmus, Desiderius 2, 109, 110, 113, 176, 177
Ergene, Boğaç 141, 185, 186
Ferdinand I 92, 96, 98, 104
Ferdinand II 91
fief 31, 84, 87, 122, 123, 124, 126, 128, 129, 144, 147, 179, 180
Florence 1, 101
Foucault, Michel 66
France 1, 4, 6, 19, 28, 31, 37, 40, 63, 73, 86, 87, 88, 91, 98, 101, 106, 107, 133, 135, 161, 169, 173, 182

Gattinara, Mercurino de 90, 110, 114, 176, 181
Giddens, Anthony 32, 158, 160, 161
Gilligan, Carol 56,
Goffman, Daniel 134, 183

Gorski, Philip 36, 161
Great Flight 124
Greif, Avner 7, 16, 21, 43, 44, 45, 46, 47, 48, 49, 52, 152, 159, 162
Grotius, Hugo 112

Habermas, Jürgen 7, 9, 15, 16, 20, 21, 43, 44, 49, 50, 52, 53, 54, 56, 57, 58, 70, 71, 80, 87, 115, 139, 140, 147, 148, 153, 154, 157, 158, 159, 162, 163, 166, 167, 168, 169
Habsburgs 2, 5, 6, 7, 9, 17, 20, 21, 23, 48, 83, 87, 88, 91, 92, 93, 95, 96, 97, 100, 101, 102, 103, 104, 105, 106, 107, 109, 111, 112, 115, 117, 118, 119, 126, 127, 128, 132, 133, 135, 136, 137, 151, 153, 154, 161, 171, 174, 175, 181, 183
Hallaq, Wael 76, 77, 167, 168
Haugwitz, Friedrich Wilhelm von 99
Hintze, Otto 33, 42, 62, 63, 161, 164, 165, 178
historical sociology 8, 15, 16, 17, 20, 22, 33, 38, 50, 86, 107, 117, 147
Hobbes, Thomas 113
Hobden, Stephen 16, 159
Hodgson, Marshall 67, 68, 69, 165
Holy Roman Empire 1, 7, 19, 21, 26, 28, 48, 62, 63, 73, 74, 80, 81, 83, 86, 87, 90, 91, 92, 94, 100, 101, 106, 107, 108, 112, 114, 115, 117, 119, 120, 125, 126, 139, 149, 150, 157, 172, 176

Hungary 92, 97, 102, 105, 173, 181, 182, 183
Hussite Wars 94

Ibn al-Muqaffa' 67, 77
Ibn Anas 76
Ibn Khaldun 67, 144, 178
Ibn Sina 141, 185
İbrahim Müteferrika 140, 144, 145, 148
Imperial Estates 74, 80, 81, 88, 89, 90, 90, 90, 91, 93, 94, 97, 100, 101, 102, 103, 105, 107, 111, 112, 113, 114, 115, 150, 173, 175
institutionalism 13, 16, 17, 20, 148, 159
Iran 77, 185
Islamic law 21, 59, 61, 63, 67, 70, 71, 72, 75, 76, 77, 78, 124, 134, 140, 146, 151, 167, 170
Istanbul 1, 3, 6, 117, 131, 132, 135, 136, 142, 182, 183

Justinian 62, 63, 64, 72, 73, 166

Kaunitz-Rietberg, Anton von 92, 93, 99, 100, 106, 146, 150, 174
Kautsky, John 25, 26, 159, 160, 178
Katib Çelebi 143
Kınalızade 141
Koçi Bey 144, 180
Kohlberg, Lawrence 54, 56
Kuran, Timur 11, 48, 61, 162, 164, 183

Legro, Jeffrey 13, 14, 158
Lewis, Bernard 66, 182, 183

life-world 20, 52, 53, 54, 55, 58
Limnaeus, Johannes 111
Luther, Martin 81, 169

Mann, Michael 16, 34, 35, 161
Maria Theresa 90, 99
Mead, George Herbert 11, 12, 158
Mehmed II 3, 120, 121, 122, 170, 185
Melanchton, Philip 81, 169
Milan 1, 101
Mohács 102
Mokyr, Joel 139, 170, 185
Moser, Johann Jacob 103
Murad I 119, 122, 178
Mustafa II 136
Mustafa Ali 144, 186
Mustafa Naîmâ 144, 186

Naples 1, 95, 101, 108, 114
natural law 9, 21, 38, 40, 55, 57, 58, 59, 60, 62, 63, 64, 75, 77, 78, 79, 80, 81, 82, 83, 84, 85, 92, 108, 112, 113, 114, 115, 139, 140, 145, 150, 151, 153, 162, 166, 169
neo-realism 7, 8, 9, 10, 86, 114, 147, 152 153
Netherlands 1, 90, 94, 96, 102, 109, 114, 135, 172, 173, 174
Nexon, Daniel 17, 18, 19, 20, 27, 28, 36, 37, 157, 159, 160, 161

Orhan 118, 120, 178
Osman 120

path dependence 7, 21, 30, 48, 117, 148
Peace of Cambrai 101
Peace of Nijmegen 104

Peace of Westphalia 17, 21, 83, 86, 91, 97, 103, 111, 112, 115, 150, 161, 175
Piaget, Jean 52, 56, 57
Pufendorf, Samuel 112, 113, 114, 177

Rami Mehmed Efendi 130, 184
realism 3, 7, 8, 9, 10, 15, 17, 18, 19, 36, 86, 114, 147, 152, 153, 157
Reformation 6, 19, 81, 82, 85, 90, 91, 93, 108, 139, 150, 164, 173
Reinking, Dietrich 111
Renaissance 1, 2, 3
Reynolds, Susan 55, 163, 164, 165
Roberts, Michael 33
Rosenberg, Justin 17, 159
Rosenthal, Jean-Laurent 35, 156, 161, 174

Saint Augustine 65
Savafids 6
Schroeder, Paul 8, 157
Seckendorff, Leit Ludwig von 111
Seljukids 3, 178, 179
sovereignty 3, 10, 11, 19, 22, 23, 25, 31, 32, 34, 38, 41, 50, 51, 58, 63, 63, 64, 66, 74, 81, 103, 107, 108, 109, 110, 111, 112, 113, 115, 127, 131, 132, 135, 159, 173, 175
Spain 2, 3, 4, 28, 31, 90, 91, 95, 95, 95, 109, 114, 175, 182
Spruyt, Hendrik 17, 157, 159, 164
state formation 5, 6, 7, 9, 14, 17, 20, 21, 22, 23, 28, 33, 34, 36, 39, 40, 41, 44, 48, 50, 57, 58, 59, 69, 81, 88, 90, 91, 101, 105, 107, 114, 115, 117, 119, 141, 147, 150, 152, 153, 169, 174

state system 5, 8, 9, 10, 11, 12, 14, 15, 16, 17, 19, 22, 23, 24, 26, 30, 31, 32, 33, 34, 35, 36, 37, 39, 44, 49, 50, 51, 58, 60, 62, 63, 85, 86, 88, 91, 93, 100, 103, 107, 109, 114, 117, 118, 126, 131, 134, 135, 137, 138, 139, 142, 147, 149, 151, 152, 153, 154, 161
Süleyman I 3, 4, 6, 132, 132, 135, 139, 145, 146, 149, 154
suzerainty 3, 5, 14, 22, 23, 25, 26, 30, 38, 39, 40, 41, 50, 51, 83, 108, 109, 110, 132, 140, 150, 161
Sweden 91, 106, 112, 173

Territorial Estates 81, 90, 92, 93, 94, 95, 97, 98, 99, 100, 101, 107, 115, 120, 174
Teschke, Benno 17, 157, 159
Thirty Years War 6, 91, 98, 112, 117, 139
Tilly, Charles 16, 34, 161
Toulmin, Stephen 56, 57, 71, 163, 166, 177
Treaty of Berlin 106
Treaty of Buczacz 136
Treaty of Istanbul 6
Treaty of Karlowitz 6, 117, 130, 135, 136, 142, 151
Treaty of Küçükkaynarca 138
Treaty of Madrid 101
Treaty of Rijswijk 104, 105
Treaty of Sitvatorok 6
Treaty of Utrecht 104, 105
Treaty of Vasvar 136
Treaty of Versailles 106
Treaty of Westminster 107
Tursun Bey 140

Ullmann, Walter 108, 156, 164, 165, 166, 167, 169, 176

Valois 101
Venice 1, 8, 101, 132, 181, 182, 183

Vienna 3, 12, 98, 102, 103, 104, 105, 113, 137, 154, 175, 181, 182, 185
Vuljetus, Hermann 110, 111

Wallerstein, Immanuel 6, 16, 24
Waltz, Kenneth 8, 11, 14, 15, 17, 30, 31, 37, 59, 157, 158
Weber, Max 33, 50, 55, 70, 71, 82, 153, 158, 159, 161, 162, 163, 164, 165, 166, 169
Wendt, Alexander 10, 11, 12, 14, 15, 30, 31, 37, 59, 60, 158, 159
world-views 20, 21, 44, 49, 52, 53, 58, 139, 148, 152

Zinzendorf, Ludwig von 99

www.ingramcontent.com/pod-product-compliance
Ingram Content Group UK Ltd.
Pitfield, Milton Keynes, MK11 3LW, UK
UKHW020820240326
469204UK00019B/110